Oracle PeopleSoft Enterprise Financial Management 9.1 Implementation

An exhaustive resource for PeopleSoft Financials
application practitioners to understand core concepts,
configurations, and business processes

Ranjeet Yadav

BIRMINGHAM - MUMBAI

Oracle PeopleSoft Enterprise Financial Management 9.1 Implementation

First published: June 2011

Production Reference: 1200611

Published by Packt Publishing Ltd.
32 Lincoln Road
Olton
Birmingham, B27 6PA, UK.

ISBN 978-1-849681-46-9

www.packtpub.com

Cover Image by Dan Anderson (dan@CAndersonAssociates.com)

Credits

Author

Ranjeet Yadav

Reviewers

Tim Lin

Jennifer Sharp

Sudharsan Srinivasaraghavan

Acquisition Editor

Dhwani Devater

Development Editor

Neha Mallik

Technical Editors

Aditi Suvarna

Neha Damle

Project Coordinator

Zainab Bagasrawala

Proofreader

Lucy Henson

Indexer

Monica Ajmera Mehta

Graphics

Geetanjali Sawant

Production Coordinator

Melwyn Dsa

Cover Work

Melwyn Dsa

About the Author

Ranjeet Yadav has been working in the IT industry for more than 10 years. He possesses professional experience of more than 8 years as a functional consultant with PeopleSoft finance and supply chain applications. He has worked on PeopleSoft implementations for many world class organizations and performed various roles such as PeopleSoft consultant, Module lead, Finance track lead, and Project manager. Although his entry into the PeopleSoft world was rather accidental, he was quickly impressed by the deep impact such an ERP product can have on an organization's functioning. He finds the challenge of designing solutions for organizations' critical business problems quite exciting.

Ranjeet holds an Electronics Engineering degree and a Post Graduate Diploma in Management with specialization in Information Systems from Indian Institute of Management, Lucknow.

This book would not have been possible without the support of my parents. It was their encouragement and unwavering help through the challenging times that was crucial. It was my wife, Madhavi, who encouraged me to accept the challenge of writing this book. Managing the writing as well as the office job was certainly not easy, but she endured my working late nights and weekends for all these months. I simply wouldn't have been able to proceed without her understanding. I dedicate this book to her.

About the Reviewers

Tim Lin has 14 years' experience of functional and technical ERP systems implementation and support with PeopleSoft, JDE, Taleo, and Saba. He has been involved in all phases of systems delivery including project management, design, development, test, and production rollout and support. He has deep functional HR and Payroll knowledge coupled with strong technical and project management skills.

Tim has implemented complex, high volume HR, and Payroll systems for large Fortune 500 companies including Federal Express, Manpower International, and Fox Entertainment Group. He has been a consultant for 15 years, including six years with Accenture. Currently, he is a Director at Fox Entertainment Group.

Jennifer Sharp has international experience in both the functional and technical sides of I.T. She has worked in the aerospace, government, healthcare, hospitality, pharmaceutical, and retail industries; specifically as a Project Manager, System Administrator, Technical Writer, QA Tester, IS Analyst, and creating web-based training.

She has worked for the State of Indiana, Eli Lilly and Company, Eli Lilly UK, Lockheed Martin, and Orlando Health.

For further information, please visit her website at www.jennifersharponline.com.

I would like to thank Nathan, Logan, and Archer for their support and inspiration.

Retail-PeopleSoft Savoir-Faire, this term perfectly fits **Sudharsan Srinivasaraghavan**. Sudharsan has spent the last eight years with major retail giants of US, helping them to successfully transform business processes, implement new enterprise systems, and in upgrade of large PeopleSoft programs.

He is a Principal Consultant of Enterprise Solutions Practice at a leading Global Technology Services Company. He has close to two decade experience in managing and implementing various ERP applications. He is specialized in PeopleSoft (PS) Financials and Supply Chain Management applications though. Before entering the IT Consulting, he was leading the Accounts Payable, Asset Management, and Corporate Accounts team in a leading Construction Company of India for 6 years.

Sudharsan also presented a paper on PS Maintenance Management in Retail Industry at Oracle Annual Maintenance Summit 2010.

He has earned a Bachelor's degree in Commerce and Accounting, and he is also a Cost Accountant.

Sudharsan and his wife, Lakshmi, have a girl, Varsha. He loves to spend time with his kid.

www.PacktPub.com

Support files, eBooks, discount offers, and more

You might want to visit www.PacktPub.com for support files and downloads related to your book.

Did you know that Packt offers eBook versions of every book published, with PDF and ePub files available? You can upgrade to the eBook version at www.PacktPub.com and, as a print book customer, you are entitled to a discount on the eBook copy. Get in touch with us at service@packtpub.com for more details.

At www.PacktPub.com, you can also read a collection of free technical articles, sign up for a range of free newsletters, and receive exclusive discounts and offers on Packt books and eBooks.

http://PacktLib.PacktPub.com

Do you need instant solutions to your IT questions? PacktLib is Packt's online digital book library. Here, you can access, read, and search across Packt's entire library of books.

Why subscribe?

- Fully searchable across every book published by Packt
- Copy and paste, print, and bookmark content
- On demand and accessible via web browser

Free access for Packt account holders

If you have an account with Packt at www.PacktPub.com, you can use this to access PacktLib today and view nine entirely free books. Simply use your login credentials for immediate access.

Instant updates on new Packt books

Get notified! Find out when new books are published by following @PacktEnterprise on Twitter, or the *Packt Enterprise* Facebook page.

Table of Contents

Preface

PeopleSoft financial applications have been recognized as a leading ERP product across a wide range of industries that help organizations automate their accounting operations, cut costs, and streamline business processes. They offer industry leading solutions for organizations' global needs, however complex they may be.

PeopleSoft Enterprise Financial Management 9.1 is probably the only learning resource for a novice practitioner, who may otherwise have to rely on thousands of pages of documentation for such a complex ERP system. This book covers all the crucial elements of PeopleSoft Financials - core concepts, business processes, and configuration. This is the ideal one stop resource before embarking into the world of PeopleSoft implementation.

Beginning with the fundamentals of a generic financial ERP system, this book moves on to basic PeopleSoft concepts and then dives into discussing the individual modules in detail.

You will see how to leverage financial modules such as Billing, Accounts Receivable, Accounts Payable, Asset Management, Expenses, and General Ledger. Dedicated chapters discuss key PeopleSoft features such as application security and commitment control for budgeting. You will learn fundamental ERP concepts such as chart of accounts, used by organizations for recording and reporting financial transactions and how to implement them in PeopleSoft through chartfields, business units, and SetIDs.

What this book covers

Chapter 1, PeopleSoft Financials Fundamentals, covers important concepts and configurations such as Chart of Accounts and PeopleSoft Chartfields, Business Units, SetIDs, ledgers, and Journals. It also discusses configuring banks, specifying User Preferences, and using the Setup Manager for PeopleSoft implementation.

Chapter 2, PeopleSoft Security, gives an overview of designing user security for PeopleSoft applications. It discusses important concepts such as Permission Lists, Roles, User Profiles, and related configurations. The chapter also discusses Row Level Security and its configurations.

Chapter 3, PeopleSoft Billing module, discusses important steps in the invoice lifecycle, such as manual and automated invoice entry, billing batch processing, and performing invoice adjustments. It also discusses concepts such as Deferred Revenue Processing and Unbilled Revenue Accrual. The chapter also covers critical billing configurations needed to implement the Billing module.

Chapter 4, PeopleSoft Accounts Receivable module, covers important concepts such as pending item accounting and related configurations such as Entry Types and Entry Reasons. It covers steps in the AR business process such as Pending Item Entry, Receivables Update process, Item Maintenance, Aging, Payment Entry, and Payment Application. The chapter also discusses customer correspondence methods such as Customer Statements and Dunning Letters.

Chapter 5, PeopleSoft Asset Management module, discusses important steps in the fixed assets lifecycle such as Asset entry, Depreciation processing, Asset adjustments, Asset retirements, and creating accounting entries. It also covers critical AM configuration steps.

Chapter 6, PeopleSoft Accounts Payable module, covers the voucher lifecycle steps such as Voucher Entry, Voucher Posting, Matching, Voucher maintenance, Paycycles for processing payments and Withholding. It also discusses critical configurations such as Accounting Templates, Voucher Origins, Miscellaneous Charges, and Payment Terms.

Chapter 7, PeopleSoft General Ledger module, covers various journal entry methods such as Journal Generator, Flat file import, and Manual journal entry. It also gives an overview of journal processing steps such as Journal Edit and Journal Post. The chapter discusses concepts such as Interim and Year-end Closing as well as Allocations and related configurations.

Chapter 8, PeopleSoft Expenses module, covers processing of cash advances and expense reports along with importing Expenses data from various external sources. It covers workflow approvals – an integral part of Expenses module along with other critical configurations such as Employee Profiles, Expense Types, and Location Amounts.

Chapter 9, PeopleSoft Commitment Control, explains the basic concepts behind budget control in PeopleSoft financial applications along with relevant critical configurations. It also discusses the entry and processing of budgets and handling of commitment control exceptions.

What you need for this book

PeopleSoft applications are installed on the server by the System Administrator. The installation is a complex task and requires PeopleSoft technical skills. The intended audience for this book will not be performing this task. It is expected that they will refer to an existing demo environment of PeopleSoft applications. However, following steps can be referred to download the application from Oracle's URL. PeopleSoft applications can be downloaded as follows:

1. Visit `http://eDelivery.Oracle.com` <http://edelivery.oracle.com/>
2. On the page, click **Continue**.
3. Enter details as shown in the following screenshot:

4. Enter details as shown in the following screenshot:

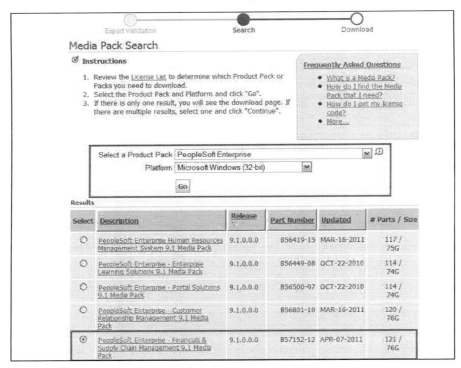

5. Download the demo version.

Who this book is for

This book is intended for functional implementation analysts planning to work on implementation teams, business analysts who support in-house PeopleSoft applications, and business users who plan to start using PeopleSoft applications.

Conventions

In this book, you will find a number of styles of text that distinguish between different kinds of information. Here are some examples of these styles, and an explanation of their meaning.

Code words in text are shown as follows: "For example, in BI_ACCT_ENTRY table, the ACCOUNTING_DT field is used to store the accounting date."

New terms and **important words** are shown in bold. Words that you see on the screen, in menus or dialog boxes for example, appear in the text like this: "The **Billing** module creates accounting entries for sales invoices for customers."

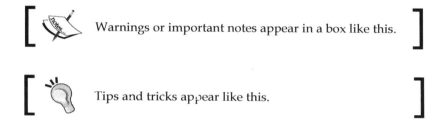

Warnings or important notes appear in a box like this.

Tips and tricks appear like this.

Reader feedback

Feedback from our readers is always welcome. Let us know what you think about this book—what you liked or may have disliked. Reader feedback is important for us to develop titles that you really get the most out of.

To send us general feedback, simply send an e-mail to feedback@packtpub.com, and mention the book title via the subject of your message.

If there is a book that you need and would like to see us publish, please send us a note in the **SUGGEST A TITLE** form on www.packtpub.com or e-mail suggest@packtpub.com.

If there is a topic that you have expertise in and you are interested in either writing or contributing to a book, see our author guide on www.packtpub.com/authors.

Customer support

Now that you are the proud owner of a Packt book, we have a number of things to help you to get the most from your purchase.

Errata

Although we have taken every care to ensure the accuracy of our content, mistakes do happen. If you find a mistake in one of our books—maybe a mistake in the text or the code—we would be grateful if you would report this to us. By doing so, you can save other readers from frustration and help us improve subsequent versions of this book. If you find any errata, please report them by visiting http://www.packtpub. com/support, selecting your book, clicking on the **errata submission form** link, and entering the details of your errata. Once your errata are verified, your submission will be accepted and the errata will be uploaded on our website, or added to any list of existing errata, under the Errata section of that title. Any existing errata can be viewed by selecting your title from http://www.packtpub.com/support.

Piracy

Piracy of copyright material on the Internet is an ongoing problem across all media. At Packt, we take the protection of our copyright and licenses very seriously. If you come across any illegal copies of our works, in any form, on the Internet, please provide us with the location address or website name immediately so that we can pursue a remedy.

Please contact us at copyright@packtpub.com with a link to the suspected pirated material.

We appreciate your help in protecting our authors, and our ability to bring you valuable content.

Questions

You can contact us at questions@packtpub.com if you are having a problem with any aspect of the book, and we will do our best to address it.

1
PeopleSoft Financials Fundamentals

Before we delve into studying the PeopleSoft Financials applications, we need to understand that it is primarily an ERP application, meant to be used as a transaction processing system. Its core philosophy is driven by the need to record, process, and report accounting transactions of an organization.

In this chapter, we'll establish the understanding of core concepts of PeopleSoft applications—such as Chart of Accounts, Business units, SetIDs, Banks, User preferences, and related configurations. We'll also learn how to use an important tool known as Setup Manager, which is used in implementing PeopleSoft applications.

Note that these concepts are not related to a specific module and serve as the foundation for all subsequent modules in this book. A PeopleSoft Financials practitioner must understand these aspects to be able to successfully maintain and implement the applications.

This book relates to the version 9.1 of PeopleSoft applications. As a result, the concepts and screenshots in this book refer to the version 9.1. Some of the screens and basic concepts may be similar to previous PeopleSoft versions.

Understanding Chart of Accounts and chartfields

Any accounting system (be it manual or automated) is built on a structure that determines how the accounting information is recorded (and ultimately reported). Each organization determines the best possible way to capture and classify the vast number of accounting transactions that take place every day. This decision is a combination of two distinct factors:

- The need to report the accounting data by various important parameters
- Feasibility and ease of recording the accounting transactions

Let's take a very simple example to better understand this.

Global Vehicles Inc. is an automobile manufacturer, selling vehicles such as passenger cars, commercial vehicles as well as scooters. Its operations are spread across multiple countries. Let's say that its annual sales from all its vehicles are $100 million. The key challenge is to know where exactly these dollars are coming from.

Implementation challenge

Design an accounting system for Global Vehicles, so that it can answer questions like the following:

- Which country is contributing the most to Global Vehicle's sales?
- Which product family is lagging in terms of revenues?
- What were the sales of passenger cars in USA?
- Which is the best selling scooter model in terms of revenue?

Did you say, "Just make sure that you record all required pieces of information when each vehicle sale takes place"? You are absolutely right if you did!

One way of recording the sale transactions can be recording the **Continent**, **Country**, **Product line**, **Vehicle model,** and **Sale Price**. Thus, its sales data for January 2011 may look something like this:

Continent	Country	Product Line	Model	Sale Price
North America	USA	Passenger Car	Alpha	USD 10,000
Europe	France	Scooter	Gamma	FRF 3000
North America	USA	Passenger Car	Theta	USD 30,000
North America	Canada	Passenger Car	Theta	CAD 33,000
North America	USA	Scooter	Gamma	USD 2,000
Europe	UK	Commercial	Zeta	GBP 40,000

As you can see, one can certainly answer the above questions if your accounting system can record all these attributes for each transaction.

Now let's go one step further. Say Global Vehicles has about 100 dealerships in the USA and wants to know the sales performance for each dealership. How can we address this additional requirement? Simple, by recording the dealership as an additional attribute for all the sales transactions.

You probably realize now that designing the structure of accounting information to be recorded is driven by how you wish to use the data. This structure (collection of all required attributes) is known as the **Chart of Accounts (COA)**. All the attributes in COA are termed **Chartfields** in PeopleSoft parlance.

You would also be able to appreciate that the number of chartfields that an organization needs, depends on its business requirements. Having few chartfields will make the recording process simpler, but will not offer much insight into the recorded accounting data. On the other hand, having more chartfields will give a more meaningful picture of the accounting transactions, but at the cost of system performance. A PeopleSoft practitioner needs to balance an organization's reporting requirements and ease of use before recommending appropriate Chart of Accounts.

PeopleSoft chartfields

PeopleSoft Financial applications offer the following 25 chartfields:

Chartfield	Length	Comments
Account	10	This is a mandatory chartfield used to record corporate accounts and cannot be used for any other attribute. For example, an organization may use account # 100000 to record fuel expenses, while account # 200000 is used to record salary expenses for employees.
Alternate Account	10	This chartfield is used only for statutory reporting to further classify accounting transactions.
Operating Unit	8	
Fund Code	5	Used primarily in education and government accounting systems.
Department	10	
Program Code	5	
Class Field	5	
Budget Reference	8	
Product	6	
Project Costing Business Unit	5	Used if Project Costing module is implemented to track projects related details.
Project ID / Grant	15	Used to track projects related details in Project Costing module.
Activity	15	Used to track projects related details in Project Costing module.
Source Type	5	Used to track projects related details in Project Costing module.
Category	5	Used to track projects related details in Project Costing module.
Subcategory	5	Used to track projects related details in Project Costing module.
Chartfield 1	10	Additional delivered chartfield by PeopleSoft. Activate it (and relabel if needed) to use.
Chartfield 2	10	Additional delivered chartfield by PeopleSoft. Activate it (and relabel if needed) to use.
Chartfield 3	10	Additional delivered chartfield by PeopleSoft. Activate it (and relabel if needed) to use.
Affiliate	5	Used for inter-unit transactions (transactions between 2 different business units) if only a single inter-unit account is used. This chartfield cannot be used for any other purpose.

Chartfield	Length	Comments
Fund Affiliate	10	Used for intra unit transactions (transactions between two separate Funds belonging to the same business unit) if only a single intra unit account is used. This chartfield cannot be used for any other purpose.
Operating Unit Affiliate	10	Used for intra unit transactions (transactions between two separate Operating Units belonging to the same business unit) if only a single intra unit account is used. This chartfield cannot be used for any other purpose.
Scenario	10	
Book Code	4	
Adjustment Type	4	
Statistics Code		

Note that some chartfields (such as Account, Alternate Account, Project Costing Business Unit, Affiliate chartfields) are reserved for specific purposes and cannot be used to record any value other than its intended purpose. For example, the Account chartfield has to be used only to record corporate accounts used in accounting. However, there are no limitations on the use of other chartfields. Thus, it is not necessary that the Product chartfield has to be used to record a product. You can very well use it to record any attribute such as 'Country' or 'Continent' in the COA example discussed earlier.

Chartfield configuration

As you can see, the given set of PeopleSoft chartfields may not really satisfy the organization's implementation requirements. This can be due to following factors:

- Delivered chartfield names cannot be used
- You may not need all of the given 25 chartfields
- Given chartfields are not sufficient and you need to add additional chartfields (although this is highly unlikely)

To achieve this, you need to perform chartfield configuration activities.

Expert tip:
As far as the number of required chartfields is concerned, always think of your system's future requirements. Remember, it is extremely complicated to add a new chartfield to the COA if the system already has data using the old COA. If you think there is a possibility of new chartfield requirements down the line, include them in your COA even if you may not use them. You can simply keep it blank until the time it is needed.

Standard chartfield configuration

The following operations can be performed on PeopleSoft delivered chartfields using standard configuration:

- Changing the display order of chartfields on pages and reports.
- Relabeling long and short names (descriptions) of chartfields.
- Deactivating or activating chartfields.
- Changing the display length of chartfields on pages and reports.
- Changing Related chartfields for IntraUnit Affiliate chartfields.

Follow this navigation to perform standard chartfield configuration:

Setup Financials/Supply Chain | Common definitions | Design chartfields | Configure | Standard configuration

The following screenshot shows the partial **Standard Chartfield Configuration** page:

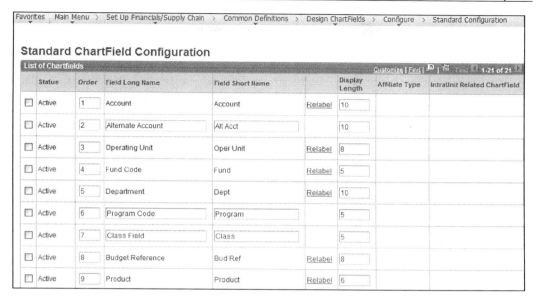

Standard ChartField Configuration

	Status	Order	Field Long Name	Field Short Name		Display Length	Affiliate Type	IntraUnit Related ChartField
☐	Active	1	Account	Account	Relabel	10		
☐	Active	2	Alternate Account	Alt Acct		10		
☐	Active	3	Operating Unit	Oper Unit	Relabel	8		
☐	Active	4	Fund Code	Fund	Relabel	5		
☐	Active	5	Department	Dept	Relabel	10		
☐	Active	6	Program Code	Program		5		
☐	Active	7	Class Field	Class		5		
☐	Active	8	Budget Reference	Bud Ref	Relabel	8		
☐	Active	9	Product	Product	Relabel	6		

The next screenshot shows a part of the bottom half of the page:

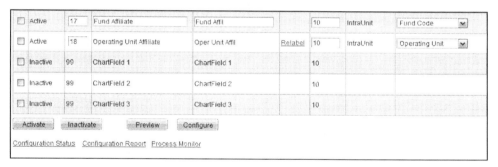

	Status	Order	Field Long Name	Field Short Name		Display Length	Affiliate Type	IntraUnit Related ChartField
☐	Active	17	Fund Affiliate	Fund Affil		10	IntraUnit	Fund Code ▼
☐	Active	18	Operating Unit Affiliate	Oper Unit Affil	Relabel	10	IntraUnit	Operating Unit ▼
☐	Inactive	99	ChartField 1	ChartField 1		10		
☐	Inactive	99	ChartField 2	ChartField 2		10		
☐	Inactive	99	ChartField 3	ChartField 3		10		

Activate   Inactivate   Preview   Configure

Configuration Status   Configuration Report   Process Monitor

In the COA example for Global Vehicles discussed earlier, we need to record the following attributes: Continent, Country, Product Line, and Model. Also, we anticipate that a new chartfield may be required in future to record 'Dealership'. Thus we need five chartfields for the COA (in addition to the Account chartfield). As you can see, PeopleSoft doesn't offer any chartfield by these names.

Therefore, we need to perform the following configuration activities:

- Ensure that necessary chartfields are activated
- Deactivate those chartfields that are not required
- Relabel the active chartfields to reflect actual intended usage

Let's say that we decide to use following chartfields for our example (based on the available chartfield lengths):

Required Chartfield	PeopleSoft Chartfield
Continent	Operating Unit
Country	Fund Code
Product Line	Department
Model	Budget Reference
Dealership	Product
Account	Account

To activate any chartfield that is inactive, select the checkbox next to it and click the **Activate** button:

- To inactivate any redundant chartfield that is currently active, select the checkbox and click **Inactivate** button.

- To change the display label of a chartfield, click the **Relabel** hyperlink. In the secondary page that opens, provide the new name to be used. For example, we need to relabel the **Operating Unit** chartfield as **Continent** as shown in the following screenshot:

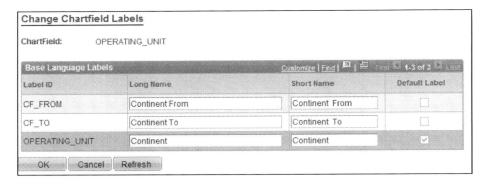

- Change display length of any chartfield in the **Display Length** column as required (provided it is not greater than original chartfield length).

- Once configuration activities are complete, click **Preview** button to see what the new COA looks like.

- Final step in the chartfield configuration process is to run the **Full Configuration** batch process. Click the **Configure** button to trigger this process.

Advanced chartfield configuration

The following operations can be performed on chartfields using advanced chartfield configuration:

- Add new chartfields
- Delete chartfields
- Resize chartfields
- Rename chartfields

Note that these changes have quite a wide impact on the PeopleSoft system, compared to standard configuration.

Follow this navigation to perform advanced chartfield configuration:

Setup Financials/Supply Chain | Common definitions | Design chartfields | Configure | Advanced configuration

The following screenshot shows the Advanced Chartfield Configuration page:

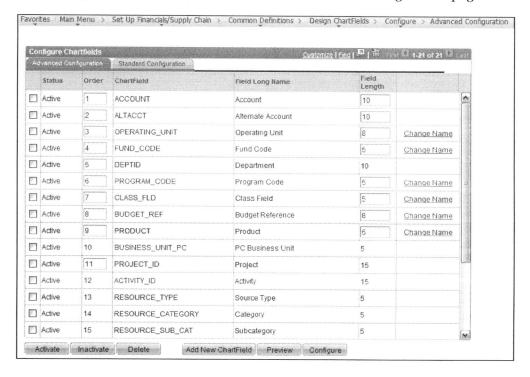

Expert tip:

Advanced chartfield configuration is not advised by PeopleSoft. Always try to achieve the desired result by its corresponding action in standard configuration.

Activate an inactive ChartField instead of adding a new ChartField.

Inactivate a ChartField instead of deleting it.

Change the display length rather than the actual field length when reducing the size of a ChartField.

Relabel a ChartField instead of renaming it.

Understanding Business Units and SetID

An ERP system like PeopleSoft financial applications needs to record and store enormous amounts of data. We need to understand the types of data that the system generates before getting into how it is done. Business Units and SetID form the basic structure of how the system records and accesses this data.

In PeopleSoft architecture, the data are categorized into the following two types:

- **Transaction data:** These are the data elements that are generated due to regular business transactions. For example, an organization like Global Vehicles may create a purchase order for one of its suppliers to buy tires for its vehicles, create a vendor invoice (also known as voucher) to acknowledge that it needs to pay its supplier for received goods or issue a sales invoice when a vehicle is sold.

  As you can see, amount of transaction data in a table that stores them, will keep on changing frequently as new transactions take place.

- **Master (Setup) data:** These are the data elements that are needed to enable the system to perform its business transactions. For example, Global Vehicles may have a group of vendors from whom it buys components for its vehicles. It also may have a group of banks where it holds its bank accounts for its financial transactions.

What key differences do you see between such master data and the transaction data elements?

The first (and somewhat obvious) is the dynamic nature of transaction data. As we saw earlier, the number of sales invoices will always keep changing from day to day. On the other hand, how frequently can we expect changes in the number of vendors? True, there will be additions or deletions of vendors, but these changes will be far less compared to transaction data.

The second difference relates to the purpose of these types of data. Master data is needed to perform regular business transactions. For example, a vendor needs to be set up in the system before we can create a purchase order (a business transaction) to buy something from it. Similarly, we need to set up rules to calculate discount before we can create a sales invoice and decide how much discount can be given to a customer.

The third key difference lies in the way these data elements can be shared or need to be separated from each other. Let's assume that Global Vehicles' business has been structured by geography. Thus, it has following operating divisions: North America, Europe, and Asia.

Now let's consider the master data first. Is it possible that all these divisions can have a common vendor or bank? The answer is yes—a single vendor can sell car seats or tires to all the divisions. Similarly, a bank with a global presence can offer banking services to all these divisions. Thus, theoretically, master data can be shared by various groups within the organizations. Note that the master data doesn't always have to be shared, but can be if needed.

Let's consider the transaction data now. When the European division sells a car, can this transaction (sales invoice) be claimed (in other words, shared) by other divisions? The answer is no—the system must segregate sales invoices of Europe from those of North America and Asia divisions, in order to keep a track of them and ultimately report on the sales performance of each.

Thus, while master data can be shared, transaction data belonging to organizational units must be segregated by the system.

Business Unit

In PeopleSoft parlance, **Business Unit** is the organizational unit. It can be any entity that needs to maintain its account balances separately from each other for reporting. In the previous examples, we can say that Europe, North America, and Asia will be the business units of the organization.

However, if Global Vehicles wants to be structured by its line of business, we can create the following Business Units: Passenger car, Commercial vehicles, and Two wheelers. Note that transaction data tables will always have Business Unit as their primary key (to identify where they belong to). In other words, sales invoices, purchase orders, accounting journals, and so on are segregated by the Business Unit.

Business Unit configuration needs to be done for each module that is to be implemented. For example, to implement Accounts Payable and General Ledger modules, the Passenger Car BU needs to be configured for both the modules.

PeopleSoft recommends using BU names that are five characters long. Any BU names having less than five characters can affect the system performance.

Tableset ID

Tableset ID (or SetID, as it is commonly known) is used to segregate the master data. Depending on how we want to group the master data, an appropriate number of SetIDs are created. It is the SetID that determines which Business Unit can access which master data elements. This is a two step process:

1. Create SetIDs and group master data elements.
2. Associate a Business Unit with an appropriate SetID to control which master data elements it can access.

Scenario 1

Assume that there are five suppliers (or vendors in PeopleSoft terms) for Global Vehicles. All these vendors need to be used by all its Business Units.

As all the master data elements (vendors) are going to be used by everybody, there is a need for only a single group (SetID) of vendors. Let's call this SetID 'GLOVH'. The Vendor table will contain the data as follows:

SetID (Primary Key)	Vendor ID
GLOVH	VENDOR1
GLOVH	VENDOR2
GLOVH	VENDOR3
GLOVH	VENDOR4
GLOVH	VENDOR5

 SetID names should be only five characters long.

Now, we need to specify which rows of master data can be accessed by each Business Unit.

Business Unit	Master data table	SetID to be accessed
Passanger Car	VENDOR	GLOVH
Commercial Vehicles	VENDOR	GLOVH
Two wheelers	VENDOR	GLOVH

Thus, each BU can now access master data defined under 'GLOVH' SetID from the Vendor table.

Scenario 2

Vendors 1 and 2 should be accessible only by Passenger Car BU, Vendors 3 and 4 should be accessible only by the Commercial Vehicles BU, while Two wheelers BU should have access only to Vendor 5.

Now we need three distinct groups of vendors. In other words, we need three SetIDs. Let's see how the data will be grouped in the Vendor table:

SetID (Primary Key)	Vendor ID
GROUP1	VENDOR1
GROUP1	VENDOR2
GROUP2	VENDOR3
GROUP2	VENDOR4
GROUP3	VENDOR5

And finally, let's specify which BU can access which data rows under Vendor table:

Business Unit	Master data table	SetID to be accessed
Passanger car	VENDOR	GROUP1
Commercial vehicles	VENDOR	GROUP2
Two wheelers	VENDOR	GROUP3

Configuring SetID

Follow this navigation to configure SetID:

PeopleTools | Utilities | Administration | TableSet IDs

The next screenshot shows the TableSet ID page, where we need to configure the new value:

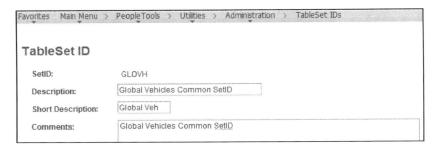

Configuring TableSet Control

TableSet Control determines which master data rows can be accessed by a BU. We saw how to do this in the previous illustration. In reality, due to the very high number of data tables, this access is given for a group of tables, rather than a single data table. Let's take a look at how this is configured.

Follow this navigation to configure Tableset Control:

PeopleTools | Utilities | Administration | TableSet Control

The next screenshot shows the TableSet Control page for a Business Unit US001:

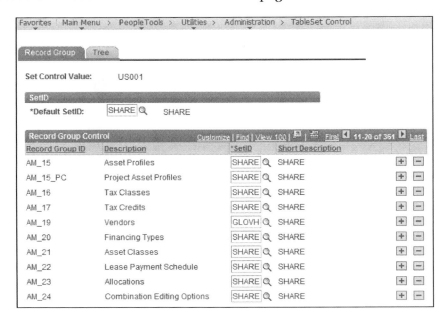

As you can see, the BU **US001** can access all master data rows defined under SetID **GLOVH** in the group of records **AM_19**. Note that this record group contains the Vendor table among others. For other record groups, **US001** will be to access master data values defined under a different SetID called **SHARE**.

Understanding accounting structure— Ledgers and Journals

The following illustration depicts a high level view of accounting entry creation and processing in PeopleSoft financial applications:

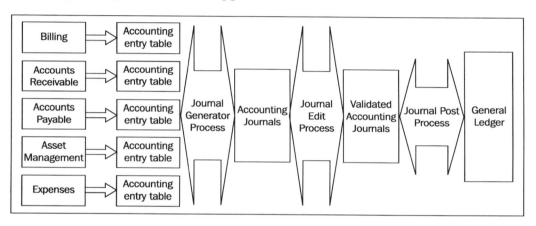

As you can observe, this illustration gives an overview of how different modules, such as Billing, Accounts Receivable, Accounts Payable, Asset Management, Expenses (also known as sub-modules or sub-systems) are integrated with General Ledger module. Each module creates accounting entries for business transactions that take place. For example, the **Billing** module creates accounting entries for sales invoices for customers; the **Asset Management** module creates accounting entries for fixed asset addition and depreciation activities, while the **Expenses** module creates accounting entries for each employee expense report that is processed. Note that these are just a few sample examples. We'll discuss the details of business transactions in respective chapters.

Once the accounting entries are created by a module, a batch process known as 'Journal Generator' performs subsequent activities. Note that Journal Generator process can create accounting journals from accounting entries generated by external non-PeopleSoft systems as well. It performs three critical tasks as part of the journal processing lifecycle:

- **Journal creation:** Journal Generator process transforms these accounting entries into 'Journals'. A journal can be considered as a collection and summarized form of multiple accounting entries.

- **Journal edit:** This process validates created journals based on the validation criteria to ensure that there are no accounting errors. If any errors are found, those journals are accordingly marked. They can be processed further only after their errors are manually resolved. Successfully validated journals are eligible for posting.

- **Journal posting:** This process ensures that amounts in the journals are posted to appropriate General Ledger accounts. In other words, the Journal Post process updates the final account balances in General Ledger. These final account balances are then reported through financial statements such as Income statement and Balance sheet by the organization.

Let's consider a simple example to understand this process. Assume that an organization uses following accounts with hypothetical General Ledger balances:

Account	Description	Balance Type	Balance Amount
100000	Trade Receivables	Debit	$50000
200000	Customer sales	Credit	-$150000

'DR' denotes a 'Debit' transaction, while 'CR' denotes a 'Credit' transaction. PeopleSoft applications always denote credit amounts by a negative sign.

Now let's say that 4 new sales invoices – for $1000, $1500, $2000 and $2500 - are created in the Billing module on a particular day. As part of the invoice processing, the following accounting entries are created:

Invoice ID	Type	Account	Amount
INVOICE1	DR	100000	$1000
	CR	200000	- $1000
INVOICE2	DR	100000	$1500
	CR	200000	- $1500
INVOICE3	DR	100000	$2000
	CR	200000	- $2000
INVOICE4	DR	100000	$2500
	CR	200000	- $2500

Each PeopleSoft module has a dedicated table to store these accounting entries. For Billing, above entries are stored in a table 'BI_ACCT_ENTRY'. Now these entries are ready to be processed by the Journal Generator process.

These entries are then consolidated into a journal as follows:

Journal ID	Type	Account	Amount
JOURNAL1	DR	100000	$7000
	CR	200000	- $7000

Let's assume that the Journal edit process successfully validates this journal by ensuring that debit and credit totals in the journal are equal. If successfully validated, it marks the journal to be picked by the Journal Post process. Now the Journal Post process picks up this journal and posts these amounts to the appropriate accounts in General Ledger.

Thus, after this journal is posted, the final account balances will be updated as follows:

Account	Description	Balance type	Balance amount
100000	Trade Receivables	Debit	$57000 (50000+7000)
200000	Customer sales	Credit	-$157000 (150000+7000)

Configuring ledgers and Journal Generator

A typical PeopleSoft financials implementation requires the following configuration activities:

- Set up a GL Business Units – We'll defer discussion of this activity to the chapter on General Ledger
- Configure ledger templates
- Configure Detail ledgers
- Configure Detail ledger groups
- Configure Ledgers for a unit
- Configure Journal sources
- Configure Accounting entry definitions
- Configure Journal templates

As discussed earlier, PeopleSoft ledgers record posted net balances for a set of chartfield values (depending on how many chartfields are activated in the configuration) for each accounting period (such as month) and fiscal year.

A **Ledger Template** can be considered to be a framework of a ledger's attributes. Rather than using a ledger template for an individual ledger, it is linked to a Ledger Group. As a result, a ledger template applies to all the ledgers in a group. It essentially specifies various records and fields for a ledger that the system needs to report from.

Usually multiple ledgers are clubbed in a **Ledger Group**. We'll discuss the need for having multiple ledgers in a ledger group in the chapter for General Ledger. For the time being, let's just note that a ledger group can have one primary ledger and (if needed) up to nine secondary ledgers.

Configuring ledger templates

Follow this navigation to configure ledger templates:

General Ledger | Ledgers | Templates

The following screenshot shows a part of the Ledger Template page.

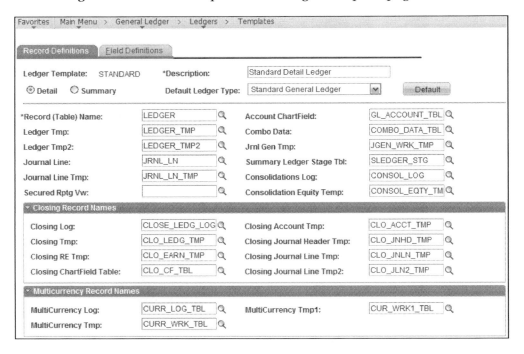

The following screenshot shows the remaining bottom portion of the Ledger Template page:

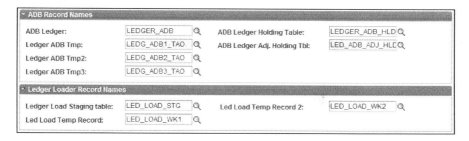

PeopleSoft delivers several default ledger templates (such as Commitment control ledgers, Standard ledgers, Average Daily Balance ledgers, and so on).

The preceding screenshot shows the ledger template used for standard detail ledgers. Each field in this screen refers to a table used for a specific purpose. Most of the fields in this definition here are used by background processes and do not affect the user transactions.

For a typical implementation, you need not change these default templates. However, we'll discuss a few important fields:

- **Record (Table) Name:** This critical table stores the final chartfield combination balances for the posted transactions. For standard ledgers, this table is 'LEDGER'.

- **Account Chartfield:** This table stores the values for the 'Account' chartfield. For standard PeopleSoft applications, it is GL_ACCOUNT_TBL.

- **Combo Data:** This table stores the data used in determining whether a given combination of chartfield values is valid. In PeopleSoft terminology, this is known as 'Chartfield Combination Editing'. For standard ledgers, this table is COMBO_DATA_TBL.

- **Journal Line:** This table stores the detailed journal line information for the journals. For standard ledgers, this table is JRNL_LN.

Expert tip:

The given tables are extremely important in the sense that majority of General Ledger processing is based on them. These tables are used by various batch processes; hence such changes have a large impact requiring many code changes. To the extent possible, avoid making changes to delivered table values. Any changes to the delivered table values in ledger template need to be very carefully analyzed. In the rare event that these values are changed, all the journal processes need to be thoroughly tested to ensure that they are not impacted by these changes.

- **Closing Record Names:** These fields specify the tables used in the closing process. The General Ledger chapter will discuss this process in detail.
- **Multicurrency Record Names:** These fields specify the tables used in the multicurrency processing.
- **ADB Record Names:** These fields specify the tables used in the Average Daily Balancing processing.
- **Ledger Loader Record Names:** While ledgers can be configured from the online pages (as we will shortly see), they can also be loaded from external non-PeopleSoft systems. These fields specify the tables used during the external ledger load process.

Click the **Field Definitions** tab to see default field values populated by the system. These defaults are dependent upon the **Default Ledger Type** value in the previous tab.

The following screenshot shows the details of **Field Definitions** tab:

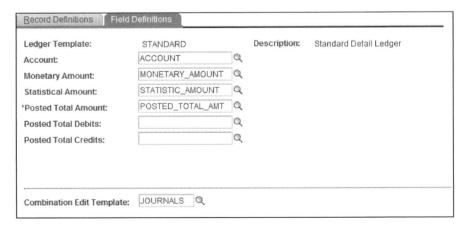

- **Account:** Denotes the field name used for the 'Account' chartfield.

- **Monetary Amount:** A journal line may contain amounts in two different currencies - Base currency of a Business Unit and Foreign currency (Transaction currency). This field stores the monetary amount in the base currency.

- **Posted Total Amount:** This field stores the net balance amount for posted transactions of a chartfield combination.

- **Combination Edit Template:** This field is mandatory for the Journal Edit process we discussed earlier. A value **JOURNALS** must be selected.

Implementation challenge

Corporate headquarters of Global Vehicles Inc. is located in the USA. Design a ledger structure to maintain its accounts and report the financial statements in USD. At the same time, it should be able to maintain all accounts in Euros and British Pounds (GBP) for internal reporting.

Solution

For the sake of simplification, we'll assume that COA for reporting in all currencies is the same. This can be achieved by maintaining three separate ledgers – one for USD balances, one for GBP balances and another for Euro balances. PeopleSoft General Ledger allows this flexibility to automatically post the journals simultaneously to multiple ledgers. We'll configure these three ledgers (named GLOBALUSD, GLOBALGBP, and GLOBALEUR respectively) and include them in a ledger group for the business unit. Let's see how to do it.

Configuring ledgers

Follow this navigation to configure ledgers: **General Ledger | Ledgers | Detail Ledgers**

The following screenshot shows the **Detail Ledgers** page:

Note that ledgers being master data elements (which can be shared by different Business Units) are defined by SetID. As we discussed earlier, a ledger needs to be linked to a ledger template. Thus, it inherits all the attributes that are defined for a ledger template.

Now our ledger is almost ready to start recording the accounting balances. The system knows which database tables and fields to refer to in order to update data from journals or retrieve data for reporting...all courtesy of the ledger template!

Configuring ledger groups

Follow this navigation to configure ledger groups:

General Ledger | Ledgers | Ledger groups

Ledger group configuration serves multiple objectives: Grouping multiple ledgers in a similar group (we'll see why we need to do this), specifying the edit tables for the relevant chartfields being used in the ledger, and specifying chartfield balancing options. Let's see each of these important functions in detail now.

We'll call our ledger group **GLOBAL**.

The **Definition** tab in the following screenshot , is where we can include multiple ledgers in a group:

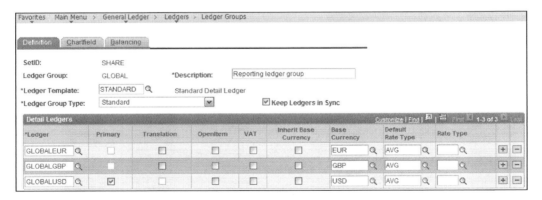

We already saw why we need three different ledgers—to address different currency reporting requirements.

Having multiple currency requirements is just one of the possible reasons we need to define multiple ledgers in a group. Commitment control ledgers groups typically have multiple ledgers. We'll discuss them in detail in the *Chapter 9, PeopleSoft Commitment Control*.

When there are multiple ledgers in a ledger group, one ledger needs to be designated as the primary ledger, while the others are designated as secondary ledgers. PeopleSoft allows up to nine secondary ledgers in a ledger group. In other words, there can be a maximum of 10 ledgers in a group. Remember, it is not mandatory to always define secondary ledgers. If an organization has very straightforward reporting requirements, they can be addressed by a single primary ledger.

Now let's discuss the important fields that you see on the **Definition** tab:

- **Ledger Template:** As discussed earlier, assign a ledger template to the ledger group so that all its ledgers inherit the template properties.
- **Keep Ledgers in Sync:** This checkbox serves a very important function. If it is checked, the system ensures that journal transactions are posted automatically to all the ledgers in the ledger group. For example, for our ledger group, when a journal entry is created, the Journal Edit process posts it to all the ledgers (GLOBALUSD, GLOBALEUR and GLOBALGBP).
- **Ledger:** Specify the ledger name that needs to be included in this ledger group.
- **Primary:** Specify which ledger in this group is the primary ledger by checking this flag.
- **Translation:** This checkbox determines if a ledger needs to be used by the currency translation process.
- **Base Currency:** Specify the base currency for each ledger.
- **Inherit Base Currency:** If we check this flag, the 'Base Currency' field is no longer available. This forces the base currency for each ledger to be the same as that of General Ledger BU.

The following screenshot shows the Chartfield tab. It is used to specify the edit tables for each chartfield being used by this ledger group:

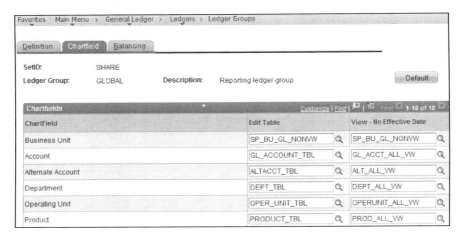

- **View – No Effective Date**: This field specifies the prompt table used for reporting prompts. Based on an organization's requirements, we can change it if needed. It'll determine which chartfield values are available for users.

The next tab on this page - **Balancing** - in the following screenshot, determines how the accounting entries are balanced:

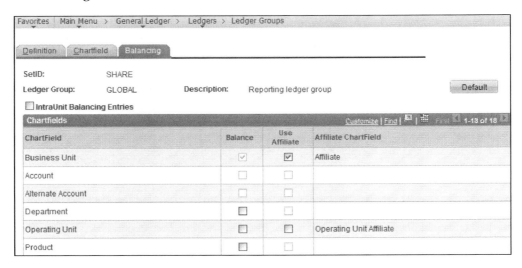

Let's first understand the concept of balancing.

A sample journal entry looks something like this:

BU	Account	Dept	Op Unit	Product	DR/CR	Amount
US001	123000	455	CPG	INT40	DR	$4500
US001	258000	155	TAX	INT40	DR	$1500
US001	215000	455	CPG	INT40	CR	-$6000

What is the most obvious thing about this accounting entry? Of course, the sum of debit and credit lines is equal. In other words, it is 'balanced'. Now can you say that debit and credit amounts are equal for each of the chartfields?

For BU US001 and Product value INT40, this is true. On the other hand, for Account, Department, and Operating Unit, accounting entries are not balanced.

Note that, no matter what happens, accounting entries have to be balanced for each Business Unit. However, if an organization maintains its balances for each Department or Operating Unit (or any other chartfield), then account balances have to be balanced for that chartfield as well.

The Balancing tab determines the chartfields by which the accounting entries must balance. Business Unit is always selected, while Account and Alternate Account are always excluded from balanced chartfields (in accounting terms, as an account can have only debit or credit balance, entries can never balance for an account). If an organization requires that, its entries should be balanced by additional chartfields, (Operating Unit, for example) the **Balance** checkbox should be selected for that chartfield. This is necessary when reporting needs to be performed by the Operating Unit.

The Journal Edit process ensures that for any journal, its accounting entries are balanced by the chartfields specified here. So, in the previous example (with entries balanced by BU and Operating Unit), our sample accounting entry would have been flagged as invalid since Operating Unit is not in balance.

Configuring ledgers for a Business Unit

Now that we have built the basic accounting structure in terms of ledgers, ledger groups, and templates, our PeopleSoft system is ready to record accounting balances. The last step is to link required ledgers to a General Ledger Business Unit.

Note that a GL BU can not only have multiple ledgers (or ledger groups) associated with it, but it can also have ledgers belonging to different types. It is possible that a BU may need to have a ledger group to maintain its budgets, another to record its accounting transactions. It also may have 2 different ledger groups to record transactions in different currencies. How many ledgers (and what types) are needed by a BU is entirely driven by the organization's processing and reporting requirements.

In addition to assigning ledgers/ledger groups to a GL BU, we also configure various processing options.

Follow the navigation to assign ledgers for a BU:

Set Up Financials/Supply Chain | Business Unit Related | General Ledger | Ledgers For a Unit

The following screenshot shows the **Definition** tab of the page. This is where we select ledgers/ledger groups for a BU:

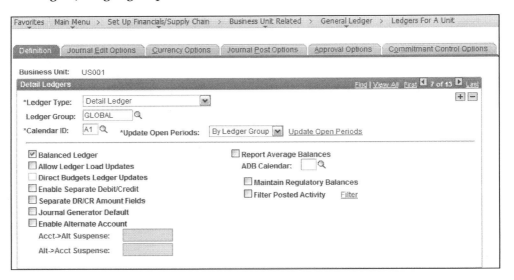

There are three types of ledgers that can be selected here: **Detail ledgers, Summary ledger,** and **Commitment control ledger**. In a nutshell, detail ledgers are used to record actual accounting transactions. Summary ledgers on the other hand record only summarized versions of detailed accounting transactions. Commitment control ledgers record control budgets. We'll discuss the commitment control in greater details in *Chapter 9, PeopleSoft Commitment Control*.

Let's discuss some of the important fields in this tab:

- **Ledger Type:** If **Detail ledger** is selected, only a **Ledger Group** field becomes available. If **Summary ledger** is selected, a **Ledger** field becomes available.

- **Balanced Ledger:** Select this checkbox to force the ledger to be balanced. As we saw earlier, this means that the system will ensure that credit and debit balances posted to this ledger group are equal.

- **Journal Generator Default:** Select this checkbox to make this ledger group the default for given BU. When Journal Generator creates journals from other sub-modules, it looks for the ledger group value on each accounting entry line. This value determines the ledger group where that entry will be posted. In case this value is missing on the accounting entry, Journal Generator will post it to the ledger group with this checkbox selected.

The following screenshot shows the next **Journal Edit Options** tab. This tab specifies how journal errors should be handled by the system:

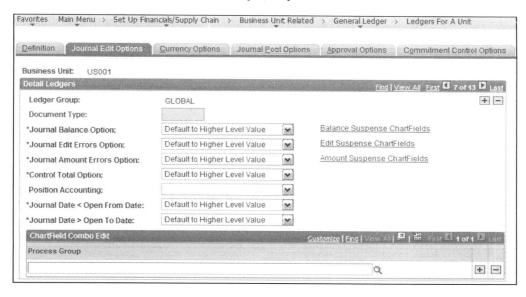

Available error processing options are as follows:

- **Default to Higher Level Value:** If this journal error is encountered, look at the processing option defined for the GL BU.

- **Suspend:** Post the error amount or the amount needed to bring journals in balance to suspense account (specified using **Suspense Chartfields** hyperlink).

- **Recycle:** If the error is encountered, mark the corresponding accounting entries as invalid and prevent them from posting until they are corrected and the journal is reprocessed by Journal Edit process.

- **Accept (only for Journal amount errors):** Ignore the error and continue processing.

The next tab on the page - **Currency Options** – is shown in the following screenshot:

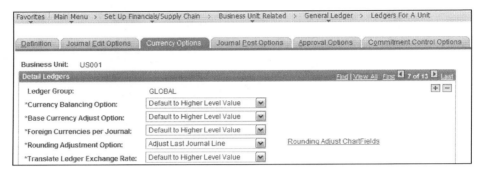

This tab specifies the default currency options for the given GL BU and the given ledger.

The next tab on the Ledgers for a Unit page is **Journal Post**. The next screenshot shows details of this tab:

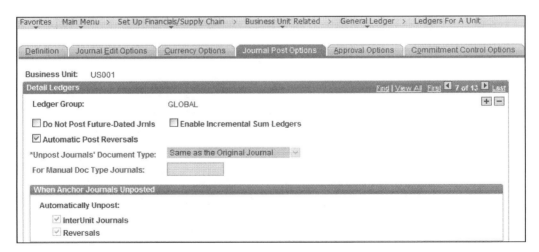

The configuration options on this tab control the posting and unposting of the journals for this ledger group:

- **Do not post Future-Dated Jrnls**: If this checkbox is selected, the system prevents a journal from posting if the journal date is greater than the journal process date. Journal process date is set during the GL BU set up.

- **Automatic Post Reversals**: Some transactions (known as accruals) generate reversing entries in the next accounting periods. If this checkbox is selected, the system automatically selects the future dated reversal entries to post when the original entries are posted.

The following screenshot shows the next **Approval Options** tab. The configuration options on this tab control the journal approval workflow process:

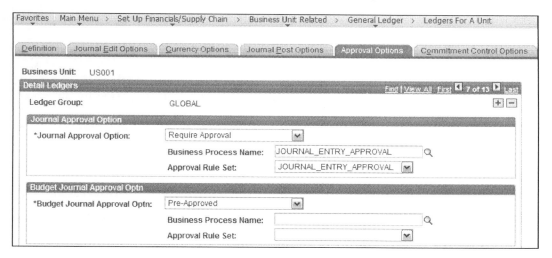

Based on organization's requirements, we can specify one of the following three options:

- **Default to Higher Level:** Use the approval option specified during the GL BU definition:

- **Pre-Approved:** If this value is selected, journal entries need not go through the approval workflow and the person entering them can post them from the journal entry page

- **Require Approval:** If this value is selected, journal entries need to be approved through workflow before they can be posted

PeopleSoft offers two different workflow methods – **Virtual Approver** and **Approval Framework**. If Virtual approver method is selected, the following fields become visible:

- **Business Process Name:** Specify the workflow business process that has been defined for journal approval
- **Approval Rule Set:** Specify the workflow approval set for the selected business process that has been defined for journal approval

If **Approval Framework** method of workflow is used, the previous two fields are not available.

> Building Virtual Framework workflow (including Business processes and Approval rule sets) requires strong technical skills. As a result, we will not discuss this area in our book.

In the example shown previously, the configuration will force regular journals to be approved, as per the business process rules defined. On the other hand, the budget journals are configured as **Pre-approved**, which means that they need not go through an approval process.

The last tab on the page is **Commitment Control Options**. It is shown in the following screenshot:

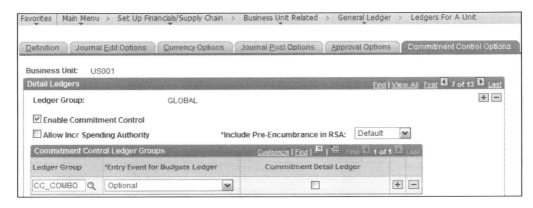

This tab enables the commitment control for the given ledger group. We'll discuss this in greater detail in *Chapter 9, PeopleSoft Commitment Control*.

Now that ledgers are ready to record Global Vehicles' accounting balances in multiple currencies, we'll turn our attention to the various sources that will generate the accounting entries and journals.

Implementation challenge

Perform necessary configurations, so that the PeopleSoft financial system can process journals created by the Billing module.

Solution

We'll need to configure (or review the PeopleSoft delivered configurations) for a journal source, accounting entry definition and journal generator templates for the Billing module.

Configuring journal sources

There are many possible sources which can create journal entries. PeopleSoft sub-modules such as Billing, Accounts Receivable, Accounts Payable, and more create their respective journals. In addition, we can create our own user defined journal sources to categorize manually entered journals. It is also possible that our PeopleSoft system receives journals created from external sources.

We can create as many journal sources as needed to tag the journal entries appropriately. For example, we can define a source 'EXT' for journals imported from an external system. There can be another source 'BI' for journals created by the Billing module.

A journal source is an important place where we can specify various processing options to handle journals from different sources differently. All the processing options we specified for a ledger are automatically inherited to journal sources. You'll see many of those options to be configured for a journal source as well. If an organization wishes to handle journals from a particular source in a different manner, we can do so by specifying that particular option at journal source level.

Note that configuration options specified at General Ledger business unit are overridden by those specified at the ledger. Options that we specify for a journal source override those specified for the ledger.

Follow this navigation to configure journal sources:

Set Up Financials/Supply Chain | Common Definitions | Journals | Source

The following screenshot shows the first tab **Definition** on the journal source page:

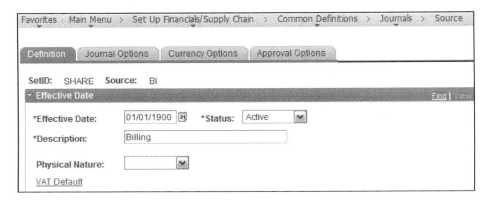

This tab is used to specify the name of the journal source and the effective date (the date from which it becomes active).

The next screenshot shows the next tab - **Journal Options**. Configuration options on this tab determine how various journal error options are handled for journals created from this source:

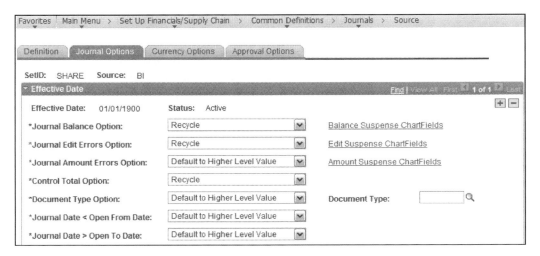

Can you recall where you have seen similar options? You are right if you answered Ledger Options For a Unit – Journal Edit Options!

If we select **Default to Higher Level Value**, the system looks at the configuration option specified for the ledger. If a particular error needs to be handled in a different way, specify the appropriate value here.

The following screenshot shows the next tab on the page - **Currency Options**:

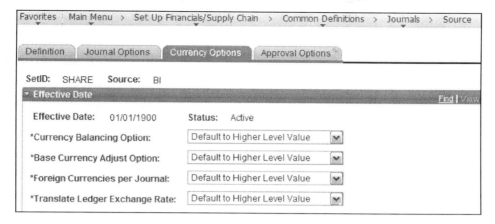

The fields on this tab are again exactly similar to those we saw for a ledger. Specify a value depending on whether it needs to be different from the ledger value or select **Default to Higher Level Value**.

The last tab on the page - **Approval Options** – is shown in the following screenshot:

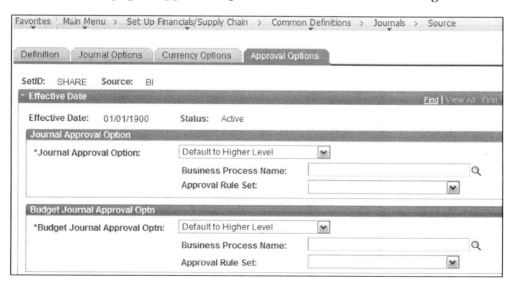

Specify how the journal approval workflow needs to be handled on this tab. If it need not be different from the configuration options for ledger, select **Default to Higher Level Value**.

Configuring accounting entry definitions

We previously discussed that that Journal Generator process picks up the accounting entries created by a sub-module and transforms them into journals. We also learnt that each sub-module has a dedicated database table to store the accounting entries. It is the Accounting Entry Definition that provides these details of appropriate tables and fields for a sub-module to Journal Generator.

Follow this navigation to configure accounting entry definitions:

General Ledger | Journals | Subsystem Journals | Accounting Entry Definition

The following screenshot shows the accounting entry definition page:

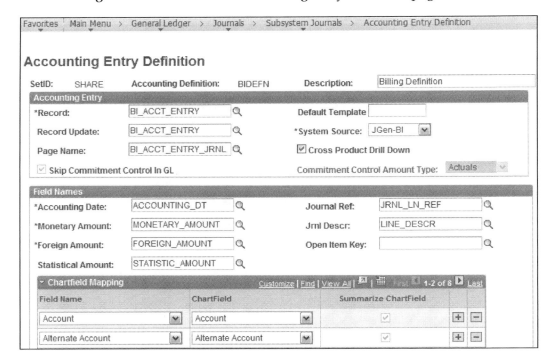

Let's familiarize ourselves with some of the important fields on this page:

PeopleSoft delivers accounting entry definitions for various sub-modules, with all the details already populated. In most of the cases, we can use the delivered definitions without making any changes.

- **Record:** This is the source table that stores the accounting entries for a particular sub-module. Journal Generator extracts the data from this table to create journals.

- **Record Update:** After Journal Generator creates the journals, it updates this table with the journal details. Usually it is the same table from which accounting entries are extracted.

- **System Source:** PeopleSoft has a pre-configured system source value for each sub-module. Ensure that the right source value corresponding to a module is selected.

- **Field Names:** In the data fields in this section, specify the appropriate field value from the source table specified previously. For example, in the **BI_ACCT_ENTRY** table, the **ACCOUNTING_DT** field is used to store the accounting date.

- **Chartfield Mapping - Chartfield:** These chartfields are used for summarizing accounting entries by the journal generator if **Summarize to All Chartfield Level** option is selected on the journal generator template page. If a chartfield is not listed here, it contains a blank value for the journals created from this accounting entry definition.

- **Chartfield Mapping - Summarize Chartfields**: If the **Summarize by Selected Chartfields** option is selected on the journal Generator template page and this checkbox is selected for a chartfield, it is summarized during journal creation by the Journal Generator.

We'll discuss chartfield summarization shortly in the journal generator template section.

Now, in addition to the PeopleSoft sub-modules, sometimes journals need to be created from the accounting entries from external non-PeopleSoft systems. For such a scenario, PeopleSoft offers an accounting entry definition called **GENERIC**.

The following screenshot shows the details of GENERIC accounting entry definition:

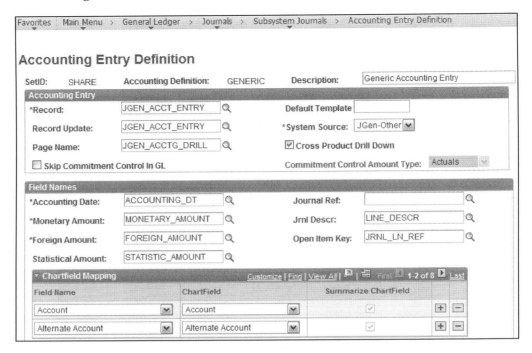

As you can see, it uses a table **JGEN_ACCT_ENTRY** to read the accounting entries from. Thus, we need to ensure that these external accounting entries are stored into this table first. Also, the value for **System Source** field must be **JGen-Other**.

It's up to us to use any of the following three options to create journals from non-PeopleSoft systems:

1. Load accounting entries into JGEN_ACCT_ENTRY table and use the 'GENERIC' definition (if the mapping between the table fields and incoming data elements is simple).

2. If needed, modify the 'GENERIC' definition by using a different table or view other than JGEN_ACCT_ENTRY (if we need to use a different table to hold the incoming accounting entry details).

3. Create a new definition and manually specify necessary fields (if organization requirements dictate that GENERIC definition cannot be used and a new dedicated definition must be used).

Configuring journal templates

Now we come to the last important step in the configuration of ledgers and journals. In order to create the journals for the Billing module, we configured a Billing journal source and Billing accounting entry definition. Thus, now the system knows where to look for the Billing accounting entries.

Typically, accounting entries created by a sub-module belong to various types. For example, in case of Billing, they can be broadly categorized as regular billing entries (when customer invoices are created) and accrual billing entries (when revenue is recognized, but the customer invoice is not created).

In case of Accounts Receivable, accounting entries can be categorized as billing entries (based on customer invoices), payment entries (when customer payment is received), maintenance entries (when an outstanding invoice is written off, among other things) and so on.

We set Journal Templates for each of such various transaction types. This template determines how the Journal Generator summarizes the accounting entries to create journals. It also controls how the reversing journal entries are created.

Follow this navigation to configure journal generator templates:

General Ledger | Journals | Subsystem Journals | Journal generator Templates

The following screenshot shows the **Defaults** tab of journal generator template page:

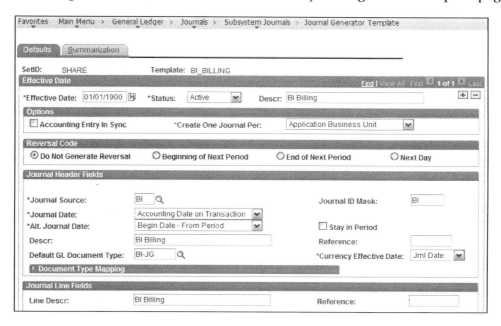

The **Defaults** tab contains several options that need to be configured as follows:

- **Accounting Entry In Sync:** Recall the **Keep Ledgers in Sync** checkbox on the Ledger Group configuration page. Checking this flag ensures that an accounting entry posted to the primary ledger in a ledger group is also simultaneously posted to other secondary ledgers as well. For example, when an accounting entry is posted to the GLOBALUSD ledger, PeopleSoft also posts this entry to GLOBALGBP and GLOBALEUR ledgers simultaneously.

- **Create One Journal For:** This field controls how accounting entries are aggregated on the journals. Each line in the accounting entry in PeopleSoft has an application business unit as well as a General Ledger business unit. There may be multiple lines in an entry and it is possible that they may have different business units. Available options for the field are **Application Business Unit** (system creates a different journal for each subsystem business unit value present in accounting entry) and **General Ledger Business Unit** (system creates a different journal for each General Ledger business unit value present in accounting entry).

- **Reversal Code:** In the case of some transactions (such as billing accrual), the accounting entries need to be reversed. This option controls if reversal entries should be created, and if so, when:
  - **Do Not Generate Reversal:** Journal Generator does not create the reversal entry, but it marks the journals with the reversal code
  - **Beginning of Next Period:** Creates a reversing entry dated the first business day of the next accounting period
  - **End of Next Period:** Creates a reversing entry dated the last business day of the next accounting period
  - **Next Day:** Creates a reversing entry dated the next business day

- **Journal ID Mask**: A unique identifier is used to distinguish journals belonging to different transaction types we discussed previously. For example, we can denote all journals for regular billing to have journals IDs starting with BIR, while the journals for billing accruals journal IDs can start with BIA. System automatically uses this prefix for the journal IDs.

Thus a journal with ID BIA45276 can be identified as a billing accrual journal, while a journal with ID BIR27675 can be identified as a regular billing journal.

Note that it is not mandatory to have different journal ID masks for different transaction types.

The following screenshot displays the **Summarization** tab of the page. This tab controls how the accounting entries are summarized on the journals:

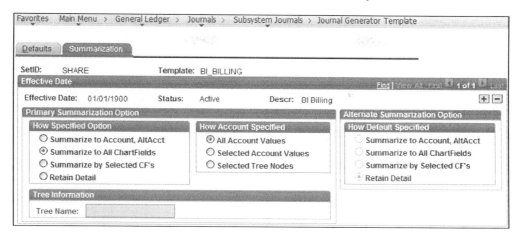

Again here we have the option to specify two different sets of summarization rules for two groups of accounts.

PeopleSoft offers the following summarization options:

- **Summarize to Account, AltAcct:** This means that accounting entries are summarized by the Account and Alternate Account (if used) in the journal, while all other chartfields are left blank

- **Summarize to All ChartFields:** This option summarizes the accounting entries to unique combinations of all the chartfields on the Accounting Entry Definition page

- **Summarize by Selected CF's:** This option summarizes the accounting entries to unique combinations of only those chartfields on the Accounting Entry Definition page that have the **Summarize ChartField** check box selected

You would be able to recall the part of the Accounting Entry Definition page in the following screenshot. This is where we specify which chartfield needs to be used for summarization:

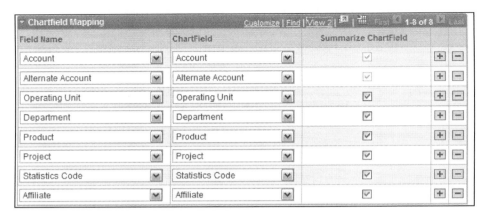

Retain Detail: This option ensures that all accounting entries are distributed to the journal without any summarization and retain all chartfield value details.

If the organization needs to have a single summarization rule for all the accounts, select the option **All Account Values** and then select the appropriate **Primary Summarization** option.

If two different summarization rules are needed for two groups of accounts, carefully analyze how these account groups are organized. For the primary group of accounts, specify their values by either the **Selected Account Values** or **Selected Tree Nodes** options and then select the appropriate **Primary Summarization Option**. For all the remaining account values, specify the appropriate summarization option under **Alternate Summarization Option**.

Example: Accounting entries containing accounts 100001, 100002, and 100003 should be summarized to all chartfields, while all other entries should retain their entire chartfield details. In this case, configuration as shown in the following screenshot, will need to be done:

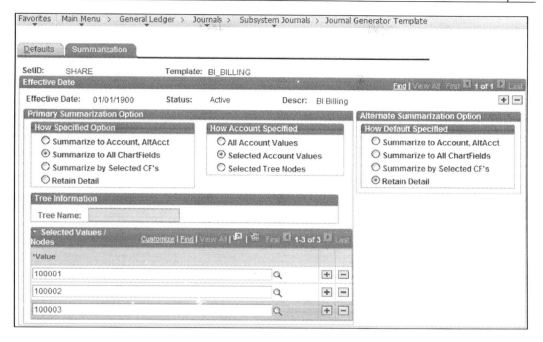

Configuring banks

Every organization needs relationships with banks to conduct its business transactions. Just like any bank account that you hold—where you receive cash and make payments—organizations too need to have bank accounts. Banks are important for PeopleSoft Financial applications to receive as well as disburse cash for various modules such as Accounts Receivable, Accounts Payable, and Treasury applications. In this section, we'll discuss the following important and mandatory configuration options that need to be in place for business processing:

- Configuring bank ID qualifier
- Configuring bank
- Configuring bank branch
- Configuring external accounts
- Configuring payment forms

Configuring bank ID qualifiers

Bank ID qualifiers are country pre-defined specific numerical values. This value drives the bank information that needs to be defined for a bank depending on the country it belongs to.

Follow this navigation to configure bank ID qualifiers:

Banking | Banks and Branches | Bank ID Qualifiers

The following screenshot shows the **Bank ID Qualifiers** page:

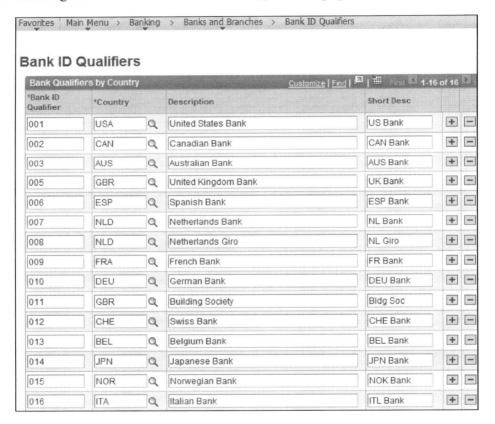

 You should not modify the delivered Bank ID Qualifiers on this page.

Implementation challenge

Global Vehicles Inc. has a banking relationship with 'US Bank' and holds a checking account at its New York branch. This account needs to be used to receive customer payments and issue checks to vendors. Perform the necessary configurations.

Solution

We will need to configure a bank, branch, and an external account. The account needs to be set up for the branch while the branch needs to be defined for the bank.

Configuring banks

As banks can be shared by multiple business units, they are set up by SetIDs.

Follow this navigation to configure a bank:

Banking | Banks and Branches | Bank Information

The next screenshot shows the Bank Information page:

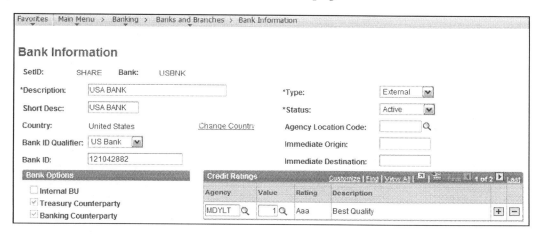

Let's understand some of the important fields on this page:

- **Type:** We can define a bank belonging to following four categories – **External** (a banking organization that is outside the organization), **Internal** (an entity such as central treasury group that is part of the implementing organization), **Netting** (used for bilateral netting between Accounts Receivable and Accounts Payable transactions), and **Origin** (an intermediate entity that holds the organization's cash before being credited to bank account).

- **Bank ID Qualifier**: As we saw earlier, bank ID qualifiers are defined for certain counties. Select the appropriate qualifier for the country of the bank.

- **Bank ID**: Each bank has a unique code that identifies it. This is used to route the electronic transactions such as EFT and ACH. The bank with which our organization needs to do business, can supply this bank ID.

Configuring bank branches

We can define as many branches for a bank as required. Let's define the New York branch for our bank.

Follow this navigation to set up a bank branch:

Banking | Banks and Branches | Bank Branch Information

The following screenshot shows the Bank Branch Information page:

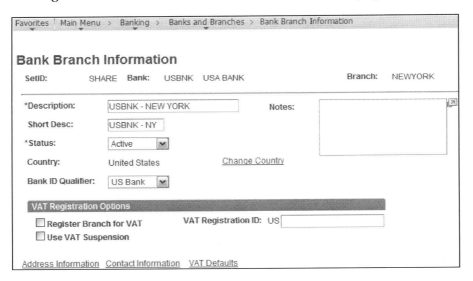

To enter the address details for this branch, click the **Address Information** hyperlink. The system opens the Address Information secondary page. The next screenshot shows this page:

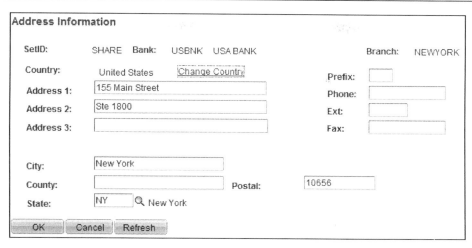

To enter the contact person details for this branch, click the **Contact Information** hyperlink on the **Bank Branch Information** page. This opens the Contact Information secondary page as shown in the next screenshot:

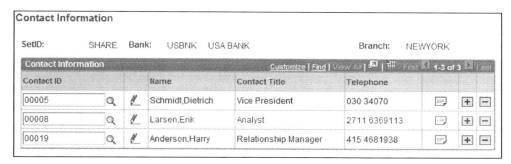

Add or remove any bank contact person details as needed by clicking + or – button.

To define the contact information, follow this navigation:

Banking | Banks and Branches | Contact Information

The following screenshot shows the Contact Information page, where relevant details of the contact person can be entered:

Configuring external bank accounts

As we saw earlier, an external bank means a physical bank with which the organization carries out its business. For example, if the organization has banking relationships with HSBC or Citibank, these qualify to be called as **external banks**. Bank accounts that an organization holds in these banks are in turn called **external accounts**.

Follow this navigation to configure external bank accounts:

Banking | Banks and Branches | External Accounts

The next screenshot shows the first tab on the **External Accounts** page:

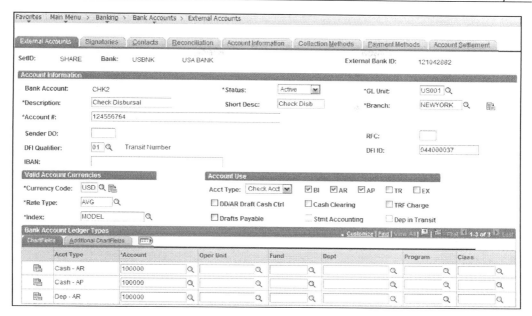

Let's familiarize ourselves with the important fields on this page:

- **Account #:** Enter the bank account number for this external account.

- **DFI Qualifier:** DFI stands for 'Depository Financial Institution', which is the bank where this account exists. We can choose to use any of the identification types for this bank (such as Transit Number, SWIFT ID and so on.) depending upon the information provided by the bank.

- **DFI ID:** Enter the unique ID for the bank.

- **BI, AR, AP, TR, EX**: These checkboxes identify the module (Billing, Receivable, Payable, Treasury, and Expenses) for which this account is being used. As we need this account for Receivable and Payable modules, let's check their appropriate checkboxes. When the **AR** checkbox is selected, the **Billing** checkbox is also automatically selected.

  Depending on the selected module, various account types get enabled or disabled in the chartfields grid at the bottom of the page.

- **DD/AR Draft Cash Ctrl**: In the Receivables module, if we wish to use the 'Draft' payment method and want to use a control account before actually receiving customer payments, we need to select this checkbox (applicable only if Billing or AR checkboxes are selected).

- **Cash Clearing:** If an organization uses cash control accounting (for AP, AR, or TR modules), this flag needs to be selected.

- **Stmt Accounting:** This flag enables the chartfields for statement accounting. If we wish to install Treasury applications and it's their related bank statement accounting functionality, we can specify the chartfields for bank fees and interest amounts.

- **Drafts Payable:** If we use the 'Drafts' payment method in the Payable module, select this checkbox.

- **Chartfields**: For the selected modules, we need to specify the actual accounts for cash accounts (such as Cash-AR and Cash-AP). The chartfield values specified here are ultimately used by the system while creating accounting entries.

For example, when a check payment is issued to a vendor, the system creates an accounting entry as follows:

- Debit Payables account
- Credit Cash account

While the payables account is extracted from the voucher being paid, the cash account is retrieved from Cash-AP chartfields specified in this tab.

The following screenshot shows the next tab on this page — **Signatories**:

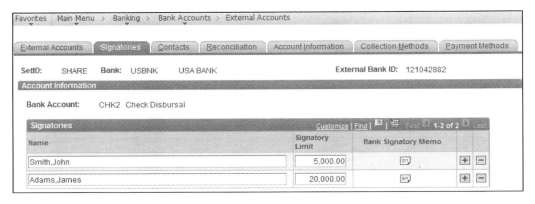

The **Signatories** tab stores the signatory person and the maximum monetary amount that he/she can approve. Note that this information is only for informational purposes and does not affect any processing.

Now let's consider the next important tab on the External Accounts page — **Reconciliation**. The following screenshot shows the details of **Reconciliation** tab:

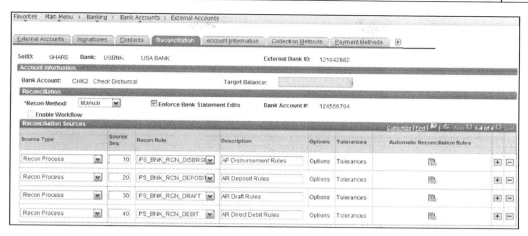

This tab is used to set up the rules for reconciling the bank statement against the cash account positions in Treasury applications. As these are not in the scope of this book, we'll not get into the details. Suffice it to say that PeopleSoft offers three reconciliation methods: **Manual**, **Semi manual**, and **Automatic**.

The following screenshot shows **Account Information** tab on the page. This tab contains various configuration options used by Receivable and Payable modules:

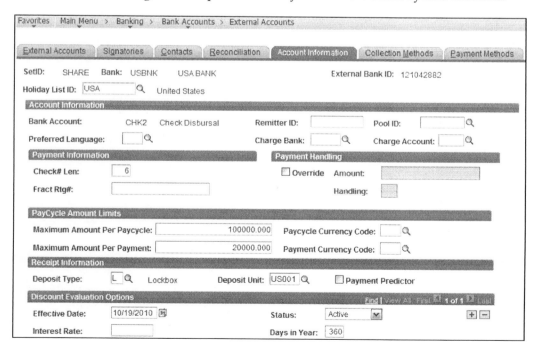

We'll concentrate on some of the important fields on this page:

- **Remitter ID**: Although not mandatory, this field stores the remitter ID that the bank assigns to this bank account. When the EFT (Electronic Fund Transfer) method is used, the system creates EFT files with payment information and transmits to another bank. The receiving bank uses this remitter ID.

- **Check# Len**: We can specify the maximum length of check numbers (up to 10 digits) that the Payable system issues.

- **Maximum Amount Per Paycycle, Maximum Amount Per Payment**: These fields are used by bank replacement feature of pay cycles in Payable module. When the limits specified here are exceeded, pay cycle uses an alternate bank to issue remainder amount above the specified limit.

- **Deposit Type, Deposit Unit**: Deposit types are configured in the Receivable module to identify categories of funds received in bank account. Deposit Unit refers to the Receivable business unit that is responsible for recording the received funds.

- **Payment Predictor**: This checkbox determines how the customer payments received in this bank account are handled by the Receivable module. If checked, these payments are processed by a batch process named 'Payment Predictor', which matches them to the outstanding customer invoices. We'll see this feature in the Accounts Receivable chapter.

The following screenshot shows **Collection Methods** tab on the page. This tab specifies various options used to receive customer payments in this bank account. Thus, these options are more relevant for the Accounts Receivable module:

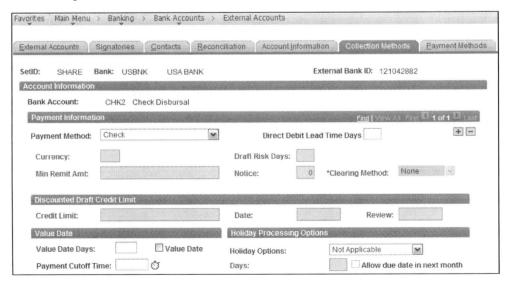

The following screenshot shows the **Payment Methods** tab on the page. This tab specifies various options used to disburse (pay) payments to external entities such as vendors or organization's employees through this bank account. Thus, this tab is more relevant for Accounts Payable module:

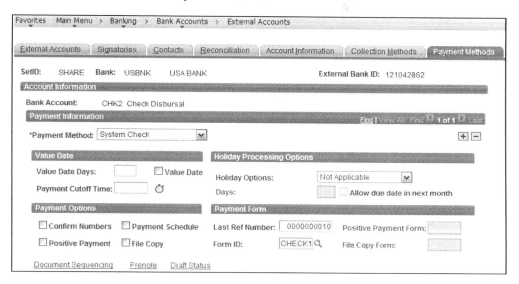

- **Payment Method:** PeopleSoft offers the following payment methods to issue payments: Automated Clearing House, Direct Debit, Draft-Customer EFT, Draft-Customer Initiated, Draft-Vendor Initiated, Electronic Funds Transfer, Giro-EFT, Giro-Manual, Letter of Credit, Manual Check, System Check and Wire Transfer.

- **Last Ref Number:** When PeopleSoft creates a payment, it assigns a unique number (known as Reference Number) to it. For example, in this case, we have specified that payments from this bank account will be issued as Checks. Now whenever the system creates a check, it assigns a check number to it. This number is always 1 greater than the value in this field.

  As you can see, when the system creates a check next time, it will be numbered 0000000011. On the other hand, if we wish to force the system to issue checks starting from 0000000050, simply change the value in this field to 0000000049.

- **Form ID**: There can be various layouts available for EFT, Check payments and Wire Transfers, depending upon the organization's requirements. For example, in case of check payments, Global Vehicles may have three or four different check layouts it uses with different banks. This field is used to specify the appropriate layout for issuing the payments. PeopleSoft delivers a few sample payment layouts for Check, EFT, and Wire transfers. We can either use them (with or without modifications) or create our own layouts.

Understanding User Preferences

So far we have seen some of the most important cross-module concepts and configurations, which serve as the foundation of PeopleSoft Financial applications. Another important system feature that controls how the system features are controlled for each individual system user is related to setting up user preferences. Technically speaking, this is more of a personalization feature that will drive which users get to do what as far as various PeopleSoft modules are concerned. Nonetheless, this is a crucial task that needs to be performed.

An important prerequisite for doing this task is of course creating user IDs in the first place. However, we'll discuss that in the PeopleSoft Security chapter.

Follow this navigation to access the User Preferences page:

Set Up Financials/Supply Chain | Common Definitions | User Preferences | Define User Preferences

The following screenshot shows the main User Preferences page. It contains hyperlinks to module specific user preference pages under Product Preference section. Hyperlinks for common user preferences are grouped under the General Preference section;

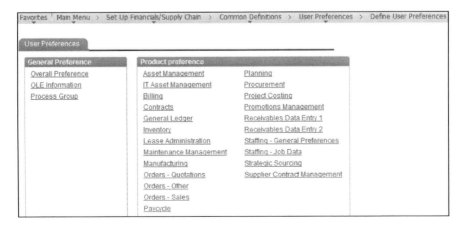

As you can see, this page allows us to define user preferences for various PeopleSoft modules as well as certain specific features such as Pay cycle. We'll quickly go through the settings for the financial modules and the cross-module preference options.

Defining Overall Preferences

Click the **Overall Preferences** hyperlink to set up cross-module preferences. The following screenshot shows the **Overall Preferences** tab. This tab specifies the default Business Unit, SetID, and the Localization Country for the given user ID:

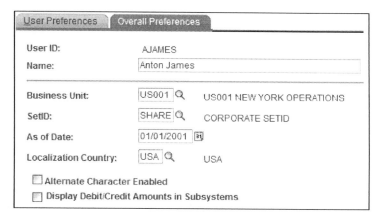

As you can see from the screenshot, for the user Anton James, the system will always use **US001** as the **Business Unit** and **SHARE** as the **SetID** whenever he accesses a PeopleSoft page to enter a new transaction or retrieve data from the database. Of course, the user can always change this value, but defaulting simplifies the job to a large extent.

Defining Process Group preferences

Click the **Process Group** hyperlink on the main User Preferences page.

The following screenshot shows the **Process Group** tab. This tab contains important configuration options for Accounts Payable and Receivable module features that can be selectively enabled for specific users:

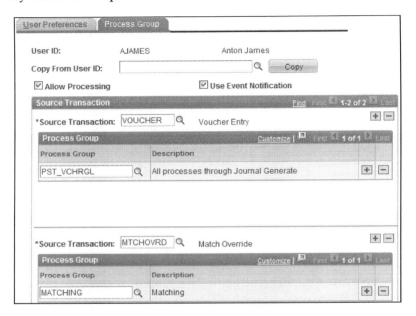

Source Transaction indicates a specific system feature from the Receivable or Payable module. PeopleSoft allows us to select from a group of 25 such system features. The screenshot shows two sample source transactions: **VOUCHER** (Voucher entry) and **ARPAYWS** (AR Payment Worksheet).

VOUCHER controls the processing options for the voucher entry function in Payable, while **ARPAYWS** controls the actions that a user can perform for Payment worksheets in the Receivable module.

In other words, we have just allowed Anton to use these two system features, while preventing him from using the remaining 23.

The **Process Group** indicates what level of privileges is granted to a user for a selected source transaction.

For example, PeopleSoft offers us the following options (Process Groups) as far as payment worksheets are concerned: **ARACTIONA** (Do not post), **ARACTIONL** (Batch standard), **ARACTIONN** (Batch priority), **ARPOST** (Post now), **ARPOSTGL** (Post now through to GL). To perform his job, Anton needs to be able to post the payment worksheets to GL. Thus, we will select the value **ARPOSTGL** in the Process Group field.

Allow Processing flag controls if on-demand processing is enabled for this user. PeopleSoft allows system users to run certain batch processes from the transaction screens. For example, a user can execute batch processes such as Voucher Post, Journal Generator, and so on. from the voucher entry page itself. He/She need not navigate to a different page just to run that particular process. This is known as on-demand processing.

Defining Billing User Preferences

Click the **Billing** hyperlink on the main User Preferences page.

The following screenshot shows the **Billing** tab.

Billing user preferences primarily control which batch processes are executed (or skipped) when they are triggered from a button on the Billing pages. Note that this doesn't apply if the batch processes are executed from their dedicated run control pages.

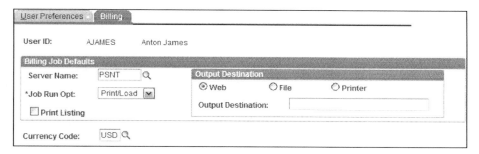

Server Name specifies the default server where the Billing processes will be executed.

Job Run Opt specifies if certain Billing processes are excluded from being executed. Selecting the 'Print/Load' option means the system runs all the processes in the multi-process job. Selecting the 'No Load' option skips the following processes: Currency Conversion, Load AR, Pre-load, Load GL, Commitment Control, and Standard Form 1080 and 1081 processes. We'll discuss these processes in *Chapter 3, PeopleSoft Billing Module*.

Defining General Ledger User Preferences

Click the **General Ledger** hyperlink on the main User Preferences page.

The next screenshot shows the **General Ledger** tab:

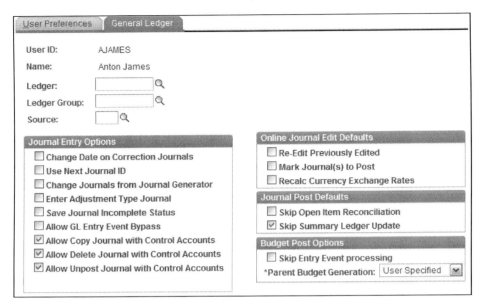

Use Next Journal ID field controls if this user can manually enter a journal ID when he/she enters a new journal. If this checkbox is selected, while creating a new journal, the system automatically disables the journal ID field and assigns the next number to the new journal. This is an important option to enforce the system generated numbering for GL users.

If the **Change Journals from Journal Generator** checkbox is selected, the user can modify the chartfields and amounts for the journals created by Journal Generator process. In PeopleSoft GL, journals can be either manually entered or created automatically by Journal Generator process. Manual journals can always be modified by system users. However limiting the capability to modify Journal Generator journals to only a select few users greatly improves the controls.

Defining Payables User Preferences

Click the **Procurement | Payables** hyperlink on the main User Preferences page.

The following screenshot shows the **Payable Online Vouchering** secondary page:

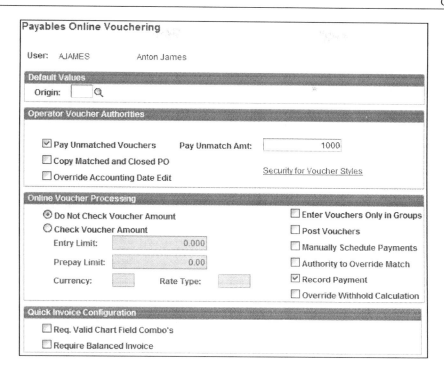

- **Pay Unmatched Vouchers and Pay Unmatch Amt**: Typically when a voucher (vendor invoice) needs to be paid, it is first matched with a valid purchase order. This ensures that vendor payment is for a genuine purchase we made. If the system is configured accordingly, it does not pay a voucher unless it is matched.

  However selecting the Pay Unmatched Vouchers checkbox allows a user to bypass the matching requirement and pay a voucher even if it is not matched. The Pay Unmatch Amt field specifies the maximum amount that can be paid without matching. As you can imagine, this is a very critical control mechanism and this privilege should be given (if at all) to only a few users.

- **Check Voucher Amount**: If a user is responsible for entering vouchers in the Accounts Payable module, a limit can be placed on the maximum amount of voucher that he/she can enter. To do so, select the Check Voucher Amount button and enter the maximum permissible amount in the Entry Limit field along with the Currency.

- **Post Vouchers**: Voucher amounts do not become part of total outstanding vendor liability until they are 'posted'. This field controls if a user can post an approved voucher.

- **Authority to Override Match**: As mentioned earlier, matching process validates if a voucher is valid by checking it against a purchase order. If an error is found, the process marks the voucher as an exception (in other words, 'invalid'). Selecting this checkbox allows a user to override it and force a voucher to skip the matching process.

Defining Receivables User Preferences

Click the **Receivables Data Entry 1** hyperlink on the main User Preferences page.

The following screenshot shows the **Receivables Data Entry 1** tab:

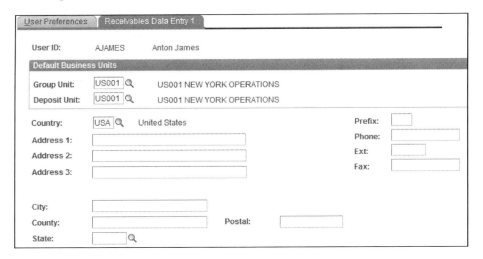

- **Group Unit**: In Accounts Receivable parlance, Group Unit refers to the business unit that tracks outstanding customer invoices (known as 'items').
- **Deposit Unit**: In Accounts Receivable terms, Deposit Unit refers to the business unit that receives customer payments.

The business unit value used in these fields is used as the default value by the system whenever the user accesses the Receivable pages. The user can of course override these default values. However this greatly reduces the data entry efforts.

Defining Receivables Write-off and Discount User Preferences

Click the **Receivables Data Entry 2** hyperlink on the main User Preferences page.

The following screenshot shows the **Receivables Data Entry 2** tab. This tab contains user preference options for the user to perform two important functions: Payment worksheets and Maintenance worksheets:

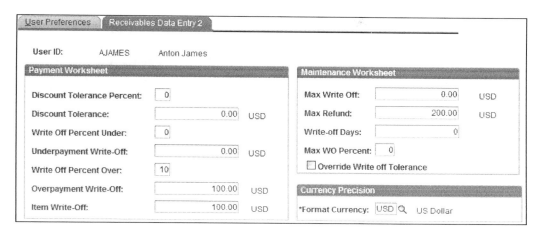

Payment worksheets are used to apply customer payment to its outstanding invoices. Maintenance worksheets are used to write off customer invoice amounts (partially or completely) and issue refunds to customers. For example, there may be an outstanding invoice for USD 1000. However it turns out that this customer may not (or will not) pay this amount (due to a variety of reasons). If he/she can pay only a part (say USD 700), we need to write off the remaining USD 300 (30% of the invoice amount). On the other hand, if the customer cannot pay anything, we will need to write off the entire amount of USD 1000.

Options under the **Payment Worksheet** section:

- **Discount Tolerance Percent, Discount Tolerance**: These fields determine the upper limit of discount that can be given to a customer (known as 'unearned discount').

- **Write Off Percent Under, Underpayment Write-Off**: When a customer pays less than the invoice amount, it is known as 'underpayment'. These fields determine the upper limit for the underpayment that can be written off.

- **Write Off Percent Over, Overpayment Write-Off**: When a customer pays more than the invoice amount, it is known as 'overpayment'. The additional amount received can be written off rather than returning it to the customer. These fields determine the upper limit for the overpayment that can be written off.

- **Item Write-Off**: This field determines the maximum amount that a user can write off on a payment worksheet.

Options under the **Maintenance Worksheet** section:

- **Max Write Off, Max WO Percent**: These fields determine the maximum amount that a user can write off using a maintenance worksheet.

- **Max Refund**: This field specifies the maximum amount that a user can refund to a customer.

- **Write-Off Days**: This field determines the minimum age of an invoice before it can be written off.

- **Override Write off Tolerance**: This powerful option enables a user to override all write off limits (specified for Business Unit, Customer and so on). Of course, the maximum write-off limits placed for the user still apply.

Understanding Setup Manager

Configuring PeopleSoft Financial applications from scratch is certainly no easy task. A typical implementation involving multiple modules typically involves hundreds of configuration activities that need to be performed in a specific sequence. In this chapter so far, we have covered some of the critical configuration activities, but discussing each of them is quite impractical. So the million dollar question is—How do we ensure that we complete all the necessary setup activities in the right order?

Let's not worry…PeopleSoft has just the right tool to help us with exactly this. It is known as the Setup Manager.

Setup Manager lists all the tasks required for implementing a product (module) in the right sequence. In addition, it shows the navigation path to the page where required configuration needs to be done. A direct link is provided so that the user can reach the appropriate page. We'll quickly see how to use it.

Implementation challenge

Configure the PeopleSoft Billing module using Setup Manager.

 Follow the navigation **PeopleTools** | **Setup Manager** | **Manage Implementation Projects**.

Follow this navigation to access Setup Manager:

PeopleTools | Setup Manager | Manage Implementation Projects

The following screenshot shows the Manage Implementation Projects page:

As you can see, we can create the implementation project either by a product (such as Billing, Accounts Receivable, and so on) or a Business Process (such as Process customer payments, Receive goods, and so on).

For our business requirement, as we need to configure the Billing module, we'll create the implementation project by Product.

Click the **Products** button. As shown in the following screenshot, the system opens a page listing all the PeopleSoft modules for which the organization holds a license:

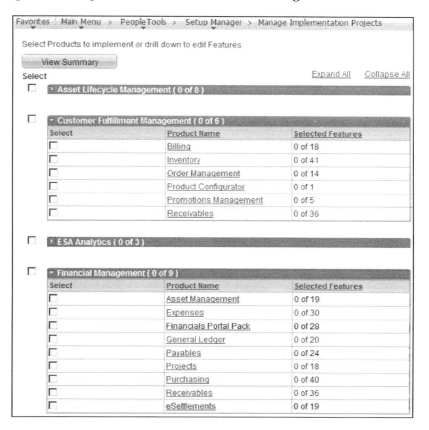

Check the **Select** checkbox next to the required module and click the **View Summary** button at the bottom of the page.

The system opens a new page with two tabs. The following screenshot shows the **Product Summary** tab:

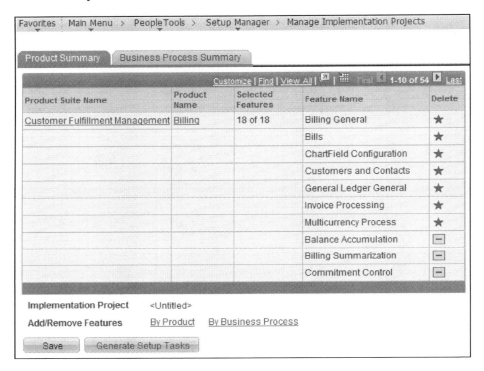

The page shows all the features offered by PeopleSoft in selected product. As part of the implementation, one of the critical tasks is to determine which of these features are really needed for the implementing organization.

Let's assume that for our hypothetical Billing module implementation, we do not need the Balance Accumulation and Billing Summarization features. Remove these features from the list by clicking the '-' button next to them.

 Features marked with a star are mandatory and cannot be removed.

Click **Save** at the bottom of the page. The system opens a new page, which is shown in the following screenshot:

Enter the **Project Name** and Description and click **OK**. As shown in the next screenshot, the system opens a page showing the implementation project with given name:

Click the **Generate Setup Tasks** button in this page to automatically create the list of configuration tasks. The following screenshot shows the process status page:

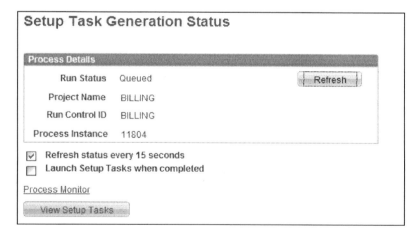

This triggers a batch process in the background with its **Run Status** as **Queued**. When the process is completed, the run status automatically changes to **Success**.

Click the **View Setup Tasks** button to see the configuration activities. The following screenshot shows the **Manage Setup Tasks** page that opens:

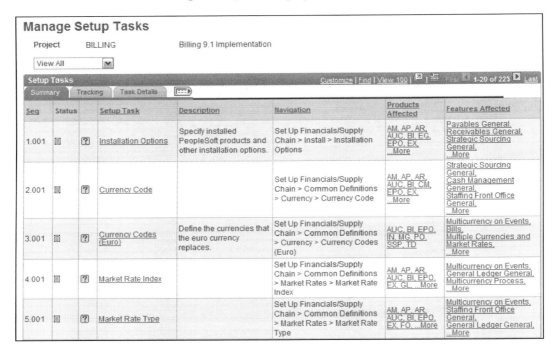

This page lists out all the necessary configuration activities in the appropriate sequence.

The Status field shows the current status for the setup task. Place the cursor over the icon to see the status: **Not started, In progress,** or **Complete**.

Setup Task: Clicking the hyperlink transfers the control to the appropriate page in order to perform the required setup activity.

Click the **Tracking** tab to record progress of setup activities. The following screenshot shows the details of Tracking tab:

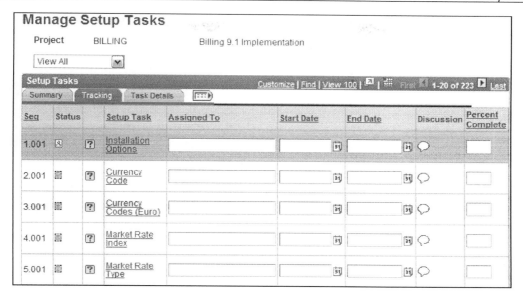

- **Assigned To**: This is a free from text field, where details of person (or persons) responsible for this task can be entered. Note that this doesn't affect who actually performs a particular task.

- **Percent Complete**: Again this field needs to be updated manually and is entirely informational. When you enter 100% in this field, the task status changes to **Complete**.

Click the **Task Details** tab. The following screenshot shows the details of Task Details tab:

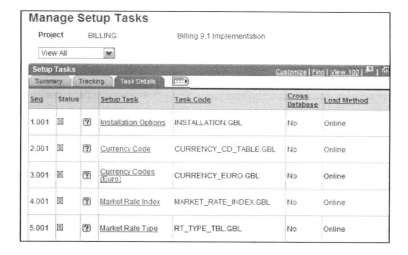

- **Cross Database**: This field indicates if a configuration option affects multiple modules.

- **Load Method**: Indicates how configuration values can be entered into PeopleSoft system. Available options are: Component Interface, ETL, Other, and Online.

Let's look at a different set of tasks. The following screenshot shows a few setup tasks for the Billing module:

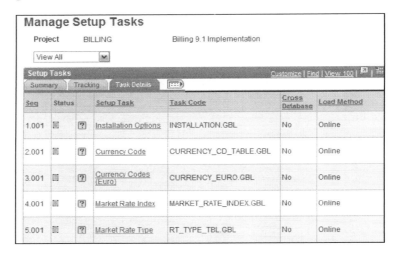

As you can see, configuring **Adjustment Type** and **Book Code** can be done by Online method alone. On the other hand, configuration for other tasks can be done either by Component Interface or Online method.

Let's understand these different configuration methods:

- **Online**: Required configuration values can be entered manually on the online pages. For example, to configure Adjustment Type, the user can navigate to the appropriate page and enter as many adjustment type values as required.

- **Component Interface**: When the volume of configuration values is quite high, this is the preferred method. PeopleSoft offers a utility called Excel to Component Interface. It essentially automates the data entry into PeopleSoft setup pages by reading data from pre-defined Microsoft Excel templates. For example, if there are 2000 Account values to be configured, it is much easier to put the data such as Account number, Description and so on, into the Excel template. The template contains all the field values that need to be entered on the PeopleSoft page. The Excel to Component Interface utility then reads these values from the template, validates them, and loads them one row after the other into the PeopleSoft component.

- **Other**: You can write a customized program to load configuration values from an external source.

So, this is what we'll need to do as we go along the configuration of a PeopleSoft module:

- Create an implementation project for a specific module. It'll show all the required configuration activities.

- In the Tracking tab, assign each task to the concerned person (it may be yourself!) along with the planned start and end dates (although it is not mandatory).

- Click the hyperlink for each task so that the system opens the required page and performs necessary system setups.

- Once a task is completed, enter 100% as percentage completed, so that task status changes to Complete.

Summary

With this we come to the end of the first chapter where we learned some critical concepts about PeopleSoft Financial applications. We also saw some of the important cross-module configuration activities needed for a working financial system. Here is what we learned.

A Chart of Accounts is the foundation of PeopleSoft financial applications. It includes various attributes that need to be recorded for each accounting transaction. These attributes are called chartfields. We can perform Standard or Advanced configuration to modify delivered chartfields according to our needs. It is always advisable to use standard configuration instead of advanced configuration.

Business Unit is an organizational unit that independently maintains its account balances. Business Units of an organization can be organized on the basis of geography, line of business or any other parameter that we choose. All the financial transaction data such as invoices, journals, and purchase orders are segregated by Business Unit. A SetID is a collection of master data elements such as vendors, customers, banks, and so on. It determines which setup values can be accessed by a Business Unit. SetIDs allow master data to be shared by multiple BUs.

A ledger is the central piece in PeopleSoft financial applications. An organization's account balances are stored in the ledger. Journals consolidate the accounting entries created by various PeopleSoft modules and post them to ledgers. A batch process known as Journal Generator automates the journal creation process. After these journals are created, the Journal Edit batch process validates them. Another batch process - Journal Post - posts valid journals to the ledger, thus completing the journal processing.

Banks are used by an organization to receive customer payments as well as make payments to its vendors. Each bank can have as many branches as needed. Each branch can have multiple bank accounts associated with it.

Configuring a PeopleSoft module involves a large number of tasks that need to be completed in the right order. PeopleSoft delivers a tool called Setup Manager to help in the setup activities. It lists tasks necessary to implement a module in the appropriate sequence. It also provides navigation paths and hyperlinks to the PeopleSoft pages where setups need to be done.

2
PeopleSoft Security

Security design is a critical part—of any implementation of PeopleSoft Financial application. By its very nature, a financial system needs robust security mechanisms to enforce appropriate controls on who can access the system and which features.

PeopleSoft security consists of multiple aspects, such as User security, Row level security, Query security, Network security, Database security, Object security, and Field level security. In keeping up with the philosophy of this book, we'll concentrate on security aspects that are typically configured by a Business Analyst or a Functional SME, that is, User-and Row-level security. Remaining aspects of security involve significant technical knowledge of PeopleSoft's application development environment (known as Application Designer) and security technologies, such as SSL.

In this chapter, we'll discuss user security components such as User Profiles, Roles, and Permission Lists. We'll also discuss how to enable and configure Row level security.

Understanding user security

Before we get into discussing the PeopleSoft security, let's spend some time trying to set the context for user security.

Whenever we think of a complex system like PeopleSoft Financial applications with potentially hundreds of users, the following are but a few questions that face us:

- Should a user working in billing group have access to transactions, such as vouchers and payments, in Accounts Payable?

- Should a user who is a part of North America business unit have access to the data belonging to the Europe business unit?

- Should a user whose job involves entering vouchers be able to approve and pay them as well?
- Should a data entry clerk be able to view departmental budgets for the organization?

These questions barely scratch the surface of the complex security considerations of an organization. Of course, there is no right or wrong answer for such questions, as every organization has its own unique security policies.

What is more important is the fact that we need a mechanism that can segregate the access to system features. We need to enforce appropriate controls to ensure users can access only the features they need.

Implementation challenge

Global Vehicles' Accounts Payable department has three different types of users – Mary, who is the AP manager; Amy, who is the AP Supervisor; and Anton, who is the AP Clerk. These three types of users need to have the following access to PeopleSoft features:

User type	Access to feature	Description
AP Clerk	Voucher entry	A clerk should be able to access system pages to enter vouchers from various vendors.
AP Supervisor	Voucher entry Voucher approval Voucher posting	A supervisor also needs to have access to enter vouchers. He/she should review and approve each voucher entered by the clerk. Also, the supervisor should be able to execute the Voucher Post process that creates accounting entries for vouchers.
AP Manager	Pay cycle Voucher approval	An AP manager should be the only one who can execute the Pay Cycle (a process that prints checks to issue payments to vendors). Manager (in addition to the Supervisor) should also have the authority to approve vouchers.

Note that this is an extremely simplified scenario that does not really include all the required features in Accounts Payable.

Solution

We will design a security matrix that uses distinct security roles. We'll configure permission lists, roles, and user profiles to limit user access to required system features.

PeopleSoft security matrix is a three-level structure consisting of Permission lists (at the bottom), Roles (in the middle) and User profiles (at the top). The following illustration shows how it is structured:

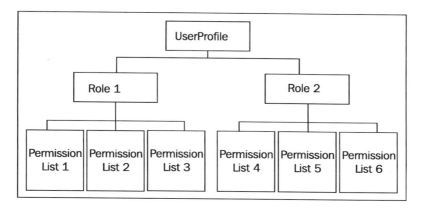

We need to create a **User Profile** for each user of the system. This user profile can have as many Roles as needed. For example, a user can have roles of Billing Supervisor and Accounts Receivable Payment Processor, if he/she approves customer invoices as well as processes customer payments. Thus, the number of roles that a user should be granted depends entirely on his/her job responsibilities.

Each role can have multiple permission lists. A Permission list determines which features can be accessed by a Role. We can specify which pages can be accessed, the mode in which they can be accessed (read only/add/update) in a permission list.

In a nutshell, we can think of a Role as a grouping of system features that a user needs to access, while a Permission list defines the nature of access to those system features.

Expert tip

Deciding how many and which roles should be created needs quite a bit of thinking about. How easy will it be to maintain them in future? Think of the scenarios where a function needs to be removed from a role and added to another. How easy would it be to do so? As a rule of thumb, you should map system features to roles in such a way that they are non-overlapping. Similarly, map system pages to permission lists so that they are mutually exclusive. This simplifies user security maintenance to a large extent. Note that although it is advisable, it may not always be possible. Organizational requirements are sometimes too complicated to achieve this. However, a PeopleSoft professional should try to build a modular security design to the extent possible.

Now, let's try to design our security matrix for the hypothetical scenario presented previously and test our thumb rule of mutually exclusive roles and permission lists.

What do you observe as far as required system features for a role are concerned? You are absolutely right if you thought that some of system features (such as Voucher entry) are common across roles.

Which roles should we design for this situation? Going by the principle of mutually exclusive roles, we can map system features to the permission lists (and in turn roles) without overlapping them. We'll denote our roles by the prefix 'RL' and permission lists by the prefix 'PL'. Thus, the mapping may look something like this:

Role	Permission list	System feature
RL_Voucher_Entry	PL_Voucher_Entry	Voucher Entry
RL_Voucher_Approval	PL_Voucher_Approval	Voucher Approval
RL_Voucher_Posting	PL_Voucher_Posting	Voucher Posting
RL_Pay_Cycle	PL_Pay_Cycle	Pay Cycle

So, now we have created the required roles and permission lists, and attached appropriate permission lists to each of the roles. In this example, due to the simple scenario, each role has only a single permission list assigned to it.

Now as the final step, we'll assign appropriate roles to each user's User profile.

User	Role	System feature accessed
Mary	RL_Voucher_Approval	Voucher Approval
	RL_Pay_Cycle	Pay Cycle
Amy	RL_Voucher_Entry	Voucher Entry
	RL_Voucher_Approval	Voucher Approval
	RL_Voucher_Posting	Voucher Posting
Anton	RL_Voucher_Entry	Voucher Entry

Now, as you can see, each user has access to the appropriate system feature through the roles and in turn, permission lists attached to their user profiles.

Can you think of the advantage of our approach? Let's say that a few months down the line, it is decided that Mary (AP Manager) should be the only one approving vouchers, while Amy (AP Supervisor) should also have the ability to execute pay cycles and issue payments to vendors. How can we accommodate this change? It's quite simple really – we'll remove the role RL_Voucher_Approval from Amy's user profile and add the role RL_Pay_Cycle to her profile. So now the security matrix will look like this:

User	Role	System feature accessed
Mary	RL_Voucher_Approval	Voucher Approval
	RL_Pay_Cycle	Pay Cycle
Amy	RL_Voucher_Entry	Voucher Entry
	RL_Pay_Cycle	Pay Cycle
	RL_Voucher_Posting	Voucher Posting
Anton	RL_Voucher_Entry	Voucher Entry

Thus, security maintenance becomes less cumbersome when we design roles and permission lists with non-overlapping system features. Of course, this comes with a downside as well. This approach results in a large number of roles and permission lists, thereby increasing the initial configuration effort.

The solution that we actually design for an organization needs to balance these two objectives.

Expert tip

Having too many permission lists assigned to a User Profile can adversely affect the system performance. PeopleSoft recommends 10-20 permission lists per user.

Configuring permission lists

Follow this navigation to configure permission lists:

PeopleTools | Security | Permissions & Roles | Permission Lists

The following screenshot shows the **General** tab of the **Permission List** set up page. We can specify the permission list description on this tab.

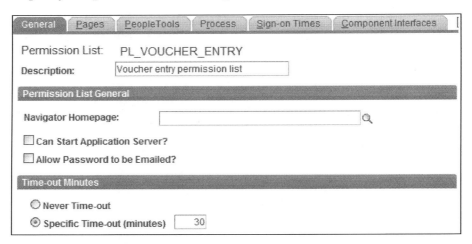

We'll go through some of the important configuration activities for the Voucher Entry permission list discussed previously.

- **Can Start Application Server?**: Selecting this field enables a user with this permission list to start PeopleSoft application servers (all batch processes are executed on this server). A typical system user does not need this option.

- **Allow Password to be Emailed?**: Selecting this field enables users to receive forgotten passwords through e-mail. Leave the field unchecked to prevent unencrypted passwords from being sent in e-mails.

- **Time-out Minutes – Never Time-out and Specific Time-out**: These fields determine the number of minutes of inactivity after which the system automatically logs out the user with this permission list.

The following screenshot shows the **Pages** tab of the permission list page. This is the most important place where we specify the menus, components, and ultimately the pages that a user can access.

In PeopleSoft parlance, a component means collection of pages that are related to each other. In the previous screenshot, you are looking at a page. You can also see other related pages used to configure permission lists – General, PeopleTools, Process, and so on. All these pages constitute a component. A menu is a collection of various components. It is typically related to a system feature, such as 'Enter Voucher Information' as you can see in the screenshot.

Thus, to grant a page access, we need to enter its component and menu details.

Expert tip

In order to find out the component and menu for a page, press *CTRL+J* when it is open in the internet browser.

- **Menu Name**: This is where we need to specify all the menus to which a user needs to have access. Note that a permission list can grant access to multiple menus, but our simple example includes only one system feature (Voucher entry) and in turn, only one menu. Click the + button to add and select more menus.

- **Edit Components hyperlink**: Once we select a menu, we need to specify which components under it should be accessed by the permission list.

Click the **Edit Components** hyperlink to proceed. The system opens the **Component Permissions** page, as shown in the following screenshot:

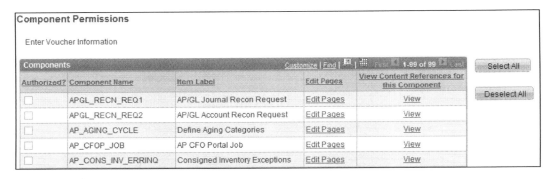

In this page, the system shows all components under the selected menu. The previous screenshot shows only a part of the component list under the 'Enter Voucher Information' menu.

Voucher entry pages for which we need to grant access exist under a component named **VCHR_EXPRESS**.

Click the **Edit Pages** hyperlink to grant access to specific pages under a given component. The system opens the **Page Permissions** page, as shown in the following screenshot:

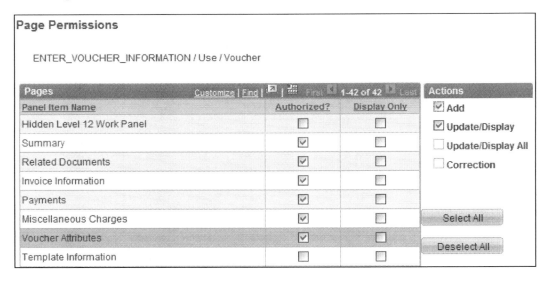

The given screenshot shows the partial list of pages under the Voucher Entry component.

- **Panel Item Name**: This field shows the page name to which access is to be granted.

- **Authorized?**: In order to enable a user to access a page, select this checkbox. As you can see, we have authorized this permission list to access six pages in this component.

- **Display Only**: Clicking this checkbox allows the user to get read-only access for the given page. He/she cannot make any changes to the data on this page.

- **Add:** Selecting this checkbox enables the user to add a new transaction (in this case new vouchers).

- **Update/Display**: Selecting this checkbox enables the user to retrieve the current effective dated row. He/she can also add future effective dated rows in addition to modifying them.

- **Update/Display All**: This option gives the user all of the privileges of the **Update/Display** option. In addition he/she can retrieve past effective dated rows as well.

- **Correction**: This option enables the user to perform all the possible operations; that is, to retrieve, modify or add past, current, and future effective dated rows.

Effective dates are usually relevant for master data set ups. It drives when a particular value comes into effect. A vendor may be set up with effective date of 1/1/2001, so that it comes into effect from that date. Now assume that its name is slated to change on 1/1/2012. However, we can add a new vendor row with the new name and the appropriate effective date. The system automatically starts using the new name from 1/1/2012. Note that there can be multiple future effective dated rows, but only one current row.

The next tab **PeopleTools** contains configuration options that are more relevant for technical developers. As we are concentrating on business users of the system, we'll not discuss them.

Click the **Process** tab. As shown in the following screenshot, this tab is used to configure options for **Process groups**.

A process group is a collection of batch processes belonging to a specific internal department or a business process. For example, PeopleSoft delivers a process group ARALL that includes all Accounts Receivable batch processes. PeopleSoft delivers various pre-configured process groups; however, we can create our own process groups depending on the organization's requirements.

Click the **Process Group Permissions** hyperlink. The system opens a new page where we can select as many process groups as needed. When a process group is selected for a permission list, it enables the users to execute batch and online processes that are part of it.

The following screenshot shows the **Sign-on Times** tab. This tab controls the time spans when a user with this permission list can sign-on to the system. We can enforce specific days or specific time spans for a particular day when users can sign-on.

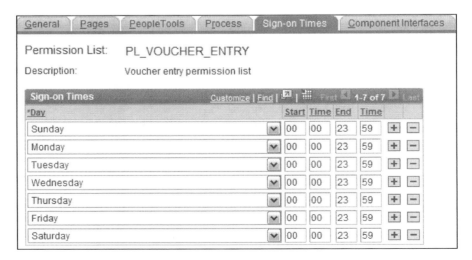

In the case of our permission list, there are no such limits and users with this permission list will be able to sign-on anytime on all days of the week.

The next tab on this page is the **Component Interface**. In *Chapter 1, PeopleSoft Financials Fundamentals*, we saw that the component interface is a PeopleSoft utility that automates bulk data entry into PeopleSoft pages. We can select component interface values on this tab, so that users with this permission list have access rights to use them.

Due to the highly technical nature of the activities involved, we will not discuss the Web Libraries, Web Services, Mass change, Links, and Audit tabs.

Oracle offers exhaustive documentation on PeopleSoft applications at the following URL: http://www.oracle.com/pls/psft/homepage. Documentation for technical topics such as web services can be found under the 'PeopleTools' section. Documentation for functional modules, such as Billing, Accounts Receivable, and so on, can be found under the **Financials Supply Chain Management (FSCM)** section.

The next important tab on the permission list page is **Query**. On this tab, the system shows two hyperlinks: **Access Group Permissions** and **Query Profile**.

Click the **Access Group Permissions** hyperlink. The system opens the **Permission List Access Groups** page, as shown in the next screenshot. This page controls which database tables can be accessed by users to create database queries, using a PeopleSoft tool called Query Manager.

- **Tree Name**: A tree is a hierarchical structure of database tables. As shown in the screenshot, the tree **QUERY_TREE_AP** groups all AP tables.

- **Access Group**: Each tree has multiple nodes called access groups. These access groups are just logical groups of tables within a tree. In the screenshot, **VOUCHERS** is a group of voucher-related tables within the AP table tree. With this configuration, users will be able to create database queries on voucher tables in AP.

Using the **Query Profile** hyperlink, we can set various options that control how users can create queries (such as if he/she can use joins, unions, and so on in queries, how many database rows can be fetched by the query, if the user can copy the query output to Microsoft Excel, and so on).

Configuring roles

Before we proceed, recall that a role can have multiple permission lists, while multiple roles can be granted to a user profile. Thus, a security role connects a user profile with actual page level access details, which are defined using permission lists.

Follow this navigation to set up security roles:

PeopleTools | Security | Permission & Roles | Roles

The following screenshot shows the **General** tab of role set up page, where we specify the role name.

Click the **Permission Lists** tab to attach the required permission lists to this role. The following screenshot shows the **Permission Lists** tab.

We will attach the permission list that we set up for voucher entry access to the role.

Click the **View Definition** hyperlink to open the permission list page and see details of the selected permission list. Add as many permission lists as required by clicking the + button.

The next two tabs (**Members** and **Dynamic Members)** show the details of static and dynamic members respectively. Let's first try to understand what that means.

We mentioned earlier that roles need to be assigned to user profiles to establish a link between profiles and permission lists. If this assignment of roles to profiles is done manually through PeopleSoft pages, selected users are known as static role members. This approach is fine with a small to medium user base, but what happens when the user base runs into thousands? Assigning various roles to all these users manually becomes a huge task. For such scenarios, we can programmatically assign roles to users based on predefined rules. In this case, the users are known as dynamic role members.

Click the **Members** tab to see if there are any static role users for this role. The following screenshot shows details of the **Members** tab.

For our illustrative example, let's assume that we manually assigned the **RL_VOUCHER_ENTRY** role to Anton. As a result, Anton comes up as a static role member in the **Members** tab.

Click the **Dynamic Members** tab to view how rules can be defined to programmatically assign this role to a large number of users. The following screenshot shows the **Dynamic Members** tab.

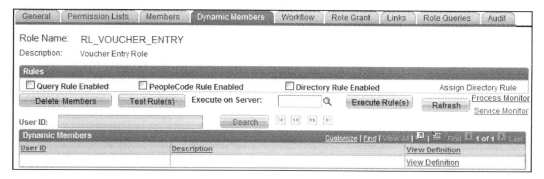

As you can see, there are three ways in which we can define the rule: using PeopleSoft Query, where a database query specifies criteria for the users who need to be assigned this rule, writing code in PeopleCode (this is the programming language used by PeopleSoft), or using the Lightweight Directory Access Protocol (LDAP) directory.

- **Query Rule Enabled:** Select this option if we specify the target user base through PeopleSoft query. This option enables a field where we can specify the query name.

- **PeopleCode Rule Enabled:** Select this option if the criteria for selecting the target user group is coded programmatically in PeopleCode. This option enables fields to specify the PeopleSoft record (table) name, field name, field event name, and name of the function that contains the required code.

- **Directory Rule Enabled:** Select this option if the criteria for selecting target user group is defined through a LDAP directory rule. This option enables the **Assign Directory Rule** hyperlink, allowing us to specify the appropriate rule.

We'll limit our discussion of security roles to these basic tabs.

Configuring user profiles

Each user that needs to access the PeopleSoft system requires a user profile. As you already know, a user profile needs to be assigned the required roles to enable that user to access certain system features.

Follow this navigation to set up user profiles:

PeopleTools | Security | User Profiles | User Profiles

The following screenshot shows the **General** tab of the User Profile page.

 Access to this page is highly restricted and usually limited to the system administrator function.

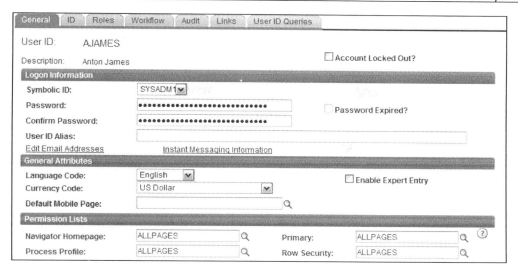

- **Account Locked Out?:** If this checkbox is selected, the user cannot sign in to the system. Thus, it is important to have it unchecked to allow a user to access the system.

- **Password and Confirm Password:** Specify the password for this user to log in to the system.

- **Primary, Row Security:** Assign a permission list for the row-level security to control the actual values of key fields (such as BU, SetID, and so on).

Click the **ID** tab to specify the type of system user (such as Employee, Customer, Vendor and so on) and specify relevant attributes (such as Employee ID, Customer ID, Vendor ID, respectively) as shown in the following screenshot:

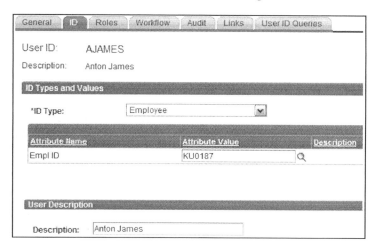

Click the **Roles** tab to assign security roles to the user. As we discussed earlier, this will mean that the user is a static role member. The next screenshot shows the **Roles** tab.

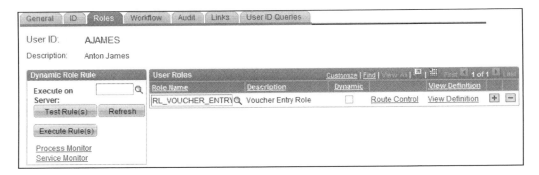

We'll assign the **RL_VOUCHER_ENTRY** role we configured earlier to this user profile. This will enable Anton to access necessary voucher entry pages through the **PL_VOUCHER_ENTRY** permission list.

- **Dynamic**: If dynamic role assignment is used for this role, this checkbox is automatically selected.

- **Dynamic Role Rule**: We already discussed that role assignment rules can be defined while setting up security roles. Options in this section help in testing the assignment and execution.

- **Test Rule(s)**: When this button is clicked, the system generates a report that shows which dynamically-defined roles will be assigned to this user in addition to the manually-assigned rules. Remember that this is just a preview for the role assignment and the roles will not be really assigned.

- **Execute Rule(s)**: Click this button to run the dynamic role assignment process.

Click the **Workflow** tab to set up workflow configuration options for this user, as shown in the following screenshot.

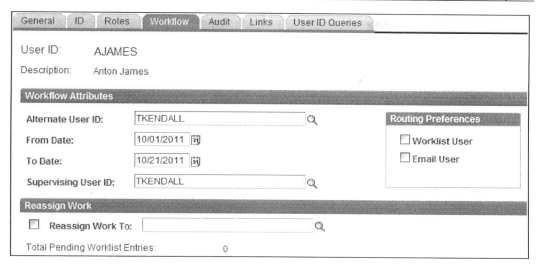

- **Alternate User ID, From Date, To Date:** Specify an alternate user ID, who should receive all workflow items that the original user receives, between the dates specified in the **From Date** and **To Date** fields. This feature is useful when a user is temporarily away due to a vacation or similar occasions. In the given example, all workflow notifications for Anton will be routed to the user ID TKENDALL between 1st and 21st October, 2011.

 Note that assignment of workflow items is applicable only for new items. Any items that were already assigned to the user are not reassigned.

- **Total Pending Worklist Entries:** This field shows the workflow items that are currently assigned to the user and are not completed.
- **Reassign Work To:** This option enables reassignment of currently assigned pending items to a different user.

Understanding row-level security

So far we have discussed security access being controlled using permission lists and roles to specify which application pages can be accessed by users.

In addition to the page security, PeopleSoft offers another level of security called Row level security. This method is useful to control access to specific rows of data using either specific User IDs or permission lists.

To understand this concept, let's continue our example of Anton, who can enter vouchers in the Accounts Payable module. We already saw configuration options that allowed us to limit his system access to voucher entry pages. But can we restrict his access to vouchers for only one Business Unit, (BU) say US001? We certainly did not see such options while configuring user profiles, roles, or permission lists. This is where row-level security comes in.

If we wish to limit Anton to seeing vouchers in the system for US001 BU alone, we essentially want to limit his access to only those database rows belonging to US001 BU.

Row-level security can be implemented for database rows that are controlled by the following fields:

- Business unit
- SetID
- Ledger (and ledger group)
- Book
- Project
- Pay cycle
- Planning Instance

We just discussed how to control access to data with a specific Business Unit. If needed, we can limit user access to data for a specific SetID, Ledger or any of the fields in the given list.

 Note that even if we decide to use row-level security, it is not mandatory to use all the fields mentioned previously for access control. For example, we may wish to use row-level security for only business unit and SetID, while users are free to access data for any pay cycle, ledger, and so on.

There are two ways of configuring row-level security:

- User ID level security
- Permission list level security

User ID level security

In this method, we need to specify which values of Business Unit, SetID, and so on, can be accessed for each user. Thus, a sample configuration may look like this, assuming we have enabled row level security only for Business Unit and SetID fields:

User ID	Business Unit access	SetID access
AJAMES	US001	GLOVH
	FRA01	
TKENDALL	US001	GLOVH
	FRA01	SHARE
	GBR01	

This approach works well if the user base is small. As you can imagine, configuring it for a large user base running in the thousands is not practical. This is where we need to use the permission list level security.

Permission list-level security

In this method of row-level security, key field values are assigned to a permission list rather than an individual user ID. This permission list is assigned to multiple users as the Primary Permission List (recall the General tab on the User Profile page).

Assuming that there are 500 users who need to access data for BUs US001 and FRA01 and SetID GLOVH, we can use the following configuration:

Pernission List	Business Unit access	SetID access
ALLPAGES	US001	GLOVH
	FRA01	

Later, this permission list is assigned to all the users as primary permission list.

Now let's say that all these users need to access an additional BU GBR01, we need to do it only for the given mapping and it will be reflected for all the 500 users.

Specifying row-level security options

Follow this navigation to specify system security options:

Setup Financials/Supply Chain | Security | Security Options | Security Options

The following screenshot shows the **Security Options** page where we can specify the security type and the important fields for which access needs to be restricted.

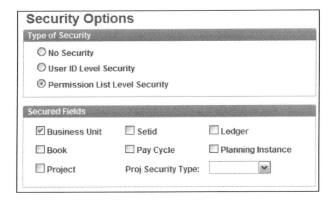

- **No Security:** If this option is selected, users can access data belonging to all business units, ledgers, or any other key field.
- **User ID Level Security:** This enables security by individual User ID. We need to assign permissible values to user ID profiles on other pages.
- **Permission List Level Security:** This enables security by Permission List. We need to assign permissible values to permission lists on other pages.
- **Secured Fields:** As you can see, the system shows the key fields listed previously. We need to select the fields that we need for row-level security access. Based on the fields we select, we need to assign permissible values to appropriate User ID or Permission list.

In the example shown in the previous screenshot, we have enabled row level security for Business Unit and selected Permission level security. Therefore, we'll have to assign the BU values to be accessed to the appropriate permission list. We'll see how to do it a little later.

Applying security options

The security options that we specified previously do not come into effect, unless we execute the **Apply Security Setups** batch process.

Follow this navigation to apply security options:

Setup Financials/Supply Chain | Security | Apply Security Setups

The following screenshot shows this page. Note that this process does not need any input parameters.

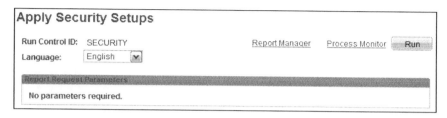

Click the **Run** button to execute the process.

Defining row-level security values

As we discussed previously, we need to assign the values for the enabled fields to appropriate User ID or Permission lists.

PeopleSoft provides the following 10 pages to assign various key field values to User IDs or Permission lists:

- Unit Security by Permission List
- Unit Security by User ID
- TableSet Security by Permission List
- TableSet Security by User ID
- Ledger Security by Permission List
- Ledger Security by User ID
- nVision Ledger Security
- Pay Cycle by user ID
- Pay Cycle by Permission list
- Project Security

We'll discuss only the Unit Security pages, as most of the other pages are similar.

Unit Security by Permission List

Follow this navigation to assign BU values to a permission list:

Setup Financials/Supply Chain | Security | Unit by Permission List

The following screenshot shows the Business Unit Security by Permission List page.

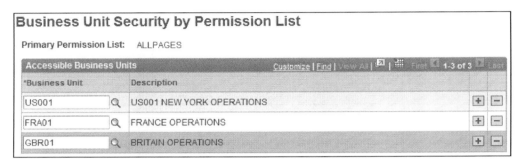

In this example, BU values **US001**, **FRA01** and **GBR01** are assigned to a permission list **ALLPAGES**. Any user with this permission list as the primary permission list on his/her user profile will be able to access data for only for these BU values.

Unit Security by User ID

Follow this navigation to assign BU values to an individual User ID:

Setup Financials/Supply Chain | Security | Unit by User ID

The following screenshot shows the Business Unit Security by User ID page.

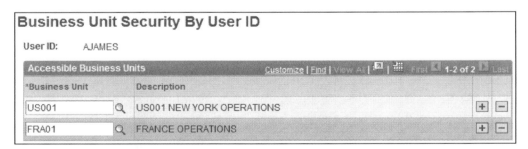

In this example, BU values **US001** and **FRA01** are assigned to a user ID **AJAMES**. This user will be able to access data only for these two BU values.

Summary

PeopleSoft security performs a critical task of controlling the access of system features to appropriate users. User security is a three-level hierarchical structure consisting of User Profiles, Roles, and Permission Lists. Permission Lists control which pages can be accessed and the mode of the access. A Role is assigned as many permission lists as needed. It can be considered a collection of system features. A user profile is created for each system user and is assigned as many roles as needed by the user.

While the user security controls which system pages can be accessed by a user, the Row-Level Security controls which rows of data can be accessed by a user. It limits the data retrieved by a user to specific values of a Business unit, SetID, Ledger, Book, Project, Pay cycle, or a Planning Instance. Row-level security options can be implemented by User ID (suited to a small user base) or Permission List (ideally suited for large user base with similar access requirements). In other words, we can specify which values of the given key fields can be accessed either for a user ID or a permission list.

3
PeopleSoft Billing Module

The PeopleSoft Billing Module performs the important function of generating customer invoices for the goods or services sold by an organization. It is an important part of the 'Order to Cash' business process. This module allows an organization to seamlessly receive data from various PeopleSoft modules to create customer invoices. It allows us to create multiple formats to generate invoices based on business needs. Various batch processes in the Billing module enable the complete automation of the entire invoicing process. Users can manually create invoices as well if required.

PeopleSoft Billing can perform necessary calculations for **Sales and Use Tax (SUT)** and **Value Added Tax (VAT)**. It also allows adjustments to generated invoices, creates accounting entries, and interfaces the invoice data to other PeopleSoft modules.

In this chapter, we will discuss the invoice lifecycle and various Billing batch processes. We'll gain an understanding of concepts such revenue accrual and deferred revenue processing. We'll also discuss important configurations in the Billing module.

Understanding the invoice lifecycle

In the PeopleSoft Billing module, you will frequently hear the terms "bill" and "invoice". To put it simply, while an invoice is the final document to be sent to a customer, a bill can be considered a 'raw' version of the invoice.

The following illustration shows a high-level process for invoice processing:

The billing process begins with the entry of bills, either manually or through delivered interfaces from other PeopleSoft modules. We'll discuss these concepts in greater detail a little later. Once these bills are in the PeopleSoft system, they can be reviewed and approved (if necessary). Reviewing the bills can be implemented through printing draft invoices, called **pro-forma invoices**. You can print pro-forma invoices using a batch process as many times as needed to review how the invoices would look. If any changes are needed, they are made to the bill.

Once the bill is deemed appropriate, a batch process is executed to 'finalize' the bill. This transforms a bill into the final invoice. Additional batch processes then print the invoices in desired formats or transmit them electronically to the customer.

There may be various occasions when an invoice needs to be modified after it is sent to the customer. This is done through invoice adjustments. These adjustments can be made to specific lines on the invoices or the entire invoice itself. After making any adjustments, an invoice needs to go through the finalization process again.

Finally, another batch process creates accounting entries for the invoices. Additional batch processes then send the accounting entries to the General Ledger, invoice data to Accounts Receivable for tracking them and inter-unit invoices to the Accounts Payable module.

We'll discuss each of these stages in detail in subsequent sections.

Entering bill data

As we briefly saw in the invoice lifecycle, bills can be entered into the PeopleSoft system manually or through an interface from other PeopleSoft modules or non-PeopleSoft systems. We'll now discuss these approaches in detail. Note that manual bill entry is appropriate when the bill volume is relatively small. Usually for large organizations, the bill data volume is quite high and originates from other sources. For such situations, manual entry is certainly not an option and an automated interface needs to be employed.

Receiving bill data from other modules or external sources

PeopleSoft offers a set of interface tables to store bill data from external sources (PeopleSoft/non-PeopleSoft) and a batch process named **Billing Interface (BIIF0001)** to load the data from these staging tables into billing tables.

Of course, you may be wondering how the bill data will be loaded into the interface tables in the first place. As far as bill data from other PeopleSoft modules (such as order management, inventory, contracts, project costing, and so on) is concerned, each of those modules offers a delivered program to load data from that respective module to billing interface tables.

For example, the order management module sends sales order data to Billing interface tables through a batch process called **Populate Billing**.

The bill data in the Billing module essentially contains a bill header and its individual lines. For example, if an organization has sold three different products to a customer, the bill would have a bill header and three bill lines. This is just a sample example; in real life, this bill would typically have other details such as tax, accounting entries, notes, and so on.

In the Billing interface, the bill data that are brought in belong to the following categories known as **Transaction types**:

Transaction type	Description
LINE	This transaction type indicates an individual bill line. In the previous example, there would be three separate data rows with this transaction type.
AE (Accounting entry)	This transaction type indicates an accounting entry. Note that this transaction type is valid only if the source system sends accounting entries and is not mandatory. There can be multiple accounting entries for each bill line.

Transaction type	Description
NOTE	This transaction type indicates a comment for the entire bill header or an individual bill line. Again, populating data with this transaction type is not mandatory. Each bill line can have multiple notes.
DS	This transaction type indicates a discount or surcharge (additional charge for the bill line amount) for the bill line. Populating data with this transaction type is not mandatory. Each bill line can have multiple discount or surcharge lines.
DDS	This transaction type indicates a deferred discount or surcharge for the bill line. If the bill is using deferred revenue accounting (which we'll see in a later section) and has a DS line type, then it also has a DDS line representing the accounting information.
AHDR	This transaction type indicates an adjustment header. This is needed when we are bringing in adjustments for existing bills.
EXSD	This transaction type indicates excise, sales tax and VAT information.
TAX	This transaction type indicates sales tax information.

Billing interface tables

If we are bringing in the billing data from another PeopleSoft module, the population of these tables is handled by the delivered interface program from that source module. For example, the PeopleSoft Order Management module includes a batch process that loads the customer order details into the Billing interface tables. However, if we bring in the data from a non-PeopleSoft system, a customized interface program needs to be developed to populate these tables. Let's say that an organization uses a non-PeopleSoft system to capture customer orders. To import these order data into PeopleSoft Billing, we will have to analyze the data format in the source systems, map the data with PeopleSoft Billing interface tables and develop a customized interface program to reformat the source data and load it into the interface tables.

Note that it is not mandatory to insert data in to all of these tables. The organization's requirements, the information sent by the source system, and so on, will determine which tables need to be populated.

The following table describes the set of billing interface tables:

Table name	Description
INTFC_BI	This is the primary interface table and must be populated for each bill line that is brought into the PeopleSoft Billing module. It can contain bill lines belonging to LINE, NOTE and AHDR types.
INTFC_BI2	This interface table is an extension of the INTFC_BI table and contains extended tax and ship to address information. It can contain only bill lines belonging to LINE type.
INTFC_BI_AEDS	This interface table holds the accounting entry and discount/surcharge information. It can contain bill lines belonging to AE, DS and DDS types.
INTFC_BI_NOTE	This interface table holds the notes and comments information. If a line in INTFC_BI table has NOTE transaction type, then this table needs to have a row.
INTFC_BI_HDR	This interface table holds a single row for the entire bill. It can contain bill lines belonging to only LINE type.
INTFC_EXSD	This interface table holds excise, sales tax and VAT details that are relevant for Indian taxes only. It can contain bill lines belonging to only EXSD type.
INTFC_BI_TAX	This interface table holds sales and use tax details. It can contain bill lines belonging to only EXSD type. It can contain bill lines belonging to only TAX type.

So for a hypothetical organization based in the USA which does not have to pay sales tax on its invoices and does not have any invoice comments, only the INTFC_BI and INTFC_BI_HDR tables will need to be populated.

Understanding Bill By Identifier

As we discussed earlier, the Billing Interface (BIIF0001) process reads the bill data from interface tables and loads them into Billing tables. In order to do that, we need to configure an important option known as **Bill By Identifier**.

A Bill By Identifier consolidates the bill lines in interface tables based on the unique combinations of defined parameters to create new bills. If it finds that an un-invoiced bill already exists with that combination, it adds the bill line to that bill. Let's take an example to understand this concept before discussing how to configure it.

Assume that an organization has brought in billing data from an external source that consists of bill lines for various customers and different orders that they had placed. Now it wishes to create invoices in such a way that bill lines belonging to the same customer order and sales person who brought the order are consolidated on a single invoice. The following table shows the hypothetical bill line data for a customer in interface tables:

Line	Customer No.	Order No.	Sales person	Amount
1	18890	56645	Jim	$1000
2	18890	56645	Jim	$500
3	18890	67741	Tom	$2100
4	18890	67741	Tom	$900
5	18890	67741	Jim	$1200
6	18890	67741	Jim	$750
7	18890	67741	Jim	$3000

As you can see, salesperson Jim was responsible for bringing in order # 56645 and selling three items in the order # 67741. Salesperson Tom was instrumental in selling two items in the order # 67741.

Now we need to configure a Bill By Identifier with two consolidation parameters: Order Number and Sales Person. When this is used by the Billing Interface process, it will create the following bills:

Bill 1:

Line	Amount
1	$1000
2	$500

Bill 2:

Line	Amount
1	$2100
2	$900

Bill 3:

Line	Amount
1	$1200
2	$750
3	$3000

Follow this navigation to configure a Bill By Identifier:

Setup Financials/Supply Chain | Product Related | Billing | Setup | Bill-by Identifier

The following screenshot shows the Bill By Identifier configuration page:

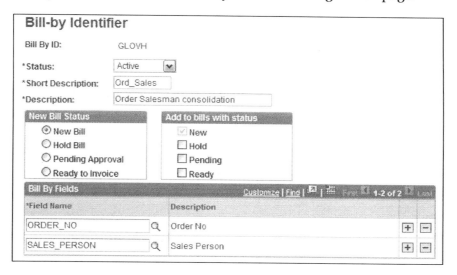

- **New Bill Status:** This value is used by the Billing Interface process to assign a status for the newly created bill. Possible options are: **New Bill** (a bill is recently created and awaiting further processing), **Hold Bill** (a bill is prevented from further processing unless its value is changed to Ready), **Pending Approval** (a bill that needs to be reviewed and approved) and **Ready to Invoice** (a bill that is eligible to be picked by the batch process and invoiced).

- **Add to bills with status:** As mentioned earlier, if the Billing Interface process finds that a combination of defined parameters already exists, it adds the bill line to that bill rather than creating a new bill. This field determines the status of the bill to which this new interface line will be added.

- **Bill By Fields:** Fields added in this section determine the consolidation criteria for bill lines in the interface tables. Based on our example, the fields are Order Number and Sales Person.

 Parameters such as Business Unit, Customer ID, Bill Source and Bill Type are already implied in the Bill By Identifier and need not be specified. In other words, the system will always create separate bills belonging to different customers, BUs, bills sources and bill types.

A Bill By Identifier can be assigned to a bill-to customer, bill source, bill type or a billing business unit.

Billing Interface (BIIF0001) process

Now that the billing data has been loaded into the interface tables and the Bill By Identifier has been configured, it's time to run the Billing Interface process to load the data into Billing tables and create new bills.

Follow this navigation to run the Billing Interface process:

Billing | Interface Transactions | Process Billing Interface

The following screenshot shows the run control page from where the Billing Interface process can be run:

From Interface ID, To Interface ID: Each transaction in the interface tables has an interface ID associated with it. Select the range of interface transactions to be processed and loaded into Billing tables. We can review the transactions in the interface staging area and see their interface IDs on the **Review Pending Transactions** page.

Click the **Run** button to initiate the process.

To access the Review Pending Transactions page, follow this navigation:

Billing | Interface Transactions | Review Pending Transactions

Entering online bills manually

Manual bill entry using online pages is suitable only for a small number of transactions. Most organizations with high bill volume do not use this feature or only use it occasionally. Before proceeding with our discussion, let's understand the various bill statuses and their significance, as shown in the following table:

Bill status	Description
New	This is the status of a bill when it is entered. In this status, it is not processed by any batch process.
Pending Approval	This status applies to the bill that is submitted for approval after its creation. This is relevant only if we mandate that bills need to be approved before they are processed further.
Ready	This status needs to be assigned to a bill to indicate that it is ready to be invoiced. Billing batch processes select only those invoices with this status.
Invoiced	This indicates that all the processing for a bill has been completed and it is now a final invoice that can be sent to the customer.

Now we'll briefly review some important pages used to manually enter bills.

Follow this navigation to enter a new bill:

Billing | Maintain Bills | Standard Billing | Header – Info 1

The following screenshot shows the Bill Header tab where we need to enter details common to the entire bill:

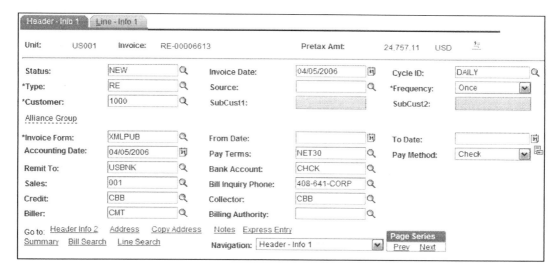

As you can see, this information pertains to the entire bill. We'll briefly discuss some of the fields here.

Status: When a bill is manually created, it is assigned a status of **New**. As long as it has this status, it is not processed by any batch processes. Once all the details are entered and it is ready to be processed, we need to change its status to **Ready**, so that it can be picked up by the batch processes. Once all the processing is complete and it is converted into an invoice, the status automatically changes to **Invoiced**.

Click the **Line – Info 1** tab to enter bill lines.

The following screenshot shows the Bill Line tab where details of bill lines are entered:

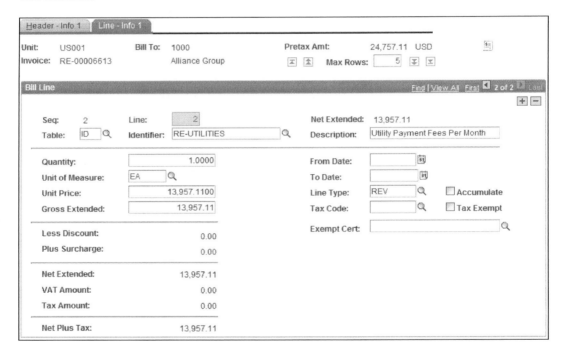

- **Table:** This field identifies the type of bill line. Available options are: **D** (discount), **ID** (identifier) and **S** (surcharge). Value ID denotes goods or services provided to the customer which is being billed.

- **Identifier:** This field denotes the actual product or service being billed. For example, we can define various identifiers such as Consulting Services, Catering Services, 32" LCD TV, 29" LCD TV, and so on, to identify the type of service or goods that needs to be billed.

- **Line Type:** This field is used to categorize the bill line. Some of the available values are **REV** (revenue line), **FRGT** (freight charges), **DISC** (discount), **SUR** (surcharge), and so on.

Now let's see how the bill accounting details are specified.

From the **Navigation** dropdown at the right hand bottom corner of the page, select the **Acctg – Rev Distribution** option.

The following screenshot shows the **Acctg – Rev Distribution** tab where revenue accounting details of selected bill lines are entered:

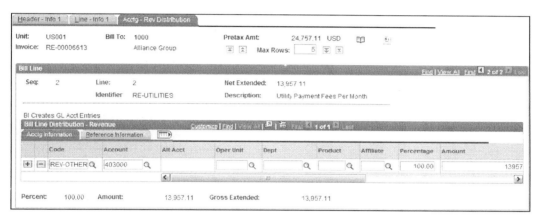

Code: This field specifies the distribution code for recording the revenue generated from this bill line. A distribution code is a pre-defined combination of chartfields. It is used to avoid entering all chartfield values manually. In the previous example, the revenue will be recorded in the account **403000**.

We'll see how to configure distribution codes in the section on configurations. If required, we can add multiple revenue lines by using the **+** button to split the revenue from this bill line. For example, let's say that revenues from a sale need to be shared between two different departments equally. To continue with the previous example, we can have two revenue lines as shown next by using different distribution codes:

Code	Account	Department	Percentage	Amount
REV-DIST1	403000	ABC	50.00	6978.55
REV-DIST2	403000	XYZ	50.00	6978.55

Online bill entry consists of many pages, all of which cannot be discussed here due to the pagespace constraints of this book. However the pages discussed previously should give you a fair idea about the information that goes into manually creating a bill.

Understanding billing batch processes

Based on our discussion of the invoice lifecycle, you have now gained some idea of how the billing batch processes play an important part in invoice processing. It would not be wrong to say that these batch processes handle almost every aspect of invoice processing. In this section, we'll explain these processes.

The following table lists the billing batch processes in the order they need to be executed. Note that not all of these processes are mandatory for invoice processing.

Process	Description	Purpose
BIIF0001	Billing interface	As discussed earlier, this process loads the bill data from interface tables into the billing tables and creates new bills. It is not required if bills are manually created.
BIPVAT00	Process VAT defaults	This process applies the Value Added Tax (VAT) default values for the bill header and bill lines based on the VAT setups. It is required only if VAT is applicable to the organization's invoices. VAT is usually used in European countries.

Bills are now brought into the system or manually entered. They are reviewed and found to be appropriate. The billing user changes their status to **READY**. Now they are eligible for further processing.

The following batch processes are used to create final invoices and make them ready to print:

Process	Description	Purpose
BIIVC000	Bill finalization	This process selects bills with **READY** status. It performs the tax calculations for all bill lines based on the tax codes assigned to them. Once a bill is successfully validated, it changes the bill's status to **INVOICED**. This process is mandatory for invoice processing. No more changes can be made to the invoice now, unless it is canceled.

Process	Description	Purpose
BI_IVCEXT	Invoice extract	This process extracts data for printable bills to the temporary print extract tables. Subsequent print processes read the data from these temporary tables and print invoices.

Now the final invoices are ready to be printed. PeopleSoft offers more than 30 batch processes to print invoices for various specific purposes. We can decide which print process to execute after BI_IVCEXT, depending on the organization's requirements. We'll assume that we will use the most appropriate batch process to print our invoices.

The following processes are used to interface the billing invoice data with other modules.

Process	Description	Purpose
BICURCNV	Billing currency conversion	This process calculates the bill amounts in base currency (of the business unit) as well as euro currency in addition to the transaction currency. This process is mandatory even if we use only a single currency.
BIPRELD	Billing pre-load	This process creates accounting entries for the invoices and loads them in accounting entry staging tables. It also performs chartfield combination editing for the accounting entries. This process is mandatory to execute subsequent processes to interface billing data with other modules.
BIGNAP01	Generate AP vouchers	When the billing module processes inter-unit bills (where one business unit bills another unit), the selling unit issues an invoice to the other unit which may have purchased something. This paying unit needs to pay the invoice amount by creating a AP voucher. This process creates AP voucher data in the three AP staging tables VCHR_HDR_STG, VCHR_LINE_STG, VCHR_DIST_STG. This process is required only if the organization uses inter-unit bills.
BILDAR01	Load AR pending items	This process interfaces invoice data to the Accounts Receivable module. It loads the data into AR pending items staging table, so that it can be picked by an AR batch process called AR UPDATE to be loaded into AR tables.
BILDGL01	Load GL interface	This process creates accounting entries based on the data in the staging tables created by the BIPRELD process. The accounting entries are stored in the BI_ACCT_ENTRY table. It also creates reversal entries for accrual entries.

This completes the invoice lifecycle with all necessary billing data being interfaced with downstream modules.

Performing invoice adjustments

In a typical invoicing process, it is fairly common that an invoice sent out to a customer will need to be modified. Consider the following scenarios:

- An invoice for customer A is accidentally created for customer B. Now customer B contacts us and wants us to cancel the bill.

- A customer complains that he received an invoice for something that he never purchased.

- A customer purchases products A, B and C but finds that we have sent him an invoice for products A, B and D. Now we need to correct the bill line with product D and change it to product C.

- A discount of 10% was promised to a customer on purchase of a certain product. However, when he receives the invoice, he finds that he did not receive the discount. He now wants us to apply the promised discount on the invoice amount and resend the corrected invoice.

These are only a few possible situations where we need to make adjustments to customer invoices.

PeopleSoft Billing offers two ways of adjusting invoices:

- Adjust the entire bill
- Adjust specific bill lines

We'll quickly go through these methods to understand how to perform invoice adjustments.

Adjusting the entire bill

Consider the first scenario from our previous list, where the invoice for customer A was accidentally billed to customer B. What would be the corrective action for this case? You are right if you answered - "Cancel the invoice sent to customer B and create a new invoice for customer A".

Now how can we handle the second scenario in the list? Of course, we would check if the customer had really purchased something from us. If he/she had not purchased anything, we would have to cancel the invoice that we had sent.

We can use the adjustment for entire bill option for such scenarios.

Follow this navigation to adjust an entire bill:

Billing | Maintain Bills | Adjust Entire Bills

The following screenshot shows the **Adjust Entire Bills** page:

- **No Bill Action**: When this option is selected, the system doesn't take any action.

- **Credit Entire Bill**: With this option selected, the system credits (reverses) the selected bill. The newly created credit bill is created in READY status, so it can be picked up by the Bill Finalization process. For example, if we wish to credit a bill with amount of $500, a new bill for the same customer is created with an amount of -$500, which in effect cancels the original bill. As you can see, this option is ideal for the second scenario listed previously.

- **Credit & Rebill**: When this option is selected, the system creates a credit bill for original bill and then creates a copy of the original bill with a status of NEW, which you can edit as required. For example, if we wish to credit and rebill a bill with amount of $500, a new bill for the same customer is created with an amount of -$500. In addition, another bill similar to the original bill ($500) is created. Now we can correct the customer on this newly created bill. This option is ideal for the first scenario listed previously.

- **Adjustment Reason**: It is mandatory to provide a reason for adjustment.

- **Adjustment Results**: This section shows the invoice ID that the system will assign to the newly created credit bill and Rebill bill. In the previous screenshot, the system automatically assigns the next invoice number.

Adjusting selected bill lines

Consider the third scenario from the previous list. In this case, we do not need to cancel the entire invoice and reissue a new one. We can simply change the bill line three to reflect the correct value.

For the fourth scenario, again, we can simply adjust the line and add the appropriate discount.

Follow this navigation to adjust specific lines on the bill:

Billing | Maintain Bills | Adjust Selected Bill Lines

The following screenshot shows the **Adjust Selected Bill Lines** page:

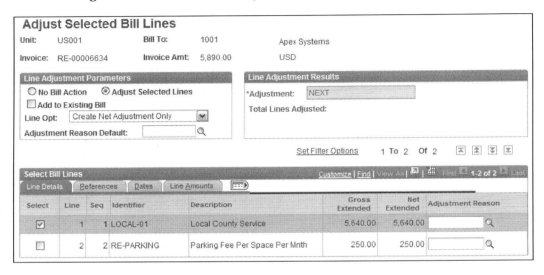

- **No Bill Action:** When this option is selected, the system doesn't take any action.

- **Adjust Selected Lines:** Select this option to modify any bill lines. Check the **Select** checkbox next to any bill line(s) to adjust it.

- **Add to Existing Bill:** Select this checkbox to add a new line to the existing bill.

- **Line Opt:** This option determines how the selected line needs to be adjusted. The available options are:
  - **Create net adjustment only**: System creates only one adjustment line
  - **Create reversal and rebill**: System creates two new lines – one to credit the selected line and the other to make any adjustments (recall the entire bill adjustment options)
  - **Credit line**: System credits the selected bill line

For the third and fourth scenario, we can use the **Create reversal and rebill** option for invoice line for product D, so that it is canceled. Then we can use the correct product C in the new line that is generated.

For the fourth scenario, we can either use the **Create net adjustment only** option to add the missing discount or use the same option as the third scenario.

The system creates a new bill containing the line adjustments.

Deferred revenue processing and unbilled revenue accrual

The most straight-forward scenario in customer invoicing includes the following steps:

- An organization sells some goods/services to a customer
- An invoice is created and sent out
- The customer pays the invoice amount and the invoice is closed in Accounts Receivable

In this case, a typical accounting entry for the invoice is as follows:

- DR Accounts Receivable
- CR Revenue

In other words, we recognize the revenue and record the receivable (from the customer) at the same time. However, there are many situations where this is not possible due to various reasons.

Sometimes, even if we invoice a customer, we cannot recognize the revenue and need to defer (postpone) the revenue recognition. This is known as deferred revenue processing. On the other hand, sometimes, we need to recognize the revenue, even if we have not invoiced the customer. This is known as unbilled revenue accrual.

Deferred revenue processing

Consider a customer invoice for the amount of $1000 is created with 1/1/2011 as its accounting date. As seen previously, under normal circumstances, Billing would create the following accounting entry:

Accounting date	Debit/Credit	Account	Amount
1/1/2011	DR	Accounts Receivable	$1000
1/1/2011	CR	Revenue	-$1000

Thus, we have recognized the entire revenue in one go.

Now let's assume that, due to contractual terms, we need to recognize the revenue equally over four months, on the first day of each month. In other words, we need to recognize $250 every month for four months. In such a scenario, in the first month we can recognize only partial revenue, while the remaining amount needs to be recorded using another account called **Deferred Revenue account**. We then progressively go on recognizing remaining amounts of revenue from the deferred revenue account.

The deferred revenue accounting entries for this scenario are created as follows:

Accounting date	Debit/Credit	Account	Amount
In month 1, out of $1000, only $250 is recognized as revenue, while the rest is recorded as deferred revenue.			
1/1/2011	DR	Accounts Receivable	$1000
1/1/2011	CR	Revenue	-$250
1/1/2011	CR	Deferred Revenue	-$750
In month 2, further $250 revenue will be recognized by reducing the amount of deferred revenue.			
2/1/2011	DR	Deferred Revenue	$250
2/1/2011	CR	Revenue	-$250
In month 2, further $250 revenue will be recognized by reducing the amount of deferred revenue.			
3/1/2011	DR	Deferred Revenue	$250
3/1/2011	CR	Revenue	-$250
In month 4, remaining $250 revenue will be recognized, completing revenue recognition.			
4/1/2011	DR	Deferred Revenue	$250
4/1/2011	CR	Revenue	-$250

This is just one of the various methods by which recognized revenue is prorated (spread) across 4 months (equally for each period). PeopleSoft Billing provides following revenue proration methods:

- Spread by days within range
- Spread evenly across all periods
- Spread evenly using a mid-period rule
- Spread partial periods by days with remainder spread evenly
- User-defined proration

In order to use deferred revenue processing for invoices, we need to configure deferred revenue distribution codes.

Entering bills for deferred revenue processing is similar to regular bills. The only additional steps required are as follows:

1. Specifying the revenue recognition basis date such as ship date, order date, and so on.
2. Providing the respective date or date range
3. Specifying the deferred revenue distribution codes

Unbilled revenue accrual

Consider a scenario where we are executing a three month long contract for a customer. We'll be completing 1/3 of total work in each month. According to contract terms, we can invoice the customer only after the work is completed at the end of the third month. Let's say that the total contract value is $3000. Now, according to accounting convention, we can recognize revenue as the work is delivered. In other words, we can recognize $1000 at the end of the first month, $1000 more at the end of the second month and $1000 more at the end of the third month.

At the end of each accounting period, we recognize the revenue but record it to the Unbilled AR account instead of the regular AR account. In each subsequent period, we then reverse these accounting entries as they are not invoiced. In the final accounting period, we recognize the entire revenue and record it to the actual AR account.

This revenue is called **Unbilled Revenue**, as we are not going to bill it to the customer. The unbilled revenue accounting entries for this scenario are created as follow:

Accounting date	Debit/Credit	Account	Amount
At the end of 1st month, we recognize $1000			
1/31/2011	DR	Unbilled AR	$1000
1/31/2011	CR	Revenue	-$1000
At the beginning of 2nd month, reverse the earlier entries			
2/1/2011	DR	Revenue	$1000
2/1/2011	CR	Unbilled AR	-$1000
At the end of 2nd month, we recognize additional $1000, that is, $2000 revenue			
2/28/2011	DR	Unbilled AR	$2000
2/28/2011	CR	Revenue	-$2000
At the beginning of 3rd month, reverse the earlier entries			
3/1/2011	DR	Revenue	$2000
3/1/2011	CR	Unbilled AR	-$2000

Accounting date	Debit/Credit	Account	Amount
At the end of 3rd month, we recognize the entire revenue i.e. $3000 and record it to actual AR account, as we'll issue the invoice to the customer.			
3/31/2011	DR	AR	$3000
3/31/2011	CR	Revenue	-$3000

In order to use the unbilled revenue accrual, we need to configure, unbilled AR distribution code and associate it with regular AR distribution code. The batch process **Load GL – Unbilled Revenue Accrual (BIACCRUE)** is executed to create accrual accounting entries. We'll see other necessary setup options for this in the next section. Follow this navigation to execute the Load GL – Unbilled Revenue Accrual process:

Billing | Generate Invoices | Accrue Unbilled Activity | Non-Consolidated Bills | Accrue Unbilled Revenue

Understanding important billing configurations

So far we have familiarized ourselves with the basic business process and the system features used by the PeopleSoft Billing module. Now we will understand some of the important configurations that enable these business processes. We'll discuss the following configuration options, which are not necessarily set up in the same order:

- Invoice number IDs
- Bill types
- Bill sources
- Invoice formatting and printing options
- Distribution codes
- Billing charge codes
- Discounts and surcharges
- Billing business unit

Configuring invoice number IDs

PeopleSoft Billing offers a flexible invoice numbering structure that enables the creation of various conventions for invoice numbers.

Let's assume that Global Vehicles Inc. needs to number its invoices in the format GV-US-XXXXXXXXXX. The first part of the invoice ID is static where GV denotes Global Vehicles. The second segment indicates the geography (such as the US) and the last segment will denote the 10-digit invoice ID.

Billing allows us to structure invoice IDs with up to three segments. Only one of these segments can be auto-sequenced (a term which means the system automatically increments the number). The total length of the invoice ID cannot exceed 22 digits.

Follow this navigation to configure the invoice number ID:

Set Up Financials/Supply Chain | Product Related | Billing | Setup | Invoice Number ID

The following screenshot shows the **Invoice Number ID** configuration page:

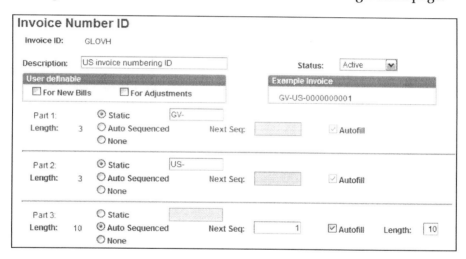

- **User definable:** Selecting a checkbox in this section allows a user to assign an invoice ID to new bills or bills that need adjustments. Leaving it unchecked means that the system forces the invoice ID by incrementing the last invoice ID.

Expert tip:

It is advisable to leave these checkboxes unchecked so that users cannot assign inconsistent IDs to invoices and create invoice IDs with gaps or different lengths.

- **Static/Auto Sequenced/None:** If a segment is not required, select **None**. Select **Static** for a segment where the value remains the same or **Auto Sequenced** to let the system automatically increment it.

Configuring distribution codes

A distribution code is a pre-defined collection of chartfield values. We specify a distribution code so that the system knows which chartfields to use while creating accounting entries. For example, we can specify a distribution code for an AR account, one for a deferred revenue account, unbilled revenue and so on.

Follow this navigation to configure distribution codes:

Set Up Financials/Supply Chain | Common Definitions | Distribution Accounting | Distribution Code

The following screenshot shows the **Distribution Code** configuration page:

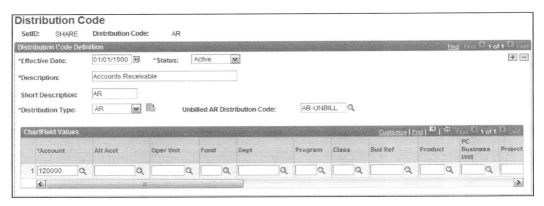

This example shows the distribution code for an AR account to be used in billing accounting entries.

- **Distribution Type:** This dropdown menu specifies the type of distribution code. Some of the values include **Revenue** (to be used for revenue accounts), **Discount** (to be used to specify distribution codes for bill discounts), **Unbill AR** (for unbilled revenue accrual), and so on.

- **Unbilled AR Distribution Code:** If we use the unbilled revenue accrual, we need to link the AR distribution code with an unbilled AR distribution code. Specify that value in this field.

- **Chartfield values:** Specify actual chartfield values used to record the amounts for this type of accounting entries.

The following screenshot shows the deferred revenue distribution code.

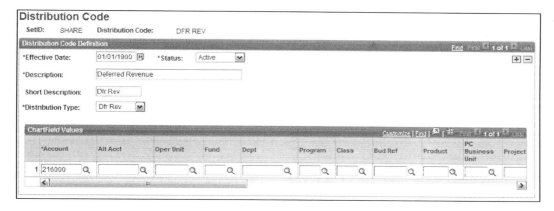

 Note that we can define multiple distribution codes for revenue, AR, deferred revenue, and so on, and use them as needed.

Configuring invoice formatting options

Invoice printing is an important activity and each organization has its own unique needs regarding what the invoice should look like. Invoice requirements cover various parameters, such as:

- **Layout**: Should the invoice be printed in the portrait or landscape mode?
- **Grouping**: How should the bill lines be grouped (such as by product ID)?
- **Summarization**: Should a summary invoice be printed along with the detailed invoice?
- **Discount, surcharge and tax**: Should the invoice display discount, surcharge and tax information on the invoice? If so, where should this information be printed?
- **Notes**: Where should the invoice header and line notes (comments) be printed?

All of these and more options are configured using Invoice Formatting Options.

Follow this navigation to configure the invoice formatting options:

Set Up Financials/Supply Chain | Product Related | Billing | Setup Invoice Options | Invoice Formatting Options

The following screenshot shows the **General** tab of the invoice formatting configuration page:

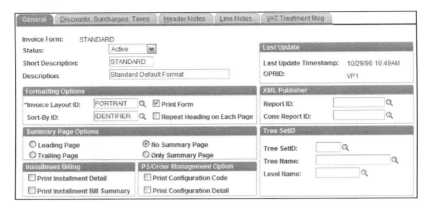

- **Invoice Layout ID:** Select one of the layout IDs delivered by PeopleSoft. Some of the values include **PORTRAIT, LANDSCAPE, CA51** (used for Contracts billing).

- **Print Form:** This checkbox controls if the invoice with this format should be printed by the system. Select this box to enable printing or leave unchecked to prevent printing.

- **Sort-By ID:** Select the parameter by which invoice lines should be sorted on the printed invoice.

- **Summary Page Options:** This option determines how or if the invoice summary page should be printed.

The following screenshot shows the **Discounts, Surcharges, Taxes** tab of the invoice formatting configuration page. This is used to control printing options for discount, surcharge, and tax amounts on the invoice.

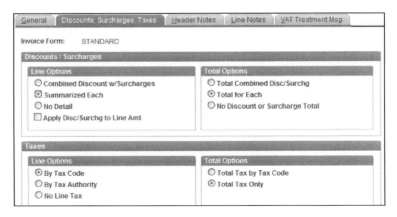

- **Discounts / Surcharges – Line Options:** This section determines how discount and surcharge amounts are printed on invoice, for example. if these amounts should be printed, if these they should be added to or deducted from the bill line amount or if they should be printed separately for each bill line.

- **Discounts / Surcharges – Total Options:** This section determines how discount and surcharge amount totals are printed on invoice, for example if the net amount is shown in one bill total, separate totals for discount and surcharge are shown or no totals are shown.

- **Taxes – Line Options:** This section controls how or if the bill line tax amounts are displayed on invoices.

- **Taxes – Total Options:** This section controls how the total tax amount is displayed on invoices.

The following screenshot shows the **Header Notes** tab of the invoice formatting configuration page. This tab is used to control header notes printing options.

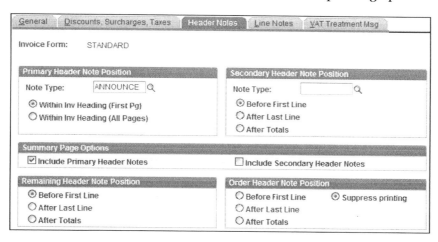

Header notes are used to record comments about the entire invoice. For example, we may print a note on each invoice that instructs the customer about a new discount scheme that is going on. Note types are configured separately before setting up invoice formatting options.

Specify the appropriate note type for primary or secondary notes. We can have multiple invoice header notes.

The **Line Notes** tab is used to control line notes printing options.

The **VAT Treatment Msg** tab contains options to control where the VAT message is printed on the invoice.

Configuring billing charge codes

We saw how billing charge codes are entered on the billing entry page. In many cases, the billing module receives data from the Order Management, Project Costing or Contracts modules in the form of customer orders. In this case, the product or service ID being sold comes from the interface. However, if bills are entered manually, we need to specify the activity which needs to be billed. This is where we need to configure charge codes.

Follow this navigation to configure billing charge codes:

Set Up Financials/Supply Chain | Product Related | Billing | Setup | Charge Code

The following screenshot shows the **Charge Code** tab of the configuration page:

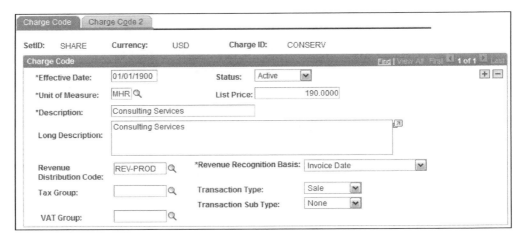

- **Unit of Measure:** This field specifies the unit of measure for the given product or service activity.

- **List Price:** Specify the price per unit of this product or service activity.

- **Revenue Distribution Code:** Specify the distribution code to record the revenue from this activity. Recall our earlier discussion on how to configure distribution codes.

- **Revenue Recognition Basis:** This field is used to specify the revenue recognition basis for deferred revenue process. If the basis value is **Invoice Date**, deferred revenue processing is not done. Any other value, such as **Ship Date,** instructs the system to perform deferred revenue processing with the selected value as revenue recognition basis.

- **Charge Code 2** tab contains the options to control VAT processing.

Configuring discounts and surcharges

In the course of regular business processing, discounts are offered or surcharges (additional charges on invoice amounts) are applied to invoices. A discount will reduce the invoice amount, while a surcharge will increase it. We can define as many discount or surcharge codes as required. These can be defined as are fixed amounts or as percentages of bill amounts. Follow this navigation to configure codes for discounts and surcharges:

Set Up Financials/Supply Chain | Product Related | Billing | Setup | Discount & Surcharge

The following screenshot shows the **Discount & Surcharge** configuration page:

- **Distribution code:** Specify the distribution code to record the discount or surcharge amount
- **Type:** Specify if this is a discount or surcharge
- **Computation Basis:** As discussed earlier, we can specify if this needs to be a fixed amount (such as $50) or a percentage of the invoice line amount to which it is applied (5% in this example)

Configuring billing business unit

Billing business unit represents an entity within an organization that needs to maintain its own invoices. This can be a country for a global organization, a separate business line, or any other entity as required.

Before we proceed to understanding how to configure a business unit, let's first understand the hierarchy of Billing setups. The following table shows the hierarchy levels for billing:

Hierarchy	Configuration
Level 1 (Top)	Business unit
Level 2	Bill type
Level 3	Bill source
Level 4	Customer
Level 5 (Bottom)	Bill entry

What this means is that configuration options set up at the business unit level are inherited by all the levels below. If the system doesn't find a configuration value at any of the lower levels, it looks for that option at the higher level. Thus if the system doesn't find a value on the bill, it looks for it at the customer level. If it is not found there, it looks for it at the bill source level and so on. A configuration option specified at a lower level always supersedes the value specified at the higher level.

Expert tip:
Take advantage of the configuration hierarchy by specifying the default options that will be used in most of the cases, at the highest level (that is, Business Unit). All levels below will inherit it. This avoids repeating configurations at all the levels. If the configuration value needs to be different at a particular level, we can specify it for that specific level.

Follow this navigation to configure billing business unit:

Set Up Financials/Supply Chain | Business Unit Related | Billing | Billing Definition

The following screenshot shows the **Business Unit 1** tab of the business unit configuration page:

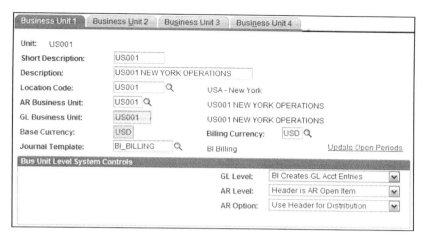

- **AR Business Unit:** Specify the AR BU that receives the billing data for tracking

- **GL Business Unit:** This value is automatically populated based on the selected AR business unit

 The AR and GL business units must be configured before we start configuring the billing business unit.

- **GL Level:** This option controls the creation of accounting entries for billing invoices. Available values are as follows:

    ° **No GL Acct Entries:** If selected, no accounting entries are created by the Billing module.

    ° **BI Creates Acctg Entries:** If selected, PeopleSoft Billing (Billing pre-load batch process) creates accounting entries for invoices. When billing data is interfaced to Accounts Receivable, accounting entries are loaded along with invoice details.

    ° **AR Creates Acctg Entries:** If selected, the Accounts Receivable module creates accounting entries for invoices based on pre-defined accounting defaults. The Billing module does not store any accounting information.

- **AR Level:** This option drives how billing invoices are tracked in the AR module. The available values are as follows:
  - ◦ **Header is AR Open Item:** If selected, the AR module creates an open item for each bill for tracking. For example, for an invoice containing 3 lines for $100, $200 and $300, AR creates a single item of $600 for follow up with the customer.
  - ◦ **Bill Line is AR Open Item:** If selected, the AR module creates an open item for each bill line for tracking. In the previous example, AR creates 3 open items for $100, $200 and $300 for follow up with the customer.
- **AR Option:** This field controls how the accounting distribution details are passed on from Billing invoices to AR open items. Available values are as follows:
  - ◦ **Use Header for Distribution:** This value can be selected only if we select **Header is AR Open Item** for the **AR Level** field. As we saw, this means that there is only one open item for the entire invoice and the bill header accounting information is sent to AR.
  - ◦ **Use Line for Distribution:** This option can be selected for both of the values of AR Level field. If selected, the bill line accounting information for each bill line is sent to AR.

The following screenshot shows the **Business Unit 2** tab of the business unit configuration page:

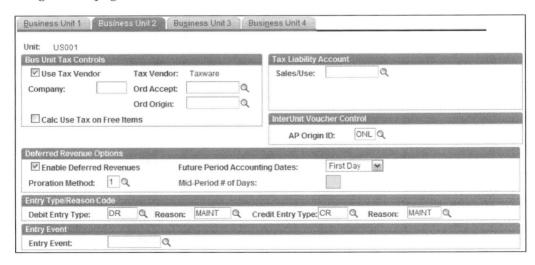

- **Bus Unit Tax Controls:** This section is visible only if a third party product (Taxware or Vertex) is installed to calculate taxes on bill lines. If Billing does its own tax calculation and these products are not required, an installation option needs to be configured accordingly.

- **Tax Liability Account:** This field stores the distribution code for recording amounts arising from tax liability on invoices. This section is visible only if we use Vertex or Taxware.

- **Enable Deferred Revenues:** We have discussed the concept of deferred revenue an the earlier section. To enable the system to process deferred revenue, this checkbox has to be selected.

- **Proration Method:** Specify one of the proration methods to be used to calculate how much revenue can be recognized and the amount that needs to be deferred.

- **Future Period Accounting Dates:** This option determines what accounting date needs to be used for future dated accounting entries. Recall that deferred revenue processing creates such entries.

- **Entry Type/Reason Code:** When the AR module creates the accounting entries for invoices, it needs to know the chartfields (including accounts) to be used for debit and credit entries. In order to do that, we configure entry types and entry reasons in the AR module. The Load AR Pending Items process needs to provide these values while sending the data from Billing to Accounts Receivable. If the invoice itself does not contain the necessary accounting details, it looks at the accounting defaults specified in this section.

Here we need to specify the values for debit as well as credit entries. We'll see how to configure entry types and entry reasons in the Accounts Receivable chapter.

The following screenshot shows the **Business Unit 3** tab of the business unit configuration page:

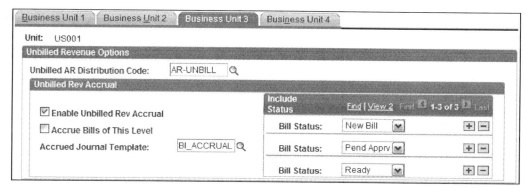

This tab contains configuration options for the unbilled revenue accrual process. They are as follows:

- **Unbilled AR Distribution Code:** Specify the default distribution code to be used for Unbilled AR account (recall the unbilled AR entries from the previous section).

- **Enable Unbilled Rev Accrual:** Select this checkbox if we need to use unbilled revenue processing.

- **Accrue Bills of This Level:** PeopleSoft offers the option to accrue bills at the business unit or bill type level. Select this checkbox if accrual needs to happen at business unit level.

- **Include Status:** We can decide the status for bills that need to be included in the accrual process. For example, if only those bills which have completed all the processing need to be accrued, select the value **Finalized**.

The following screenshot shows the **Business Unit 4** tab of the business unit configuration page:

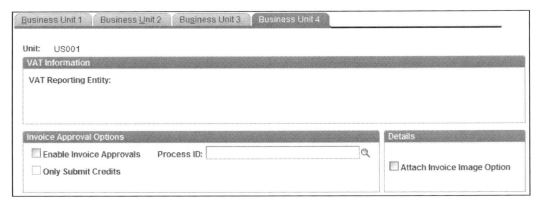

- **VAT Information:** This section is visible only if the business unit processes Value Added Tax (VAT). It contains information such as VAT Reporting Entity, whether the BU sells goods or services, the location where services are performed, and so on.

- **Invoice Approval Options:** If an organization decides to use workflow for invoice approvals, select the Enable Invoice Approvals flag and provide the process ID that specifies the workflow rules. Note that this workflow needs to be customized using Application designer.

- **Attach Invoice Image Option:** If selected, an image of the printed invoice is attached to the invoice.

Configuring bill types

A bill type categorizes the billing transactions to segregate them on separate bills. The bill type allows various processing options to be configured that determine how bills from that particular bill type are processed. Bill type is the second level of the billing hierarchy and inherits all options defined for the business unit.

Let's try to understand how bill types can be used. Consider an organization which is part of a group of companies. It sells its products to external customers as well as sister companies in the same group. Now if it wishes to separate the invoices issued to group companies from the invoices issued to external customers, it can use the bill types to do so. It can configure two separate bill types (let's say INTERNAL and EXTERNAL) for this purpose. It can also configure various options to process these differently if needed. This is just one example of how bill types can be used. Assume that this firm sells products as well as performing professional services. If needed, it can define two bill types: such as PRODUCTS and SERVICES to segregate items on different invoices.

Follow this navigation to configure a bill type:

Set Up Financials/Supply Chain | Product Related | Billing | Setup | Bill Type

The following screenshot shows the **Bill Type 1** tab of the bill type page:

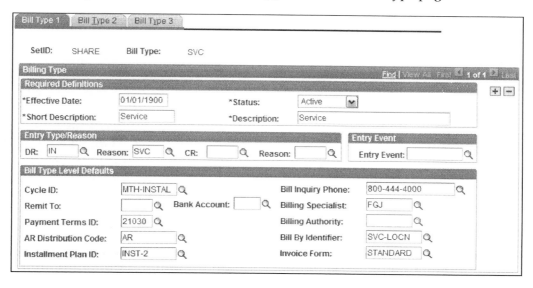

- **Entry Type/Reason:** We saw that default entry type and reason values are defined for business units. If these need to be different for invoices from this bill type, specify the same here.

- **Bill By Identifier:** Specify the bill by identifier to be used for summarizing bill lines from the interface.

- **Invoice Form:** This field specifies the pre-defined invoice formatting options that we saw earlier.

- **AR Distribution Code:** This field specifies the distribution code for Accounts Receivable chartfields to be used for invoices having this bill type.

The following screenshot shows the **Bill Type 2** tab of the bill type page:

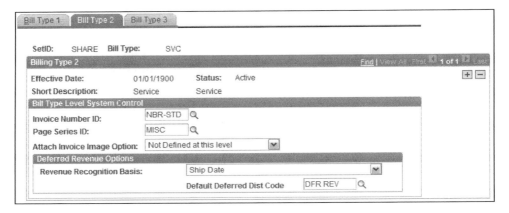

- **Invoice Number ID:** This field specifies the invoice numbering scheme to be used for this bill type.

- **Page Series ID:** The billing entry component contains a large number of pages. Using a page series definition, we can specify the order in which these options should be displayed by the system. Specify the page series ID in this field.

- **Attach Invoice Image Option:** We saw this configuration option at the business unit level. If we wish to specify a value to enable or disable invoice imaging for this bill type, select the appropriate value.

- **Deferred Revenue Options:** If deferred revenue processing is being used, specify the revenue recognition basis (when the revenue can be recognized in future) and provide the distribution code to record deferred revenue.

 If the revenue recognition basis is Invoice Date, the system assumes that deferred revenue is not applicable.

The following screenshot shows the **Bill Type 3** tab of the bill type page.

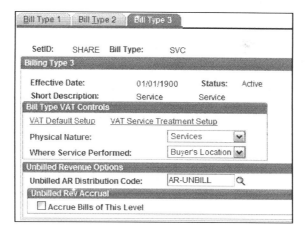

We saw that all these options existed at the business unit as well. If they need to be different for this bill type, specify the appropriate values in this tab.

Configuring bill sources

Bill data can originate from various sources. An organization may receive bills from a non-PeopleSoft system or other PeopleSoft modules such as Order Management, Contracts, and so on. A bill source enables us to track the origin of each bill and assign default configuration values.

Bill source is the third level of billing hierarchy and it inherits the configuration options from the business unit and bill type levels. Follow this navigation to configure a bill source:

Set Up Financials/Supply Chain | Product Related | Billing | Setup | Bill Source

Note that you'll notice that most of the configuration options on these pages will be seen on the bill type pages as well. The following screenshot shows the **Bill Source** tab of the bill source page.

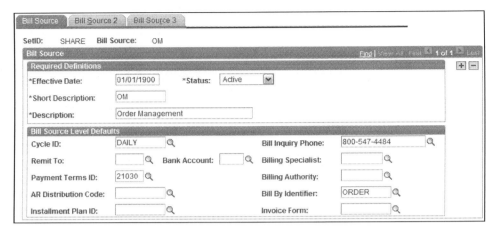

All of the configuration options inherit values defined from higher levels of the hierarchy. If we wish to specify a different value for this bill source, we can do it here. For others, we can simply leave the fields blank, so that the system can pick it up from the bill type.

The following screenshot shows the **Bill Source 2** tab of the bill source page.

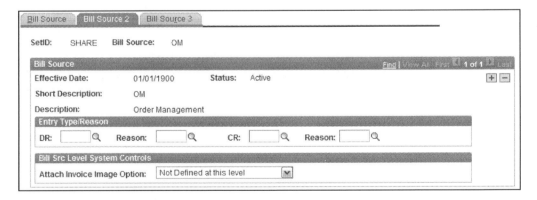

Leave these fields blank if the configuration values are same as that of the bill type.

The following screenshot shows the **Bill Source 3** tab of the bill source page.

Specify a different value for VAT controls for this bill source, if required.

Now that we have familiarized ourselves with the Billing business processes and important configurations, let's us consider some typical situations that arise during Billing implementation.

Implementation challenge 1

An organization wishes that invoices for one of its customers should not be printed, while for others, invoice printing should take place. Assume that all the customers use same bill type.

Solution

Recall the invoice formatting configuration we discussed earlier. The **General** tab contains a **Print Form checkbox**. Leaving this checkbox unchecked ensures that the invoice will not be printed. We'll need to perform the following configurations to achieve this objective:

- Configure an invoice form with Print Form field checked to enable invoice printing. Let's call this invoice form **PRINT**.

- Configure another invoice form with Print Form field unchecked to disable invoice printing. Let's call this invoice form **NOPRINT**.

- Attach the **PRINT** invoice form to the bill type to be used.

- Attach the **NOPRINT** invoice form to the customer whose invoices should not be printed.

- For all other customers leave the invoice form field blank.

We know that in billing hierarchy, the customer comes at a level lower than that of the bill type. As a result, any configuration value defined at customer level overrides the value defined for the bill type. Thus, for all the regular customers, when the system does not find an invoice form value, it uses the value PRINT defined for the higher level: bill type. On the other hand, for all invoices belonging to the specific customer, it uses the value NOPRINT and the system automatically prevents the printing of its invoices.

Implementation challenge 2

An organization sells two types of products: diagnostic equipment and surgical supplies. It receives the bill data for these from an external non-PeopleSoft system. It needs to ensure that bill data for surgical supplies are summarized by Customer and Order number, while the bill data for diagnostic equipment are summarized by Customer and Contract number. Invoices for diagnostic equipment and surgical supplies should be printed in the portrait and landscape formats respectively.

Solution

We need to perform the following steps for this requirement:

- Configure two bill types. Let's call them SURGICAL and DIAGNOSTIC.
- A customized interface program needs to be developed to load the bill data into Billing interface tables. The code should populate the values SURGICAL and DIAGNOSTIC for appropriate bills in the bill type field of interface table.
- Configure two Bill By Identifiers. Let's call them CUST_ORDER and CUST_CONTRACT.
- Specify Customer ID and Order Number as summarizing parameters for CUST_ORDER bill by identifier.
- Specify Customer ID and Contract Number as summarizing parameters for CUST_CONTRACT bill by identifier.
- Configure two invoice forms: LANDSCAPE and PORTRAIT. Specify the appropriate print layouts for both.
- Now attach the invoice form and bill by identifier to the bill type as shown:

Bill type	Invoice form	Bill by Identifier
SURGICAL	PORTRAIT	CUST_CONTRACT
DIAGNOSTIC	LANDSCAPE	CUST_ORDER

Thus, when the Billing Interface batch process encounters a bill for surgical supplies in the interface table, it reads the bill type value SURGICAL. When it refers to this bill type definition, it retrieves PORTRAIT as the invoice form and CUST_CONTRACT as the bill by identifier. Thus it knows that the bill lines need to be summarized by Customer ID and Contract number, while the invoice needs to be printed in PORTRAIT layout

Summary

Bills can be entered into the system manually or brought in through the Billing interface. PeopleSoft offers a set of interface tables which act as a staging area for bills coming from other PeopleSoft modules such as Order Management, Contracts, and so on or external non-PeopleSoft systems. A batch process known as Billing Interface reads the data from interface tables, performs the validations and creates bills in the Billing system. This option is suitable for high volumes of billing data.

A set of batch processes perform various operations such as finalizing the bill, printing invoices, creating accounting entries, and interfacing the bill data to other PeopleSoft modules such as General Ledger, Accounts Receivable, and Accounts Payable.

If created invoices need to be modified, PeopleSoft offers two methods to do so: crediting entire bill or crediting specific bill lines. In Billing module, we can handle various scenarios such as Deferred Revenues (where revenue recording can be deferred to future accounting dates) and Unbilled Revenue Accrual (where revenue is recognized even though an invoice is not created).

4
PeopleSoft Accounts Receivable Module

Accounts Receivable is an important module in the 'Order to Cash' business process. It comes into the picture after the Billing processes that we have discussed in the previous chapter. At any given time, a typical organization has a large number of outstanding invoices, which are not yet paid by its customers. Ensuring that they are tracked regularly, payments are received from customers within promised timelines, and corrective actions are taken if payments are delayed is critical for the organization's functioning. This task has a direct impact on its cash flows. Accounts Receivable (or AR, as it is commonly known) performs these critical functions and presents a picture of outstanding amounts owed by the organization's customers. In a nutshell, the AR module is responsible for the entry of items (outstanding invoices), handling customer payments, managing customer invoices, and creating customer correspondence such customer statements and dunning letters.

In this chapter, we'll gain an understanding of important AR processes and configurations that are required.

Understanding Accounts Receivable process flow

Before we start our discussion of Accounts Receivable processes, let's first understand two most commonly used AR terms: pending items and items. We said earlier that customer invoices are interfaced from the Billing module (although it is not the only source for AR). When these transactions (from various sources) enter the AR system, they are known as **pending items**. They are still not part of the total customer balance. A batch process known as **Receivables Update** later posts these pending items to the customer accounts and updates the outstanding balance. Now these transactions are referred to as **items**. In other words, a transaction that is part of a total customer account balance is an **item,** while a transaction that is still waiting to be posted to a customer account is a **pending item**.

Let's consider a simple example to understand this. Assume that the total outstanding balance for a customer is $1000. Now the Billing module sends two more invoices: INVOICE 1 for $100 and INVOICE 2 for $200 to AR. The **Load AR Pending Items (BILDAR01)** process creates two pending items in the AR system for these invoices. Even after they are created, the customer balance is still $1,000, as these invoices are not yet posted to the customer account. Now let's assume that the Receivable Update process picks up INVOICE 1 and posts it. Thus, the customer outstanding balance is now $1,100. In other words, INVOICE 1 is now an item, while INVOICE 2 is still a pending item, waiting to be posted. When the AR UPDATE process picks up INVOICE 2 and posts it, the customer balance is updated to $1,300. Now both INVOICE 1 and INVOICE 2 are items in AR. In the PeopleSoft AR module, pending items are always entered as part of a group, known as a pending item group. A pending item can never be a stand-alone entity.

The following schematic shows the typical AR steps:

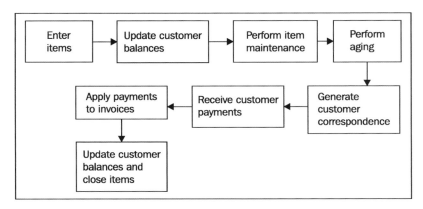

Note that the previous diagram is a simplified illustration of AR activities in a logical sequence. It is not necessary that the displayed activities have to occur in the exact same sequence as shown. Some activities can take place in parallel as well. For the sake of simplicity and due to the page constraints, we will only discuss certain AR processes.

The AR process begins with the pending item entry, either manually or through an automated interface. Pending items can be brought in from other PeopleSoft modules such as Billing, Purchasing, and so on using, delivered PeopleSoft programs or from non-PeopleSoft systems using a customized programs. PeopleSoft AR also offers an option to enter pending items manually.

As discussed previously, the Receivable Update (AR UPDATE) batch process is executed to validate and post these pending items to the appropriate customer account. Note that this process needs to be executed after performing any transaction (such as application of a payment to close an item, write off an item, and so on) that results in change of customer balance.

Once the pending items are transformed into items and customer balance is updated, there are various transactions that may need to be performed. These transactions include writing off an item (partially or completely) due to various reasons, matching a debit item with a credit item, transferring an item to a different customer, and so on. Such activities are known as item maintenance. A utility known as the **Maintenance Worksheet** is used to perform item maintenance manually.

One of the important functions of the AR module is performing aging of items. This means tracking how long an item is outstanding after its creation. PeopleSoft offers a batch job to categorize items in various user-defined categories such as 0-30 days / 30-60 days / 60-90 days, and so on, and process them as required. Note that these categories are created based entirely on an organization's requirements. This process is critical to generating various aging reports to get a snapshot of how effective an organization is in collecting payments from its customers.

We can generate customer correspondence such as customer statements (listing outstanding invoices and received payments), dunning letters (to notify that a customer has exceeded the due date for an invoice), or follow-up letters.

The AR module is responsible for handling the payments from customers for the invoices sent to them. PeopleSoft offers the ability to enter payments manually or electronically using methods such as lockbox (payment file from a bank), EDI, Electronic Fund Transfer (EFT) and through spreadsheets. As you can imagine, manual payment entry is suitable only for small payment volumes. In PeopleSoft AR module, payments (manual or electronic) are always entered as part of a group, known as deposits. Thus a deposit can contain one or more payments. A payment can never exist without a deposit.

Finally, when customer payments are received, they need to be applied to the open (outstanding) invoices. There are two methods to achieve this. A utility known as Payment Worksheet is used to manually apply payments to open items. A batch process known as Payment Predictor is used to automate the payment application based on the rules configured for the same. Once payment is applied to an item, it is considered closed, the outstanding amount from the customer is closed and it is not tracked any more. Note that this is only one of the many possible ways to close an item.

Now we'll take a detailed look at the steps and configurations involved in each of these processes.

Understanding pending item accounting

We briefly discussed that pending items can be manually entered or loaded into PeopleSoft through an automated interface. In order to process these pending items, we first need to establish the necessary structure in the form of system function IDs, entry types and entry reasons. We'll explain these configurations now.

System function ID

PeopleSoft delivers a group of system functions to specify all the different activities that can be performed within the AR module. Each system function specifies the accounting entries created by the system for a particular transaction. The following table shows the system function types:

System function type	Description
DD	Direct debit: This is a form of receiving customer payments electronically
DM	Draft management: This is another form of customer payments
FC	Finance (Overdue) charges: These are the additional charges applied to a customer in the case of a late payment
IT	Item entry: This relates to the entry of customer invoices/debit memos (which increase customer outstanding balance) or credit memos (which decrease customer outstanding balance)
MT	Item maintenance: These transactions include item refunds, write-offs, and so on using maintenance worksheets or Automatic Maintenance batch process

System function type	Description
TR	Transfer worksheet: This relates to transferring an item from one customer to another
WS	Payment processing: These transactions include payment applications, pre-payments, discount processing and so on using worksheets and Payment predictor

As you can see, these system function types cover all of the possible AR activities that can create accounting entries. There are multiple system functions belonging to each group. For example, the IT system function type contains following system function IDs:

- IT-01: Create an Invoice/Debit Memo
- IT-02: Create a Credit Memo

 The accounting entry structure for each system function ID is defined by the system and cannot be changed.

Follow this navigation to review system function ID configuration:

Setup Financials/Supply Chain | Product Related | Receivables | Options | System Functions

The following screenshot shows the **System Function 1** tab of the page:

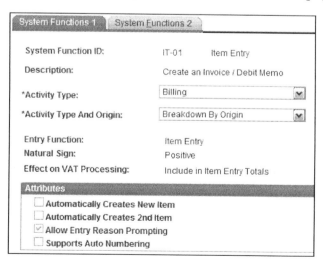

- **Entry Function**: This is a system-defined field, that cannot be changed. Two of the possible values in this field are Auto Entry and Item Entry. These indicate the two different categories of entry types. Automatic entry types indicate those items that are created by the system in the background, while Item Entry types indicate the items that are manually created or brought into AR by an external interface. We'll discuss this in more detail in the next section.

- **Natural Sign**: This field shows the sign to be used for the item using this system function. For example, an item belonging to IT-01 system function will have positive amount (which will increase the customer's outstanding balance), while an item with IT-02 system function will have negative amount (which will decrease the customer's outstanding balance).

The following screenshot shows the **System Function 2** tab of the page:

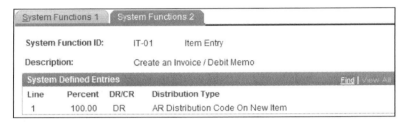

This tab shows the accounting entry that the system creates for an item belonging to this system function. Some system functions have both the debit and credit accounting lines defined. In these cases, the system creates the complete accounting entry. On the other hand, some system functions have only one accounting line (either debit or credit) defined by the system. The other line is user-defined and needs to be specified during configuration of item entry or automatic entry type.

Each AR item needs to have an item entry type or automatic entry type. Each item entry type or automatic entry type in turn is linked to a system function ID. This is how the system generates appropriate accounting entries for items.

Understanding entry types and entry reasons

Entry types are one of the most critical building blocks of AR module. An entry type is used to categorize items. We have already seen various categories used by the system functions. Entry types essentially build on that foundation. Each AR item must have an entry type.

For example, we can have an entry type such as **Invoice** used for invoices coming in from Billing systems. It will be linked to the IT-01 system function. We may have another entry type named **Debit Memo** used for additional charges created for a customer. As it is similar in function to an invoice (it increases a customer's outstanding balance), it can be again linked to IT-01 system function. As another example, we may need an entry type called **Credit Memo** for invoice credits coming from Billing (recall our discussion on credit invoices). It can be linked to the IT-02 system function. It is immaterial what name we use for these entry types.

The decision about how many and which entry types are needed depends entirely on which PeopleSoft AR features we need to use. For example, if we wish to handle customer payments, we need the entry type **Payments**. As you can imagine, this entry type will be based on a system function from the WS category of system functions.

Entry reasons are used to further categorize the items belonging to an entry type. For example, if we have an entry type called Invoice, we can define various entry reasons to specify different types of invoices, such as Consulting, System integration, Hardware sales, and so on.

Configuring entry types and entry reasons

PeopleSoft delivers various pre-defined entry types. We can decide to use them as delivered or modify them as needed. Follow this navigation to configure entry types:

Set Up Financials/Supply Chain | Product Related | Receivables | Options | Entry

Type | Entry Type

The following screenshot shows the **Entry Types** tab of the configuration page:

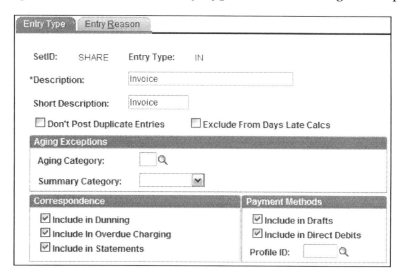

- **Don't Post Duplicate Entries**: In AR processing, the same item can have multiple entry types during its lifecycle. For example, an item numbered 1000 can have an entry type IN (Invoice) when it is created. Later, when it is paid, system creates the item ID 1000 with an entry type of PY (Payment). If the system encounters same items with different entry types, the one with this option selected takes precedence while posting.

 You should select this option only for the entry types representing Invoices.

- **Aging Exceptions**: We briefly saw how the aging process categorizes the items in defined categories. Specify the aging category options if you wish to age items with this entry type differently from the normal aging process. We'll discuss this in detail in the aging section.

- **Correspondence**: Specify if the item with this entry type should be included in the dunning letters, customer statements or overdue charging process.

The following screenshot shows the **Entry Reasons** tab of the configuration page:

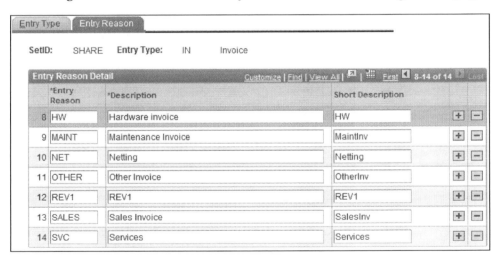

As mentioned earlier, entry reasons are used to further categorize items with an entry type. We can specify as many entry reasons as we wish. These are used by the automatic entry types and item entry types. **Entry Types** and **Entry Reasons** combinations are used to derive the accounting details for AR transactions.

Item entry types and automatic entry types

Item entry types and automatic entry types represent the two subsets of entry types. During the item processing, the system creates certain pending items automatically in the background, while some pending items are manually entered (or brought into the system from external sources). For example, when we apply a customer payment to an item, the system automatically creates a pending item with 'Payment' entry some type. We cannot really enter a pending item with this entry type. Such entry types are known as **Automatic entry types**. On the other hand, we can manually enter pending items such as invoices, debit items or credit items. Such entry types are known as **Item entry types**.

When we configure the item entry types and automatic entry types, we are essentially marking the existing entry types appropriately using the item entry or automatic entry type page.

Configuring item entry types

We need to set up an item entry type by linking an existing entry type to an appropriate system function ID and specifying other accounting entry options.

Follow this navigation to configure item entry types:

Set Up Financials/Supply Chain | Product Related | Receivables | Payments | Item Entry Type

The following screenshot shows the **Selection** tab of the configuration page:

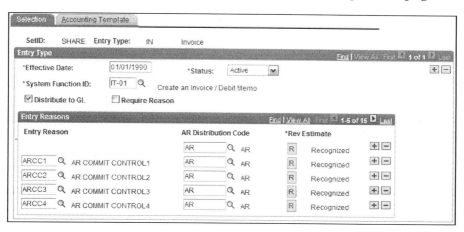

- **System Function ID:** Link the item entry type to a system function. Only two options are available for item entry types: **IT-01** and **IT-02**.

We can create as many item entry types (of course we need to create entry types first) as we wish and link them to the same system function. For example, we can have three item entry types IN (Invoice), DR (Debit memo), and CC (Customer charge), which all represent additional charges to the customer and link them to IT-01 system function.

 Deciding which item entry types to configure is one of the most critical aspects in an AR implementation. We need to thoroughly analyze an organization's reporting requirements to understand how it wishes to segregate the items and handle their accounting treatment. This drives the different item entry types and their accounting options.

- **Distribute to GL**: If this checkbox is selected, accounting entries created for this item entry type are distributed (sent) to General Ledger. Leave it unchecked if an item entry type is created for a specific purpose and its accounting entries should not be posted to GL.

- **Entry reasons**: Specify the entry reasons in these rows that need to be used for this item entry type.

- **AR Distribution Code**: Specify the chartfield combination to be used for the system generated accounting line.

Recall that the IT-01 system function creates only the debit side of the accounting entry using the AR distribution code, while the credit side is user-defined.

We can specify different AR distribution codes for different entry reasons. For each entry reason's user-defined side, specify the accounting details on the **Accounting Template** tab.

The following screenshot shows the **Accounting Template** tab where the credit side of the accounting entry is defined:

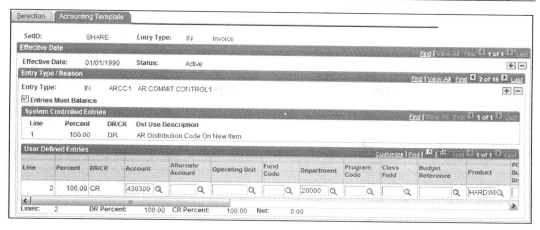

To sum it up, when the system encounters a pending item with IN item entry type and ARCC1 entry reason, it will do the following to create the accounting entry:

1. It looks at the system function IT-01 to get the structure of accounting entry.

2. It knows that the debit side needs to use chartfields as defined on the item entry type page for the given entry reason. In this case, it concludes that the distribution code AR needs to be used and uses the chartfields defined as part of this distribution code.

3. From the system function definition, it deduces that credit side of the accounting entry is user defined. It looks for the chartfield values on the Accounting Template and uses them to complete the accounting entry.

 Note that a user can override these values on the item and manually specify different chartfields.

Implementation challenge

An organization needs to enter and account two different types of invoices: Hardware sales and Software sales. Hardware invoices should be recorded to the Receivables account 250000, while the Software invoices should be recorded using a different Receivables account 350000. The revenue generated from Hardware and Software invoices needs to be tracked using different revenue accounts: 100000 and 900000 respectively. For the sake of simplicity, we will not consider chartfields other than ACCOUNT.

Solution

Let's sum up the accounting requirements discussed previously in the following table:

Hardware Invoices	DR Receivables (250000)
	CR Revenue (100000)
Software Invoices	DR Receivables (350000)
	CR Revenue (900000)

Here we need an Item entry type to manually enter these different invoice transactions. Based on our previous discussion, we can use the IT-01 system function and configure an Item Entry Type called IN. Now as there are two types of invoice transactions with different accounting requirements, we'll need two entry reasons. Let's name them HW and SW.

Now how will these entry reasons derive the AR side of the accounting entry? The answer is—'using AR distribution code'. As there are two different AR accounts, we'll need two distribution codes as well. We'll name them ARHW (distribution code for hardware invoices) and ARSW (distribution code for software invoices). These distribution codes will be configured as shown next:

Distribution code	Account
ARHW	250000
ARSW	350000

Once we assign the appropriate distribution code to the entry reason, it'll point to the correct AR account.

Finally, we'll specify the right revenue account for entry reasons on the Accounting Template tab. Thus, the final configuration for entry type and entry reason will be as shown in the following table:

Item Entry Type	Entry Reason	Distribution Code	Accounting Template
IN	HW	ARHW	100000
IN	SW	ARSW	900000

Configuring automatic entry types

As part of configuring an automatic entry type, we need to select a system function and link it to an entry type. Similar to item entry type, we need to specify the chartfields to be used to create accounting entries.

Follow this navigation to configure automatic entry types:

Set Up Financials/Supply Chain | Product Related | Receivables | Payments | Automatic Entry Type

The following screenshot shows the **Selection** tab of the configuration page:

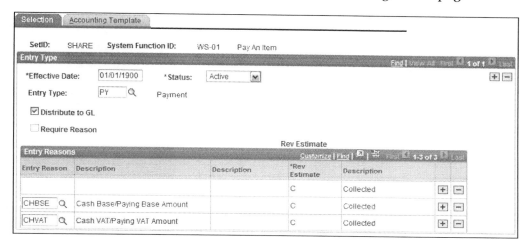

Once a system function is selected, we can assign a previously enabled entry type to it in the Entry Type field. Similarly to item entry type, we can decide what entry reasons need to be used for this automatic entry type. Note that the fields on this tab vary according to the selected system function.

Specify the chartfields to be used for accounting entry creation on the Accounting Template tab.

The following screenshot shows the **Accounting Template** tab:

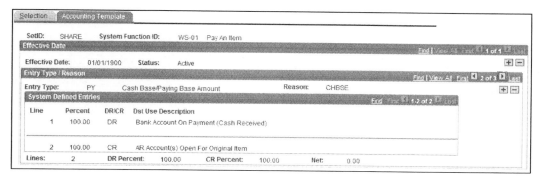

In the given example, we can see that both the debit and credit lines of the accounting entry are created by the system, which is the case with most of the system functions. However, for some system functions (and in turn, some automatic entry types) one of the two lines is user-defined and we need to provide the default chartfield values for that user-defined line.

Understanding pending item entry

Pending items can either be entered manually using online pages or loaded through an interface. We'll briefly discuss these methods here.

PeopleSoft offers the following staging tables to store pending items:

Table	Description
GROUP_CONTROL	Mandatory: This table holds the details of the pending item groups such as the number of pending items, total amount, and so on
PENDING_ITEM	Mandatory: Each row in this table indicates a pending item
PENDING_VAT	Optional: If VAT processing is applicable, this table holds the VAT information for pending items
PENDING_TAX	Optional: This table is used to hold India tax information
PENDING_TAX_DTL	Optional: This table is used to hold India tax information
PENDING_DST	Optional: This table holds the accounting information for the pending items

If other PeopleSoft modules send transactions to AR, a dedicated program (such as BILDAR01 for the Billing module) loads the data into these staging tables. If we wish to bring in AR transactions from a non-PeopleSoft system, we need to develop a custom program to populate these tables as required. However, irrespective of how pending items enter the AR module, they are processed by the Receivable Update process to post them. This is where the pending items are converted into items.

Entering pending items manually also loads the same tables listed previously. We'll go through a few pages used for online pending item entry.

Follow this navigation to access online pending entry pages:

Accounts Receivable | Pending Items | Online Items | Group Entry

Note that pending items need to be entered as a part of group even if there is only one pending item. The following screenshot shows the **Group Control** tab, where we specify the statistics of the pending item group, such as group currency, number of pending items, total amount, and so on.

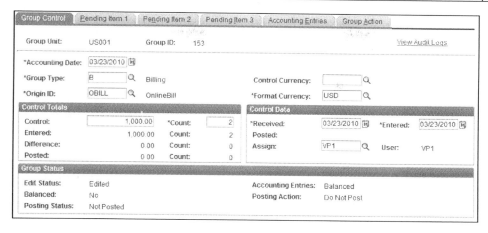

Subsequent tabs such as **Pending Item 1**, **Pending Item 2,** and **Pending Item 3** are used to enter additional details about the individual pending item, such as Item ID, amount, payment terms, reference details, and so on.

The **Accounting Entries** tab is used to create the accounting entries online for a pending item. If they are already created, they are displayed on this tab.

The last tab, **Group Action**, controls various actions for the pending item group. The following screenshot shows the buttons and options on the **Group Action** tab:

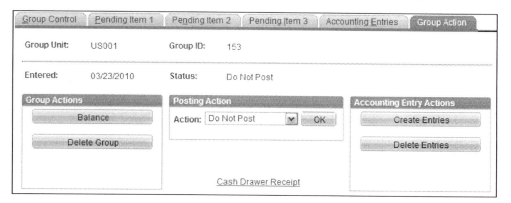

- **Balance**: When this button is clicked, the system checks if the control amount and count are equal to the entered amount and count. If they are equal, it checks if the accounting entries are balanced. If the totals are out of balance, the system shows a warning message.

- **Delete Group**: If this button is clicked, the entered pending group is deleted.

- **Posting Action**: This field controls how AR posts the pending item group.

Possible options are:

- **Do Not Post**: This system saves the changes to group and pending items, but the group is not picked by the AR UPDATE process.

- **Post Now**: This results in the Receivable Update process being triggered to post the pending item group.

- **Post Now to GL**: This results in the Receivable Update process being triggered to post the pending item group followed by the processes to create journals and post them (such as Journal Generator and Journal Post) to GL.

- **Batch Priority**: This option instructs the system to pick up this pending item group when either the Receivables Update configured to pick up the priority groups runs next time or a regular Receivables Update runs, whichever is earlier.

- **Batch Standard**: This option results in the pending item group being picked up for posting when the standard scheduled Receivables Update job runs next time.

Receivable Update process

The Receivables Update process is probably one of the most important AR processes: it needs to be run to post any pending items. These pending items could be manually entered as discussed previously or through maintenance and payment worksheets.

Note that the AR Update process does not pick up a pending item group for posting if its Posting Action is Do Not Post.

Follow this navigation to execute the Receivables update process:

Accounts Receivable | Receivables Update | Request Receivables Update

Understanding item maintenance

Now that we have successfully entered the pending items into the system and posted them using Receivable Update process, we are ready to track them. However, there are many situations where items need to be modified before we receive payments for them. Before we proceed, let's remember the conventions for the debit and credit items.

In AR terms, a debit item increases a customer's outstanding balance. For example, an invoice, a debit memo (which represents some additional charge), and so on. Such debit item amounts are always positive.

A credit item decreases a customer's outstanding balance. Examples include an invoice that was credited (recall our discussion in the Billing chapter), a discount, a write off, and so on. Such credit item amounts are always negative.

Now, let's consider the following scenarios:

- **Scenario 1**: A customer has two outstanding invoices of $100 and $300. However we have also issued a credit for $400 to correct a billing error in the past.

- **Scenario 2**: A customer's account shows a credit of $500. Now this credit amount needs to be refunded to the customer.

- **Scenario 3**: We discover that due to a dispute, an outstanding invoice for the amount of $350 will not be paid by the customer and we need to take it off the system.

In the first scenario, we can ask the customer to pay the $100 and $300 invoices while we send a check to pay for the $400 credit. However, wouldn't it be much easier if we just match the total of $400 that the customer needs to pay us with the $400 that we need to pay the customer and close the three items? This will certainly save the effort of processing 3 different transactions. This is known as offsetting the debit items ($100 and $300) against the credit items (-$400).

In the second scenario, we need to select the credit item for customer and issue a payment through the Accounts Payable module. This is known as issuing a refund.

In the third scenario, we need to cancel the invoice and remove it from the customer's account without receiving any payment for it. This is known as writing off an item. We can write off an item completely or partially.

These activities are known as item maintenance. The PeopleSoft AR module offers two methods to perform maintenance activities:

- Automatic maintenance process (AR_AUTOMNT)
- Maintenance worksheets (manual)

Automatic maintenance

We can automate the item maintenance activities in AR module by following these two steps:

1. Configure the automatic maintenance method
2. Execute the Automatic maintenance batch process

Automatic maintenance method is used to define the rules for automatic maintenance of debit and credit items. There are three ways in which we can perform this activity:

- By specifying the matching options for debit and credit items
- By using a PeopleSoft-delivered algorithm to match items
- By instructing the system to write off unmatched items with a certain entry type and entry reason

Follow this navigation to configure the automatic maintenance method:

Set Up Financials/Supply Chain | Product Related | Receivables | Credit/ Collections | Automatic Maintenance Method

The following screenshot shows the **Method Summary** tab of the configuration page. This tab is just a summary of configuration options defined on the Method Detail tab.

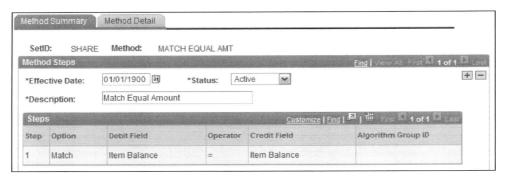

As you can see, this method instructs the automatic batch process to match debit and credit items with amounts that match exactly.

Let's take a look at the Method Detail tab to see how it is configured.

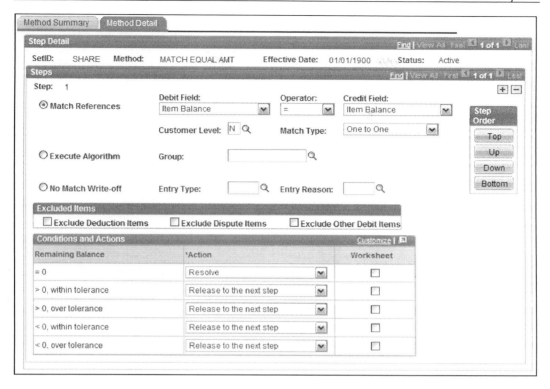

As you can see, we can choose how the maintenance should be performed.

- **Match Reference**: In this method, we can specify the matching parameters for debit and credit items. For example, we can decide to match the amounts or purchase order numbers of the items. The appropriate value needs to be selected from the Debit Field and Credit Field dropdown menus.

- **Execute Algorithm**: PeopleSoft delivers a matching algorithm called #OLDEST, which matches the open debit and credit items for a customer with oldest due dates first. If needed, we can develop our own customized algorithms to be used for maintenance.

- **No Match Write-Off**: We can instruct the system to write off any items with a specific entry type or entry reason that could not be matched by previous steps. Of course, the item amount must be less than the write-off limit.

  For the Match Reference and Execute Algorithm methods, we can also specify which actions should be taken if the debit and credit amounts don't match and there is a remaining balance. The available options are:

- **Resolve**: This option instructs the system to match the entire amount of items and close them. This option should be used only when there is no remaining balance.

- **Resolve, Write-off Balance**: This instructs the system to match the items, close them, and write off the remaining balance. This option should be used only when the remaining balance is greater than or less than zero but within the tolerance limits.

- **Resolve, Create New Item**: This option ensures that system matches items, closes them, and creates a new item for the amount of remaining balance. It uses an entry type of MD (create a new debit) if the balance is positive or MC (create a new credit) if the balance is negative.

- **Resolve, Item Balance Open**: This option instructs the system to close items but keep the item with the latest due date open. The amount for this item is changed to the remaining balance.

- **Release to Next Step**: This action simply makes the debit and credit items available to the next step.

Note that there can be multiple steps in an automatic maintenance method. For example, in Step 1, we can use the Match References method and match all debit and credit items whose amounts are equal. In Step 2, we can match debit and credit items whose purchase order numbers are the same. In Step 3, we can use No Match Write Off method and write off any unmatched items with a certain entry type.

An automatic maintenance method is assigned to the AR business unit, which is used as a default by the Automatic Maintenance process. However we can override it while running the process.

Now that we have defined the rules for automatic maintenance, we can execute the Automatic Maintenance process.

Follow this navigation to run the process:

Accounts Receivable | Receivables Maintenance | Automatic Maintenance | Request Automatic Maintenance

The following screenshot shows the run control page where we can specify the options to execute the process.

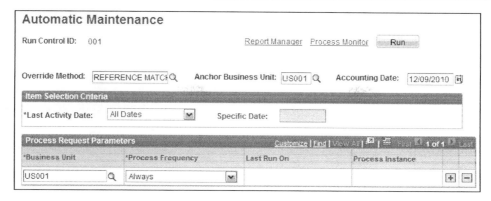

Override Method: To override the method specified at the business unit, provide a value in this field. Available options are: **MATCH EQUAL AMT** (match equal amount), **NO MATCH WO** (no match write-off), **OLDEST** (using #OLDEST algorithm) and **REFERENCE MATCH**.

The Automatic Maintenance process creates match groups for the items that are matched. The match groups also contain any new write-off items as well as new adjustment items created. These groups are automatically set to post or put on maintenance worksheets if specified on the automatic maintenance method.

Maintenance worksheets

Maintenance worksheets are used to perform offsets, write-offs (for debit as well as credit items), and refunds manually.

Follow this navigation to create a maintenance worksheet:

Accounts Receivable | Receivables Maintenance | Maintenance Worksheet | Create Worksheet

The following screenshot shows the **Worksheet Selection** tab where we specify the parameters (such as Customer ID, Accounting date, and so on) to select items that need to be processed:

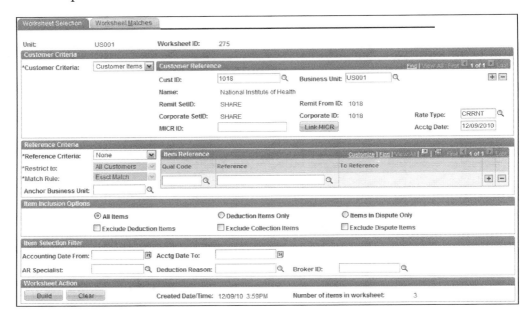

In the given example, we have given the customer ID and business unit as selection parameters, so that the system retrieves all open items for the given customer. It also shows the number of items that will be pulled onto the worksheet as number of items in worksheet.

Click the **Build** button to create the worksheet. The system automatically opens the Worksheet Application section.

The following screenshot shows the **Worksheet Application** tab where we can perform maintenance activities:

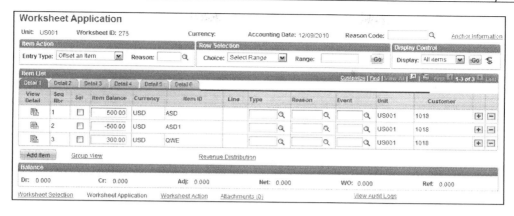

As you can see, the system pulls all the open items for specified customer and business unit on this page. The **Entry Type** dropdown menu offers the following options: **Offset an Item, Refund a Credit, Write-off a Debit, Write-off a credit**.

The **Balance** section shows the following amounts: **Dr** (Debit), **Cr** (Credit), **Adj** (Adjustment), **Net** (Remaining balance), **WO** (Write-off),and **Ref** (Refund).

Select the item or items that need to be maintained by checking the **Sel** checkbox and selecting the appropriate operation from the **Entry Type** menu.

If we decide to offset the $500 and -$500 items, the page changes as shown in the following screenshot:

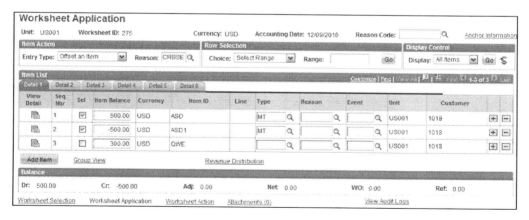

Note the changes in entry type and the amounts in the **Balance** section at the bottom of the page. Save the page.

A worksheet can be posted only when the Net balance is zero.

Click the **Worksheet Action** hyperlink to see the worksheet posting options. The following screenshot shows the options on the Worksheet Action section:

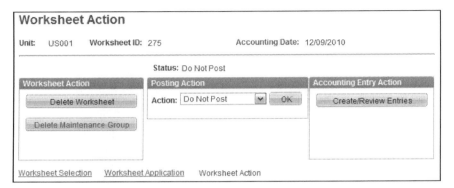

The posting options are the same as the ones we saw for the pending item group.

When the worksheet is saved, it creates match groups with the items selected on the worksheet or the ones that get created during the adjustment.

The following table summarizes various scenarios while using maintenance worksheets:

Entry Type	Description	Action	Result
MT	Offset an item	Select debit and credit items with matching amounts. Select 'Offset an item' action.	The system creates new items with an entry type of MT.
RC	Refund a credit	Select a credit item. Select 'Refund a Credit' action.	A new item is created with an entry type of RC.
WO	Write off a debit	Select a debit item. Select 'Write off a debit' action.	A new item is created with entry type of WO. The original item is closed.
WOC	Write off a credit	Select a debit item. Select 'Write off a credit' action.	A new item is created with an entry type of WOC. The original item is closed.

Entry Type	Description	Action	Result
MC	Create new credit	Select debit and credit items with the credit total larger than debit total. Specify the entry type MC to create an adjustment.	A new item with negative amount equal to the difference is created with an entry type of MC.
MD	Create new debit	Select debit and credit items with the debit total larger than credit total. Specify the entry type MD to create an adjustment.	A new item with positive amount equal to the difference is created with an entry type of MD.
RRC	Refund remaining credit	Select debit and credit items with the credit total larger than debit total. Select 'Refund remaining credit' option.	Two new items with negative amount equal to the difference are created with entry types of MC and RRC respectively. Original items are closed.
WRC	Write off remaining credit	Select debit and credit items with the credit total larger than debit total. Select 'Write off remaining credit' option.	Two new items with negative amount equal to the difference are created with entry types of MC and WRC respectively.
WRD	Write off remaining debit	Select debit and credit items with the debit total larger than credit total. Select 'Write off remaining debit' option.	Two new items with positive amount equal to the difference are created with entry types of MD and WRC respectively.

Once the item maintenance activities are completed (either using automatic maintenance or through maintenance worksheets), the Receivable Update process needs to be executed. This process posts all the new maintenance items created, thereby altering the original item balance. The AR module tracks all the operations performed on an item in a table named ITEM_ACTIVITY.

Let's see how this works with a couple of examples.

- **Scenario 1: An invoice (ID 176587) for $100 is written off completely.**

  When this invoice is originally created, the ITEM_ACTIVITY table holds a row for this transaction as shown:

Item ID	Entry Type	Amount
176587	IN	$100

When we write off this item, the system creates a new item with the same item ID but with entry type WO and amount of $-100. When this item is posted by the Receivables Update process, the ITEM_ACTIVITY table holds an additional row for this transaction, as shown:

Item ID	Entry Type	Amount
176587	IN	$100
176587	WO	$-100

The end result is that the item's status changes to **Closed** from **Open**.

- **Scenario 2: An invoice (ID 52467) for $200 is offset against a credit memo (57879) for $-200.**

   When these items are originally created, the ITEM_ACTIVITY table holds rows for these transactions, as shown:

Item ID	Entry Type	Amount
52467	IN	$200
57879	CR	$-200

When we offset these items against each other, the system creates two new items with same item IDs and amounts, but with opposite signs and entry type MT. When these maintenance items are posted by the Receivables Update process, the ITEM_ACTIVITY table holds a additional rows for these transactions as shown next:

Item ID	Entry Type	Amount
52467	IN	$200
57879	CR	$-200
52467	MT	$-200
57879	MT	$200

The status for both items changes from Open to Closed.

Understanding aging

One of the important functions of any Accounts Receivable system is to give a snapshot of how long the customer invoices are outstanding. If an organization does not know how long its customers are taking to pay the invoices, it can encounter serious cash flow problems. PeopleSoft AR offers elaborate ways in which we can review the open items, place them in appropriate categories depending on how old they are, and then generate various reports to analyze customers' payment performance. The aging business process in the AR module performs these activities.

There are three elements that constitute the customer aging in PeopleSoft AR:

- Configuration of aging ID
- Execution of aging batch process
- Aging reports

Configuring aging ID

An aging ID is the foundation of aging process. It defines the various categories that we wish to use for classifying open items based on their age. It also determines how the items in dispute, items in collection and deduction items are processed.

Follow this navigation to configure an aging ID:

Set Up Financials/Supply Chain | Product Related | Receivables | Credit/ Collections | Aging

The following screenshot shows the configuration options on the aging ID configuration page:

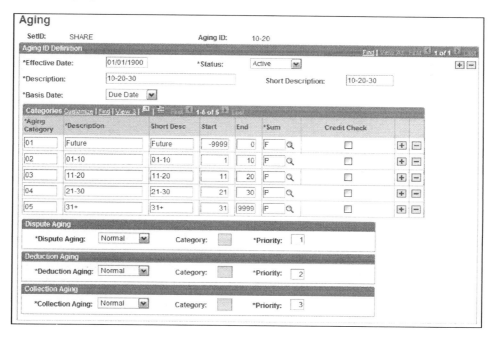

This is the page where we decide how many aging categories and corresponding age ranges we need for our reporting. In the previous example, we have configured the following aging categories: one-10 days old, 10-20 days old, 20-30 days old, and items older than 30 days.

- **Basis Date:** Specify the date to be used as basis for aging items. Possible options are **As of Date, Accounting Date, Item Date and Due Date**.

- **Start, End:** These fields specify the start and end value for the item age for a specific category.

[Irrespective of how many aging categories we configure, there must be one category with -9,999 as the start value and one category with 9,999 as the end value.]

In the previous example, as we are using **Due Date** as the basis, any item that has not reached its due date will be placed in category 01 (i.e. which is less than zero days past due). Any item that is up to 10 days past its due date will be placed in category 02 and so on.

- **Sum:** Specify a summarization option for each category. Possible options are: **Current Due, Past Due, Current Due and Other**. In this example, as all categories other than category 01 represent past due items, they have **Past Due** as summarization option.

Dispute aging, Collection aging, and Deduction aging options

If we wish, we can process the collection, deduction, and disputed items differently from the regular items. Possible options are as follows:

- **Categorize:** We can create separate categories in addition to those we saw previously. If we select this option, the **Category** field becomes active and we can specify the special purpose category, where the system will place the dispute, deduction and collection items. We can specify a single category for all of these or have different ones for each type.

- **Exclude:** If this option is selected, the aging process ignores all dispute, deduction, and collection items.

- **Normal:** If this option is selected, the aging process treats dispute, deduction, and collection items like regular items and puts them in appropriate aging categories based on the basis date.

- **Vary:** If this option is selected, the system refers to the Dispute Reason, Deduction Reason, and Collection Code configurations respectively to decide how the dispute, deduction, and collection items need to be aged.

An aging ID is assigned to the AR business unit to be used by the aging process.

Executing aging batch process

Once the aging ID is configured, the next step is to execute the ARAGE multi-process job. This batch process uses the aging ID assigned to the AR business unit, reviews all open items, and places them in the appropriate aging category depending on the defined rules.

Follow this navigation to run the aging batch job:

Accounts Receivable | Receivables Analysis | Aging | Request Aging Process:

The following screenshot shows the run control page used to run the aging process.

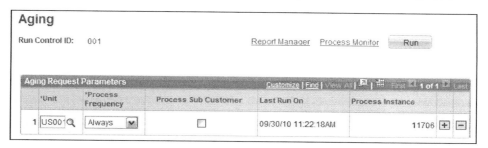

- **Unit:** Specify the business unit for which we need to run the aging process
- **Process Frequency:** Specify the value **Always**

Click the **Run** button to start the process.

Expert tip:

The aging process can be run as many times as needed. However, it needs to be executed after all the pending items (including maintenance, payment, and so on) are posted by Receivables Update process, so that it reflects the latest open items. Make sure the following sequence of processes is used: **Receivables Update | Aging | Aging Reports**

PeopleSoft AR provides the following delivered aging reports that are based on the aging categories and items placed in them by the aging process. If needed, additional reports can be developed to present the aging data.

Report name	Description
Aging detail by unit	Aged open balance for all items in a business unit
Aging detail by tree	Aged open balance for all items in a tree (a hierarchical structure for customers, and business units)
Aging summary by unit	Aged open balance for all customers in a business unit
Aging summary by tree	Aged open balance for all customers in a tree
Aging by chartfield	Aged total receivables by customer, item, and specified chartfields
Aging by reason	Aged open balance for deduction, collection, and dispute items for all customers in a business unit

Receiving customer payments

As part of its normal business operations, an organization regularly receives payments from its customers. PeopleSoft AR offers multiple methods to receive payments. Payment methods can be broadly categorized into manual and electronic (automated). We'll discuss these in the following sections.

Entering payments manually

Just as we saw that a pending item must be a part of item group, customer payments also need to be a part of payment group, known as **Deposit**. A deposit can contain multiple payments or a single payment. In PeopleSoft parlance, we can enter two types of deposits manually: **Regular deposits** and **Express deposits**. Which type of deposit is used depends on the amount of information we have for the received payment.

A payment, when received, should ideally have the customer ID (who paid this amount) and the item ID (to which this payment needs to be applied). However, in many cases, this is not true. When organizations receive the payments, some of them lack the item ID or customer ID details.

Entering regular deposits

Regular deposits are used to enter payments when they have the customer information (although it is not mandatory) and need not be applied immediately.

Follow this navigation to enter regular deposits:

Accounts Receivable | Payments | Online Payments | Regular Deposits

The following screenshot shows the **Totals** tab of the regular deposits page:

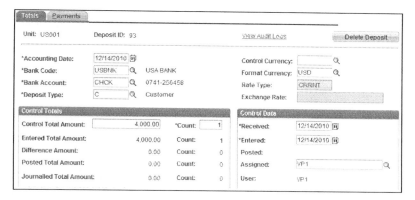

This tab is used to enter the bank and bank account where this deposit (and the payments that are part of it) will be deposited. It also records the control information, such as the total amount for all payments and the total number of payments in this deposit. The system compares these control details against the actual payments entered. Any differences are highlighted in the **Difference Amount** and **Difference Count** fields.

Click the **Payments** tab to enter the details about individual payments.

The following screenshot shows the **Payments** tab of the regular deposits page:

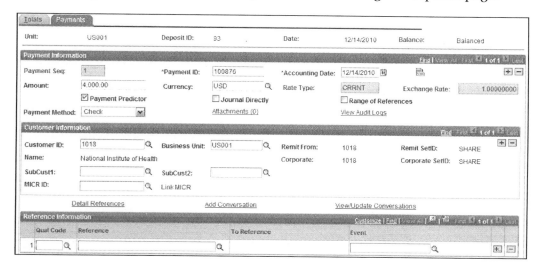

In the previous example, we have received a check payment for $4000 from a customer, the National Institute of Health.

- **Payment ID:** This field is used to record the check number or any other unique identifier for the received payment.

- **Payment Predictor:** If this checkbox is selected, the Payment Predictor process picks up this payment to be applied to appropriate customer open item. If it is unchecked, we need to manually apply this payment. Recall our discussion about setting up a bank account. If the Payment Predictor flag is enabled for a bank account, all payments with that bank account have this flag automatically enabled on this page.

- **Journal Directly:** This checkbox is used to mark a payment that is not related to a customer item. If selected, a payment cannot be processed on the payment worksheet.

- **Miscellaneous Payments:** Payments that are not related to a customer are also known as Miscellaneous Payments. It is a very useful feature to record payments such as interest paid by the bank, payments received as donations, and so on. If this checkbox is enabled, it indicates to the system that it needs to be processed in a different manner. It cannot be applied to any customer item.

- **Payment Method:** Available options are: Check, Electronic Funds Transfer and Giro-EFT (used in the Netherlands).

- **Detail References hyperlink:** Even if we don't have any item reference information on the received payment, we can specify the customer items to which this payment should be applied. Click this hyperlink to associate any open items to this payment.

The following screenshot shows the **Detail Reference Information** page that opens where we can specify the items for the payment:

In the previous example, we have manually specified two items for this customer, to which this payment can be applied. Note that it is not necessary to specify the items here. The payment predictor process is capable of searching the open items for a given customer and applying the payment to eligible items.

Reference information section

Qual Code: This field indicates the type of identifying information that the payment has. For example, when a customer sends a payment to us, he may give a reference so that we can identify what this payment is for. It can be the invoice number (item), purchase order number that the customer sent us to purchase something, sales order number that we created to record the customer's order, and so on. Select the type of reference on the payment.

Reference: This field is used to store the reference number.

> Regular deposits entered as explained previously need to be applied to items using either payment worksheets (manually) or payment predictor process. We cannot enter as well as apply the payments using regular deposits page.

Entering express deposits

Express deposits are used to enter payments as well as applying them to the specified items. This is possible when the received customer payment has the item information to which it can be applied.

Consider a scenario where a telephone company sends the monthly bill (invoice) to the customer. The customer then mails the payment check along with the invoice stub that contains the invoice number. In this case, when the check payment is received, we also know the invoice number for which this payment is made. Even if we don't know the customer, the system can still apply the payment.

Follow this navigation to enter express deposits:

Accounts Receivable | Payments | Online Payments | Express Deposit

The following screenshot shows the **Totals** tab of the express deposit page:

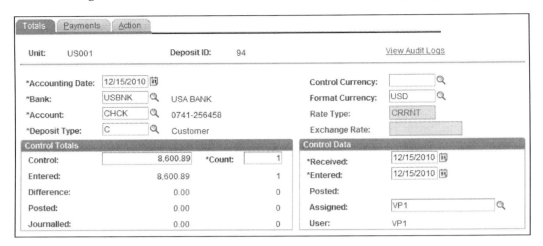

You will have noticed that this tab is similar to the one for regular deposits page.

Click the **Payments** tab to enter individual payment details. The following screenshot shows the **Payments** tab:

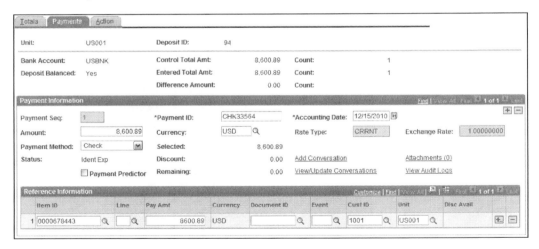

As you can see, one of the important differences here is the lack of customer information fields, as we don't need them. However, the item information is required. We can select the item or items in the **Item ID** field.

Click the **Action** tab to create and post the payment worksheet, so that the given payment can be applied.

The following screenshot shows the **Action** tab and various processing options on it:

- **Build**: Clicking this button creates payment worksheets for each payment in the deposit.

- **Delete**: This button deletes the payment worksheet but retains the deposit.

- **Batch Standard**: This button sets the payment status to Batch Standard, so that it can be picked up by the Receivables Update process next time it runs. We'll discuss the payment worksheets in detail in the payment application section.

Thus, express deposits serve a dual purpose by allowing the entry and application of a payment at the same time. However, it is useful only for a low payment volume environment.

Understanding electronic payments

When the number of payments handled by an organization is high, using regular or express deposit is not feasible. PeopleSoft offers following automated methods to enter payments in large batches:

Payment method	Description
Lockbox	This method reads a payment file sent by the bank and loads those payments using a delivered PeopleSoft program.
Excel spreadsheet	PeopleSoft provides a pre-formatted excel template, which can be used to record payments and upload them into AR system.
Electronic Data Interchange (EDI)	PeopleSoft can receive payment files in industry standard EDI formats (European as well as U.S.) and load them automatically.

Payment method	Description
Cash drawer	This method is used to load point of sale (POS) payments that are recorded in the order management module.
Bank statement	If an organization is using treasury modules, it can receive bank statements electronically. PeopleSoft delivers methods to reconcile the bank statement with the cash account in General Ledger and load the reconciled deposits into AR.
Bilateral netting	This is a feature of the PeopleSoft treasury modules. Here, the system can match the receivable (money due from an entity) and payable (money due to the same entity) balances and load the net receivable balance into AR.
Credit card	Using a PeopleSoft bolt-on, we can directly establish a connection with a credit card issuer to authorize a transaction and process a credit card payment.

In order to use electronic payment methods, PeopleSoft provides a set of staging tables (AR_LOCKBOX_EC, AR_DEPOSIT_EC, AR_PAYMENT_EC, AR_IDITEM_EC and AR_IDCUST_EC). It also delivers a batch program known as **Payment Loader** (AR_PAYLOAD) to read the payment data from staging tables and load them into AR.

We will discuss the two most commonly used methods: **Lockbox** and **Excel spreadsheets**.

Understanding lockbox payments

Many organizations utilize the services of a bank to handle customer payments. Consider a telephone company with thousands of subscribers, who send their check payments every month. Rather than handling thousands of payments every week and entering them into AR system, it can give a post office box address operated by a bank to its customers. Thus, all these check payments are received by the bank and deposited into the company's account. Now the bank prepares a data file containing details of deposited checks and sends it to the organization at regular intervals (every night, once every week, and so on). This is known as a lockbox service.

Note that a lockbox file can contain a large number of payments from multiple lockboxes from different bank accounts.

PeopleSoft can receive such payment data files (provided they are in a specific format) and load these payments using a two-step process:

1. Running the Lockbox SQR (AR25001) process
2. Running the Payment Loader (AR_PAYLOAD) process

Follow this navigation to execute the Lockbox SQR process:

Accounts Receivable | Payments | Electronic Payments | Retrieve Lockbox Files

The following screenshot shows the run control page used to specify the processing options:

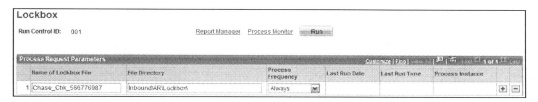

We need to specify the payment data file and its location on the server to run the **AR25001** process. Click the **Run** button to start the process.

This process reads the data from the file and loads them into the payment staging tables we discussed earlier.

The next step in the process is executing the **Payment Loader** process.

Follow this navigation to execute this process:

Accounts Receivable | Payments | Electronic Payments | Process Payment Interface

The following screenshot shows the run control page used to specify the processing options for the **Payment Loader** process:

The Payment Loader process is used to load payments that may have entered from various sources such as lockbox, EDI, and so on from the staging tables into the AR system. Various checkboxes on this page are used to instruct the payment method to payment loader process. Select the **Lockbox** checkbox to process lockbox payments.

Click **Run** button to trigger the process.

> Before implementing the lockbox feature, we need to analyze the PeopleSoft lockbox file format. It offers various types of data records, but it is not necessary to use all of them. Based on the organization's requirements, we select the record types needed in the file. For example, when we receive payment information from bank, we may not need the customer address details along with the payment. In this case, the record type for customer address in the file is no longer required. Once the required file records are identified, we need to work closely with the bank to ensure that it sends the file in exactly the same format as required. Refer to the detailed file specifications that PeopleSoft provides.

Understanding Excel spreadsheet payments

Many organizations use Microsoft Excel-based templates to record customer payments. To simplify loading these payments into AR, PeopleSoft provides a utility to upload payments from pre-defined Excel sheets.

The spreadsheet payments uploading process consists of following steps:

- Setting up the spreadsheet template
- Entering data into the template
- Posting the data from the spreadsheet to Excel payment upload tables
- Running Excel Payment Upload process
- Running Payment Loader process

The PeopleSoft-delivered spreadsheet template consists of two worksheets: **Template** and **Data Entry**. The Template worksheet shows all the individual fields that are available for payment data entry. It is not necessary for an organization to use all these fields and we can specify only those fields that we need. The fields we select here become available on the Data Entry worksheet.

The following screenshot shows a part of the **Template** worksheet:

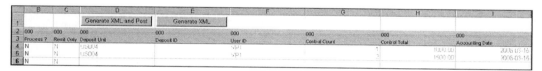

- **Record**: This row shows the Excel upload table where a particular field value will be stored.

- **Record Type**: There are four different record types, each indicating a type of payment information being entered. The available values are: **000** (Deposit information), **001** (Payment information), **002** (Customer information) and **003** (Reference information). As you can see, this structure essentially copies the regular deposit page.

- **Add to Data Sheet**: Select this checkbox to make a field available on the Data Sheet worksheet.

The following screenshot shows a part of the **Data Entry** worksheet:

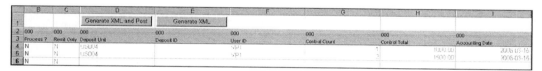

The data entry structure on this sheet is similar to the hierarchy on the regular deposit page: deposit information is followed by payment information which contains customer and possibly multiple reference lines.

Once the data entry is complete, we can use the **Generate XML and Post** button to upload the data in this tab to the Excel upload tables.

The next step is to run the **Excel Payment Upload** process which validates the data in the Excel upload tables and loads them into payment staging tables (the same tables used by the lockbox process).

Follow this navigation to run the **Excel Payment Upload** process:

Accounts Receivable | Payments | Electronic Payments | Excel Edit Request

The following screenshot shows the run control page for the process:

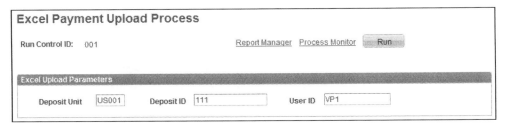

Follow these steps to upload an Excel spreadsheet containing payment details:

- Enter a value in the **Deposit Unit**, **Deposit ID** and **User ID** fields to process a specific BU or deposit ID. Leave these fields blank to process all deposits.

- Click the **Run** button to trigger the process.

- Finally, run the Payment Loader process to load these payments from the staging table to the AR system. Note that we need to check the **Upload From Excel** checkbox in order to process the spreadsheet payments.

Understanding payment application

So far, we have discussed various processes by which we can record a customer's outstanding items, and modify them as well as receiving payments from the customer. The last logical step in this cycle is applying the payment to open items. In real life, this seemingly simple task is complicated due to various factors. Consider following situations, which will give you a sense of various payment application considerations:

- A customer has three open items for $300, $250, and $400. We receive a payment for $700. As this amount can pay only two items at the most, which items should this payment be applied to? What should be done with the remaining payment amount?

- We receive a payment from a customer, but find out that currently there is no open item to which it can be applied. However, we know that a new invoice will be issued soon. What should we do with this payment?

- A customer gets a 10 percent discount on an invoice for $1,000. However, we later promise an additional five percent discount. The customer sends a payment for $850. However, the system has automatically calculated $100 as discount amount. How do we specify an additional $50 discount amount?

- What do we do if the customer pays less or more than the invoice amount that is outstanding?

PeopleSoft offers two methods for payment application:

- Payment predictor, which automatically applies payments based on the rules we configure
- Payment worksheets (manual)

Understanding payment predictor

We can automate the payment application activities in AR module by following these two steps:

1. Configure the payment predictor method
2. Execute the payment predictor batch process

Before we get into a discussion about payment predictor, let's understand a few relevant basic concepts.

Item references

We have already seen that payments carry some type of identifying information that helps matching it with the appropriate item. The reference information could be the Customer ID, Item ID, or both. As far as the payment predictor is concerned, it categorizes item references into three types.

Payment reference type	Description
Customer reference	In this case, the payment simply carries the customer ID.
Item summary reference	The payment carries the item ID to which it needs to be applied. However it doesn't say what amount should be applied.
Item detail reference	In this case, the payment carries the item ID to which it should be applied, as well as the item amount that should be paid by the payment.

Based on the type of reference information that a payment carries, the payment predictor uses the appropriate method of payment application.

Algorithm groups

PeopleSoft delivers various methods by which it can match a payment with open items. These are known as algorithm groups. Each algorithm group consists of one or more algorithms, which carry instructions to select open items that match a payment being processed. In most of the cases, delivered algorithm groups can fulfill the payment application requirements of an organization. However, some special requirements may need a modification of algorithms or even creation of a new algorithm group.

Although we can't discuss all the delivered algorithm groups individually, let's briefly take a look at a few of them, so that you can get an idea of how they work.

- **#BALANCE** is an algorithm group used for applying payments that have only customer references. When it encounters such a payment, it retrieves the customer ID, retrieves all open items for that customer and checks if the total of those open amounts exactly matches the payment amount. If it does, only then does it select those items for payment application.

- **#OLDEST1** is another algorithm group used for applying payments that have only customer references. When it encounters such a payment, it retrieves the customer ID, retrieves all open items for that customer and arranges them in decreasing order of item age. Thus it selects the oldest item and applies the payment to it. If there is a remaining balance amount, it selects the next oldest item and applies the balance to it. This is continued until the remaining payment balance is less than the item amount, for which it creates a partial amount.

- **#REFS** is an algorithm group used for applying payments with summary item references. It doesn't matter if it carries a customer reference. When it processes such a payment, it retrieves the reference information on it (nothing but the item ID) and selects the item that exactly matches this reference.

By this time you would have realized that each algorithm group performs a very specific function. Organizations have their own unique requirements for applying payments. Sometimes the same organization can have different application rules for different business units. We can use combinations of algorithm groups to satisfy these requirements.

Refer to the following table, which lists the appropriate algorithm group for each of the reference type:

Payments with no reference	Payments with summary reference	Payments with detail reference
#BALANCE	#REFS	#DETAIL
#COMBOS	#REF_ONE	#DTL_TLR
#OLDEST1	#REF_NG	#DTL_PM
#OLDESTC		#DTL_TPM
#OVERDUE		
#PASTDUE		
#STATMNT		

Configuring payment predictor method

A predictor method is a collection of instructions for the payment predictor process. It lays down the rules for payment applications under different circumstances. We can configure as many predictor methods as are required. Once a predictor method is defined, it is assigned to an AR business unit. If payments from a particular customer need to be applied in a way different from this default method, we can create a new predictor method and assign it to that customer.

Before we see how to configure a predictor method, let's consider a practical requirement.

Implementation challenge

An organization receives its payment information through lockbox and always includes the item ID as reference (summary reference). It needs a payment to be matched with specified item ID. If the underpayment (payment amount is less than item amount) is less than $50, the difference should be automatically written off. If the underpayment exceeds $50, a new deduction item for the difference amount should be created. If the overpayment (payment amount is more than item amount) is less than $50, the difference should be automatically written off. If the overpayment exceeds $50, the additional payment should be placed on customer account for later application.

However, there are a few payments that are received with only customer ID. Any such payments should be placed on a payment worksheet for a manual review.

Solution

As the payments have summary reference, we will use the `#REFS` algorithm group. We'll see the configuration options to satisfy the given requirements.

Follow this navigation to configure a predictor method:

Set Up Financials/Supply Chain | Product Related | Receivables | Payments | Predictor Method

The following screenshot shows the configuration options on the **Predictor Method** page:

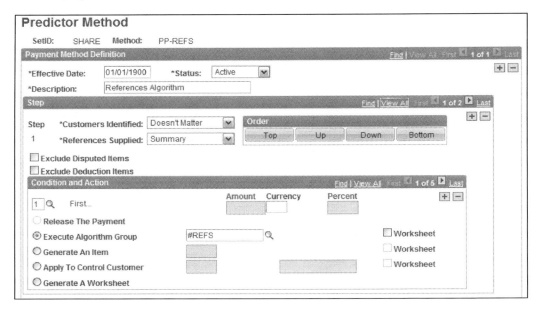

Note that a predictor method consists of one or multiple steps. Each step defines the type of reference information that can be encountered and specifies the actions that need to be taken. Thus each step has one or more actions.

- **Customers Identified**: This field specifies if a customer reference is necessary for a payment. Available options are **None, One, More Than One** and **Doesn't Matter**. For our example, if the payment has item information, it doesn't matter if customer ID is present or not.

- **References Supplied**: This field specifies what kind of item reference information is required for a payment. Available options are **Summary, Detail, No** and **Doesn't Matter**. In our example, we know that payments need to have summary information.

- **The Condition and Action** section defines all the possible conditions and corresponding actions for this combination of reference information.

PeopleSoft delivers the conditions **First, Any Overpayment, Overpayment Exceeds, Overpayment Is Less Than, Any Underpayment, Underpayment Exceeds, and Underpayment Is Less Than**. A step can have all of these conditions or only a few of them. However, there must be at least one condition for each step.

For a selected condition, the following actions are available:

- **Release the Payment:** This option instructs the payment predictor to ignore any application done for a payment and make it available for the next step.

- **Execute Algorithm Group:** If selected, the payment predictor uses the algorithm group specified in the adjoining field and tries to apply the payment. If it is successful in application, a payment group is created and set to post, so that it can be posted by the Receivables Update process.

- **Generate an Item:** This option creates a new pending item using the system function specified in the adjoining field.

- **Apply to Control Customer:** This option instructs the payment predictor to place the payment on the account of the customer specified in the adjoining field. This option is used when the customer cannot be identified for the given payment.

- **Generate a Worksheet:** This option simply creates a worksheet with eligible items to which the payment can be applied.

For the first three options, the system creates a payment group with its posting action as Batch Standard. However, if the **Worksheet** checkbox is selected, the process creates a payment worksheet, so that it can be reviewed by a user before being posted. If required, any manual changes can be done to the worksheet. In other words, it doesn't automatically post the payment groups.

Generate a Worksheet

This option creates a payment worksheet for the payment by showing all the item matches, overpayments, underpayments, and so on.

For our implementation challenge, we will configure the predictor steps and conditions and actions as follow:

Step 1

Customers Identified	References Supplied
Doesn't Matter	Summary

This step will handle the majority of the payments with summary item references. It will need to have the following conditions and actions:

Condition	Value	Action	Value
1. First		Execute Algorithm	#REFS
3. Overpayment Exceeds	$50	Generate an Item	WS-05 (Place an amount on account)
4. Overpayment is less than	$50	Generate an Item	WS-10 (Write off an overpayment)
6. Underpayment Exceeds	$50	Generate an Item	WS-08 (Create a deduction)
7. Underpayment is less than	$50	Generate an Item	WS-11 (Write off an underpayment)

This will instruct the payment predictor to select a payment with summary reference and try to apply it using #REFS algorithm group. If it finds an overpayment, it will place the extra amount on the customer account or write it off depending on the amount difference. Similarly, for an underpayment, it will create a deduction item or write it off depending on the amount difference.

Step 2

Customers Identified	References Supplied
One	No

This step will handle those remaining payments that don't have any item reference but do have a customer reference. It will need to have following conditions and actions:

Condition	Value	Action	Value
1. First		Generate Worksheet	

This will ensure that any payment with only a customer reference will be placed on a payment worksheet. A user can review the worksheet, add any open items for that customer, and then set it to post.

Running the payment predictor process

Once a predictor method is configured, the payment predictor process uses the defined application rules and applies the received payments.

Note that the **Payment Predictor** flag for the payment must be selected for it to be processed by the payment predictor.

Follow this navigation to execute the payment predictor process:

Accounts Receivable | Payments | Apply Payments | Request Payment Predictor

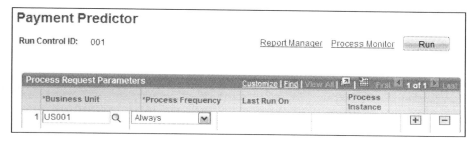

Specify the business unit for which the payments should be applied. Select Always as the process frequency and click the **Run** button.

Using payment worksheets

Payment worksheets are used to manually apply payments. We can apply a payment completely or partially, write off any underpayments or overpayments, give any additional discounts, and create adjustments. As we saw in the previous section, the payment predictor also creates payment worksheets if so instructed. The structure of payment worksheets is similar to maintenance worksheets, which we discussed in the item maintenance section. It consists of three sections:

- **Worksheet selection:** This is the place where we can specify the criteria to fetch items and build the worksheet

- **Worksheet application:** Payments are applied to items in this section

- **Worksheet action:** We can choose the appropriate posting action for the worksheet, delete the worksheet (if necessary), or create accounting entries

Follow this navigation to create a payment worksheet:

Accounts Receivable | Payments | Apply Payments | Create Worksheet

Select a payment for which the payment worksheet needs to be created. The system opens the **Worksheet Selection** tab. We'll not discuss it in detail, as it is not much different from the page for the maintenance worksheet. Click the **Build** button to create the worksheet.

The following screenshot shows the **Worksheet Application** tab:

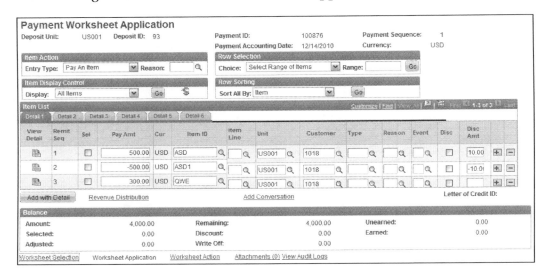

As you can see, the page shows all open items to which this payment can be applied.

Entry Type: This dropdown menu shows the actions that we can perform: **Pay An Item, Create a Deduction, and Write Off An Item**. To perform any of these actions, check the checkbox for the desired items and select the appropriate action.

Let's say we wish to pay the $300 item now. In order to do it, select it, choose the option **Pay An Item**, and click the **Refresh** button on the page. The following screenshot shows the changes to the page:

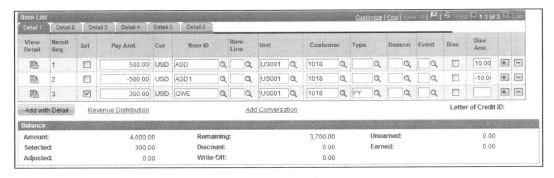

The system automatically assigns the entry type PY (representing payment) to the item. The **Balance** section at the bottom updates the **Selected** amount and shows **Remaining** balance as $3,700.

Now let's say we wish to keep the balance amount of $3700 on customer account, so that it can be applied for future payments.

 In order to adjust underpayments and overpayments or create on-account payments, we need to manually create new item using the **Add With Detail** button.

Click the **Add With Detail** button to create a new on account item. The following screenshot shows the page that the system opens:

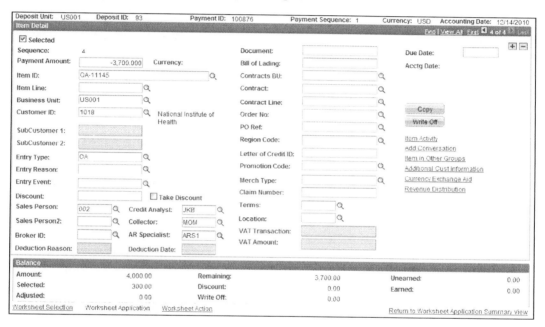

Specify the item ID for this new item we are adding, along with the amount and entry type. In our example, as we wish to create an on-account payment for $3700, we should choose OA as the entry type and -$3700 as the payment amount (recall that any item that reduces customer balance needs to have a negative sign). We can create items for various entry types on this page. Possible options are as follows:

- **Adjust remaining overpayment**: If a payment amount remains after applying to an item, we can create a new item with a negative amount for the remaining payment amount. The entry type of this item is AO.

- **Adjust remaining underpayment**: If a payment amount is less than item amount to which it is applied, we can create a new item with a positive amount for the remaining item amount. The entry type of this item is AU.

- **Write off an overpayment**: If a payment amount remains after applying to an item, we can write off this remainder rather than creating a new item for the remaining payment amount. In the background, the system creates an item with the entry type AO with a negative amount and another item with the entry type WAO with a positive amount and the same item ID.

- **Write off remaining underpayment**: If a payment amount is less than the item amount to which it is applied, we can apply the payment and write off remaining item balance rather than creating a new item for the remaining item amount. In the background, the system creates an item with the entry type AU with a positive amount and another item with the entry type WAU with a negative amount and the same item ID.

Click the **Return to Worksheet Application Summary View** hyperlink to go back.

The page now shows the changes The customer has a new item to represent its on-account payment with entry type OA. Also, the remaining amount is now zero, indicating that the payment is fully processed. Now we can go to the **Worksheet Action** section to set the worksheet to post.

Customer correspondence

As the AR system deals with tracking invoices sent to customers and receiving their payments, one of its important functions is generating effective correspondence with them. It can be in the form of customer statements (which list the open items, received payments and so on.), dunning letters (which notify the customers about their overdue items) or follow up letters. We'll discuss the most widely used features—statements and dunning letters.

Customer statements

An organization may dispatch detailed statements each month, which let the customers know their outstanding items, total balance, and so on. We can generate customer statements by following these steps:

1. Configuring a statement ID that establishes rules for statement generation
2. Running the customer statements multi-process job
3. Running the statement print multi-process job

Configuring the statement ID

Statement ID specifies which items are included in customer statements. It also specifies conditions when statements should not be created.

Follow this navigation to configure statement ID:

Setup Financials/Supply Chain | Product Related | Receivables | Payments | Statements

The Following screenshot shows the configuration options for statement ID:

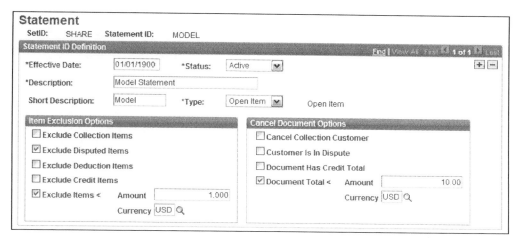

- **Type**: This important field decides the structure of the customer statement. The available values are:
    - **Open Item**: This type of statement includes all of a customer's open items
    - **Balance forward**: This type of statement shows the balance carried forward from last statement, all of the open as well as the closed items and payments in the current period, and the net outstanding balance. This is similar to the credit card statement that you receive from your card company.
- **Item Exclusion Options**: An organization may not wish to list all the open items on the statement. We can specify if the statement should exclude the collection, deduction, disputed, and credit items. We can also specify that items below a certain amount should be excluded from statements.
- **Cancel Document Options**: It may not be necessary to create statements for all customers. We can specify the conditions under which a statement for a customer should not be created. This is possible if the collection action is in process for a customer, a dispute is on-going with a customer, the total customer balance is negative (that is, we owe the customer), or if the outstanding balance is less than a certain amount.

A statement ID is assigned to the AR business unit and used by the Customer statement process. It can also be assigned to an individual customer to override the default statement ID.

Running the customer statement multi-process job

This multi-process job retrieves the eligible items data for customers based on the rules defined in a statement ID. These items are stored in a statements temporary table (AR32000_TMP).

Follow this navigation to execute the customer statement batch process:

Accounts Receivable | Customer Interactions | Statements | Create Statements | Statement Parameters

The following screenshot shows the run control page used to specify options to run the process:

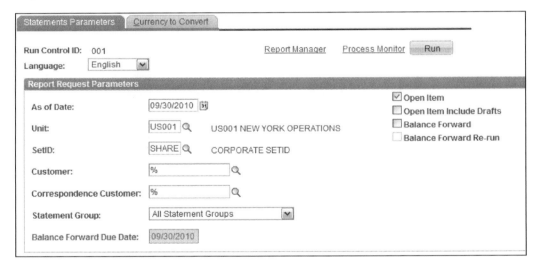

- **Unit**: If we specify a business unit value in this field, the process creates statements for all customers, with have items in the given unit.
- **SetID**: Specify the SetID for the customers for whom statements need to be created (remember that customers are grouped by SetIDs).
- **Customer**: We can specify a single customer in this field or leave it blank so that the system processes all customers under the given SetID and BU.

- **Correspondence Customer**: In PeopleSoft we can designate a customer to receive all correspondence on behalf of other customers. This is known as a correspondence customer. If this is not needed, each customer is by default its own correspondence customer. Specify a value in this field if we wish to create statements for all customers in a correspondence group.

If the Customer or Correspondence Customer fields are left blank, the system automatically populates them with the wildcard % character, indicating that the system should process all values.

Click the **Run** button to initiate the batch job. When the processing is complete, the system generates a statement number for each statement that is created. We can review these statements before printing them.

> Note that a statement ID indicates a unique statement process run. It is possible that a single run may create multiple statements for different customers. However, the statement ID is still the same for all statements in this run.

Follow this navigation to review customer statements online:

Accounts Receivable | Customer Interactions | Statements | Review Statements

Running the statement print multi-process job

This multi-process job retrieves the customer statements data rows from the statements temporary table and prints them according to the specified processing options.

Follow this navigation to execute the statement print batch process:

Accounts Receivable | Customer Interactions | Statements | Create Statements | Statement Parameters

The following screenshot shows the run control page used to specify options to run the process:

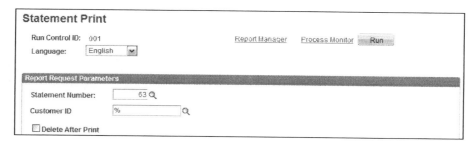

Enter the statement ID generated by the previous run and customer ID if we wish to further narrow down the scope of print process. PeopleSoft provides different reports to print different types of statements:

Process	Name	Description
AR32000	Customer statement print	Used for open items type of statements without draft items.
AR32A00	Customer statement print with Accept Giro	Used for open items type of statements without draft items. Also prints the acceptgiro attachments.
AR32001	Balance forward statement print	Used for balance forward type of statements without draft items.
AR32A01	Balance forward statement print with Accept Giro	Used for balance forward type of statements without draft items. Also prints the acceptgiro attachments.
AR32002	Draft customer statement print	Used for open items type of statements with draft items.
ARSTPRT	PS/AR Statements print	Used to print open items as well as balance forward type of statements.

Dunning letters

Dunning letters are used by organizations to notify customers about overdue items. We can generate dunning letters by following these steps:

1. Configuring letter codes and corresponding content
2. Configuring a dunning ID that establishes rules for dunning letter generation
3. Running the extract dunning letter multi-process job
4. Running the dunning print multi-process job

Configuring the letter codes

Organizations can define multiple levels of dunning letters depending upon the severity of the customer's delayed payment. For example, we may want to send a letter to a customer merely reminding him that some of his items are past due. If we don't receive the payments even after the reminder, we may send a harsher letter instructing that a late payment may be charged. The harshest letter may warn the customer that legal action may be initiated if payment is not received.

The number of levels of letters and corresponding content entirely depends on the organization's requirements.

Follow this navigation to configure statement ID:

Setup Financials/Supply Chain | Product Related | Receivables | Options | Letter Code

The following screenshot shows a sample dunning letter:

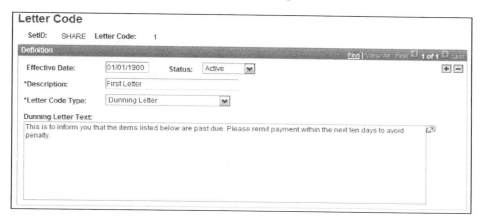

Ensure that Dunning Letter is selected in the Letter Code Type field while configuring dunning letter codes. We can define different letter codes for each level of escalation.

Configuring dunning ID

A dunning ID (or dunning method as it is sometimes called) defines the rules for the generation of dunning letters. It also determines how dunning letters are created, how many levels are used, and which letter codes are used for each level.

Follow this navigation to configure a dunning ID:

Setup Financials/Supply Chain | Product Related | Receivables | Credit/ Collections | Dunning Methods

The following screenshot shows the Dunning ID tab of the configuration page:

As you can see in this example, the item exclusion options and document cancelation options are similar to those we saw for the statement ID.

Dunning Method : PeopleSoft offers three different methods by which dunning letters can be created. The following table describes these approaches:

Dunning Method	Description
Dunning by days	The level of dunning letter is determined by the number of days by which customer items are past due. For example, we can specify that for items up to 30 days past due, a level one letter should be used, while for items between 30 and 60 days past due, a level two letter should be used.
	However, there are cases where a customer has items that fall into different categories. In such cases, the system does not generate different letters for such items. letter can contain items from different dunning levels.
	Continuing with the above example, let's assume that a customer has two items: the first item is 10 days past due (level one), while the second is 40 days past due (level two). We can instruct the system to use the lowest or highest dunning level letter for such cases. Thus the customer will receive only one letter containing both the items.
	It is not necessary for an item to move through each dunning level.

Dunning Method	Description
Dunning by level	In this method, the past due item sequentially moves through the dunning levels. The dunning levels are determined not by the age of the item, but the interval between two levels.

When the dunning process is run, it checks the level for past due items when it was executed last time. If the number of days for which the items were present in that level exceeds the defined interval, items are moved to the next level and a letter for that level is sent.

Let's say that we specify an interval of 20 days between dunning levels one and two. Assume that we run the dunning process on January 1, when two items became past due. The process creates a level one letter for those items.

When the dunning process is rerun on January 10, the process sees that only 10 days have passed since these items were included on the last letter and doesn't create a new letter. However, if a third item became past due in the meanwhile, the process creates a level one letter and includes that item.

If the process is run on 25th January, the process calculates that first two items have been in level one for more than 20 days and creates a harsher level two letter for them. However, the third item has been in level one for only 15 days and will not be included on this letter. |
| Dunning by action list | A process known as Condition Monitor automatically creates dunning letters at the appropriate level based on the collection and assessment rules. This method is used when we wish to use the condition monitor. Due to the page constraints, we will not discuss this process. |

Click the **Dunning Level** tab to define the various dunning levels and corresponding letter codes.

The following screenshot shows the **Dunning Level** tab when we use the **Dunning By Days** method:

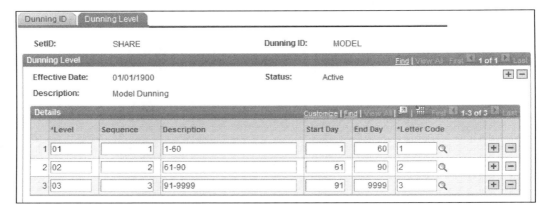

In the given example, letter code 1 will be used if items are up to 60 days past due, letter code 2 if items are between 60 to 90 days past due and so on.

The tab is slightly different when a different dunning method is used. The following screenshot shows the tab when **Dunning By Level** method is used:

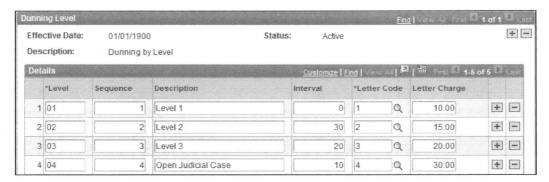

As you can see, we need to specify the interval between levels instead of a range of days. We can also specify if an additional penalty should be charged for each level in the Letter Charge field.

Running AR Dunning process

Once the dunning ID is created, the AR Dunning process uses those rules and extracts items eligible for dunning into a temporary table (AR33000_TMP).

Follow this navigation to execute the AR dunning process:

Accounts Receivable | Customer Interactions | Dunning Letters | Extract Dunning Letter Info

The following screenshot shows the run control page for the dunning process:

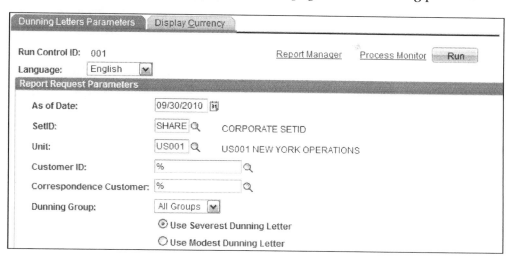

You will notice that processing options for this page are similar to those we saw for customer statement process.

- Use Severest Dunning Letter: If there are items belonging to multiple dunning levels, the system uses the letter code for the highest dunning level and puts all overdue items on that letter.

- Use Modest Dunning Letter: If there are items belonging to multiple dunning levels, the system uses the letter code for the lowest dunning level and puts all overdue items on that letter.

When the process is complete, it creates a dunning number for that specific dunning run. It needs to be used during the dunning letter print process. We can review dunning letters before printing them.

> Note that a dunning number indicates a unique dunning process run. It is possible that a single run may create multiple dunning letters for different customers. However, the dunning number is still the same for all dunning letters in this run.

Follow this navigation to review dunning letters online:

Accounts Receivable | Customer Interactions | Dunning Letters | Preview Letter

Running Dunning letter print process

This process retrieves the dunning letter data rows from the temporary table AR33000_TMP and prints them, using delivered PeopleSoft dunning letter formats. We only need to specify the dunning number to print dunning letters.

Summary

Pending items can be entered into AR manually using online pages or brought from external sources. A set of staging tables stores the pending item groups. The Receivables Update process posts these pending items, which then become items and part of the customer's balance.

Item maintenance activities include item write offs, refunds, and offsets. The Automatic maintenance process is used to automate the item maintenance activities. Maintenance worksheets are used to perform these activities manually.

The AR module is used to record customer payments through electronic methods or manually. Lockbox is one of the most widely used electronic payment methods. We can also upload payments through Excel spreadsheets. PeopleSoft provides a group of staging tables to store electronic payment data from external sources. The payment loader process reads the data from these tables and creates payments.

Received payments need to be applied to customer items. Payment worksheets are used for manual payment application, while Payment Predictor process is the automated tool for payment application.

We can create customer statements to list customer items and balances. Dunning letters are used to notify customers about their past due items. Statement ID and Dunning ID specifies the rules for correspondence creation.

With this chapter, we conclude our discussion of the Order-to-Cash business process. In the next chapter, we'll discuss the Asset Management module, which is critical for organizations that need to maintain a large number of fixed assets.

5
PeopleSoft Asset Management Module

The Asset Management module is part of the Asset Lifecycle Management solutions offered by PeopleSoft. In accounting terms, assets are categorized as current assets such as cash, accounts receivable from customers, investments, and so on, and fixed assets, such as vehicles, buildings, land, and so on. The Asset Management (or AM as it is commonly referred to) module is critical for an organization that needs to maintain and track a large number of fixed assets. It offers features that help us to add new assets, perform transactions during their useful life right through to their retirement, and record the accounting entry details in accordance with regulatory requirements.

In this chapter, we will familiarize ourselves with the following important AM topics:

- High-level overview of Asset Management processes
- Understanding important configurations, such as asset books, asset categories, asset profiles, and so on
- Capital acquisition plans
- Adding new assets using basic add, express assets, and through automated interface
- Depreciation processing
- Understanding asset adjustments
- Understanding asset retirements
- Creating accounting entries
- Loading reporting tables
- Reviewing open transactions

Asset Management processes

Before we get into the process flow in the AM module, let's take some time to understand a few basic concepts.

Accounting standards treat the fixed assets differently from current assets. For example, when an organization buys stationery items such as pens and notepads, they are considered as business expenses and are immediately recognized. Similarly, other assets such as cash, securities, and so on are called **current assets**. On the other hand, assets such as machinery, buildings, and vehicles are known as **fixed assets**. Fixed asset purchases, although paid for fully, are considered as expenses over a period of time.

Any asset (we'll be referring to only fixed assets in this chapter) has a specified useful life. This is the duration for which an organization can reasonably use that asset for its business activities. For example, a car can have a useful life of eight years, while the same can be three years for a computer. Throughout the life of an asset, its initial value continues to be reduced due to normal wear and tear. A car purchased for $20,000 may be worth only $15,000 after two years. This is known as **depreciation**. In accounting terms, this reduction in asset value can be claimed as a business expense. The rules for depreciation are dictated by regulatory requirements. When the asset reaches the end of its useful life, it may or may not have some remaining value, known as **residual value**. Various transactions may take place for an item during its life. Its value may change, it might be transferred from one business unit to the other, or it may have to be retired before the end of its useful life. Nevertheless, each asset needs to be retired at some point of time. It can be retired by scrapping, selling, or any other method. When it is retired, the asset is taken off the books. At each asset transaction, accounting entries are created and recorded.

Let's consider a hypothetical example to illustrate these concepts:

Assume that an organization buys a computer at a price of $2,400. Its useful life is considered two years with no residual value at the end of the two years (24 months). We'll assume that the organization uses the straight line depreciation method, where depreciation is calculated uniformly over the item's useful life.

When the asset is recorded in the AM system, it will be capitalized. As a result, the asset amount is not recorded to an expense account, but rather to an asset account. The initial accounting entry will be as follows:

DR	Computer assets	$2400
CR	Cash	-$2400

Now the straight line depreciation method calculates the amount by which the asset value needs to be depreciated: (Asset Cost / No. of periods in the useful life). Thus the monthly depreciation amount will be $100.

Each month, this amount is recognized as an expense and the accumulated depreciation (total depreciation amount for the asset) account is used as offset. Thus, the following entry will be created every month:

DR   **Depreciation expense** $100

CR   **Accumulated depreciation**   -$100

At the end of 24 months, the accumulated depreciation account will have a total credit balance of $2400. This means that the asset is now fully depreciated.

Note that this was a highly simplified scenario used to understand the fixed assets accounting.

The following schematic shows the important processes in the Asset Management module:

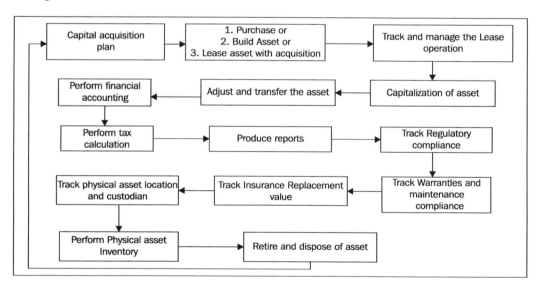

Fixed assets usually involve significant capital investments, which need careful planning and budgeting activities before being acquired. Organizations can identify their future asset purchases, estimate their costs, and put capital acquisition plans in place. PeopleSoft AM allows us to prepare such plans and track their performance. As assets are acquired, they can be assigned to a capital acquisition plan. This enables us to track the expenditure for asset purchases against the plan.

Asset Management serves as the master system to record the fixed assets. Assets can be added manually using online pages, uploaded in bulk using Excel spreadsheets, or loaded from external systems through automated interface. PeopleSoft offers three interface staging tables where external systems can load the asset data. A batch process known as Transaction Edit (AMIFEDIT) validates the staged data. Another process known as Transaction Loader (AMIF1000) loads the data into Asset Management and creates the assets.

Capitalization is the process by which capital (fixed) assets are distinguished from non-capital assets. We can set up an amount threshold, so that the system recognizes any purchase above that amount as a capital asset.

Sometimes during the life of an asset, we may have to adjust its cost. For example, a truck that was purchased for $20,000 two years ago meets with an accident. It turns out that, due to the damage suffered, its value needs to be reduced. Also, accounting standards usually dictate that assets be carried on company's books at their fair value. To ensure this, we may need to revalue these assets.

As discussed earlier, we need to depreciate the assets based on the pre-defined depreciation rates and method. PeopleSoft offers many depreciation methods to suit regulatory requirements of various countries. The depreciation process determines the amount of asset cost that can be recognized as an expense for that period. In other words, the asset value is reduced by the depreciation amount.

Like any other financial module, Asset Management creates accounting entries for various asset transactions such as asset addition, cost adjustments, retirements, and so on. A batch process known as Create Accounting Entries (AM_AMAEDIST) is used to generate accounting entries based on the accounting templates we define.

All assets will need to be retired once they reach the end of their useful life. Other events such as damage and accidents can also result in asset retirement. Assets can be retired by scrapping, sale, donation, or any other method provided by PeopleSoft. PeopleSoft allows complete or partial asset retirement. The system creates all required accounting entries once an asset is retired.

Understanding important asset configurations

Although Asset Management needs various configurations to be completed for a successful implementation, we'll consider a few critical setups in the following section. These configuration activities are:

- Configuring asset books
- Configuring asset categories
- Configuring asset profiles
- Configuring cost types
- Configuring transaction codes
- Configuring accounting entry templates
- Configuring depreciation conventions
- Configuring depreciation schedules
- Configuring depreciation limits

Configuring asset books

An asset book is used to define cost and depreciation rules for assets. In real life, organizations may need to follow multiple accounting policies and conventions due to the different countries or states in which they operate. PeopleSoft allows us to configure as many books as are needed and assigned to an asset. This approach offers flexibility to process an asset in different ways to comply with multiple regulatory requirements.

Follow this navigation to set up an asset book:

Setup Financials/Supply Chain | Product Related | Asset Management | Financials | Asset books

The following screenshot shows the configuration page:

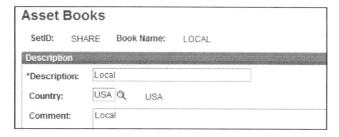

Let's say an organization headquartered in United Kingdom conducts its operations the U.S. It needs to follow accounting conventions of the U.S. and the United Kingdom for its assets. It can do so by maintaining two books: LOCAL (for the local U.S. operations) and CORP (for the corporate headquarters). The number of books required is driven by the reporting requirements of an organization. Note that PeopleSoft allows the creation and maintaining of as many asset books as needed.

Configuring asset categories

Asset categories classify assets in logically related groups. These categories are driven by the need to process accounting for various assets differently. Thus we can have asset categories such as Computing Equipment, Software, Servers, Vehicles, and so on. Of course, it is the organization's requirement which will drive this decision.

Follow this navigation to set up an asset book:

Setup Financials/Supply Chain | Product Related | Asset Management | Financials | Categories

The following screenshot shows the asset category configuration page:

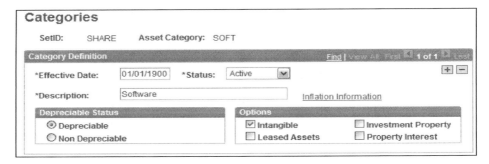

Specify the depreciation status, as well as the nature of assets such as intangible, leased, or defined as investment property or property interest according to international accounting standards.

Configuring asset profiles

Asset profile is one of the important AM configurations. A rule of thumb to follow is that we typically configure asset profiles for each of the defined asset categories. If necessary, we can also create asset profiles at a more detailed level than the asset categories.

We earlier mentioned that an asset can be assigned to as many books as needed. It is the asset profile that specifies the asset books. It also specifies the rules for depreciation and taxation. When an asset is created, it is assigned to an asset profile, thus inheriting all these rules. In a nutshell, asset profile works as the template for asset creation and processing. The configuration values provided for an asset profile will automatically default while creating an asset.

Follow this navigation to set up an asset profile:

Setup Financials/Supply Chain | Product Related | Asset Management | Profiles | Asset Profiles

The following screenshot shows the **Definition** tab of the asset profile configuration page:

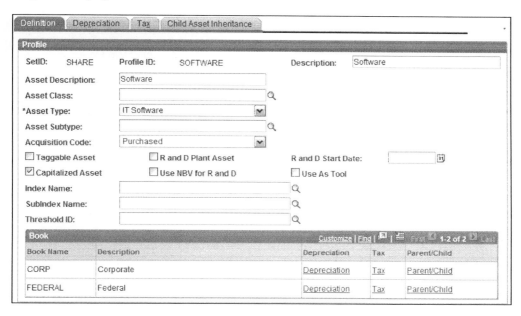

As you can see, we have defined an asset profile for the Software asset category defined earlier.

- **Asset Type:** This field specifies the Oracle-defined type of asset. The delivered values are Hardware, Software, Equipment, Property, Fleet, Machinery, Furniture, Facility, Intangible, and Other.

- **Capitalized Asset:** PeopleSoft treats the assets as Capitalized (those which possess some cost and can be depreciated) or Expensed (such as stationary items, which cannot be depreciated). The majority of the assets in AM system will be capitalized, for which this checkbox needs to be selected. However, there may be some assets which are expensed or fully depreciated, for which the checkbox needs to be blank.

- **Index Name:** You may have come across various indexes (such as Consumer Price Index, Wholesale Price Index, and so on) that are used for calculating inflation. This field specifies any index used to calculate an asset cost.

The **Book** section shows the asset books used for this profile. Books are assigned to asset profile on the next tab.

The following screenshot shows part of the **Depreciation** tab of the asset profile configuration page:

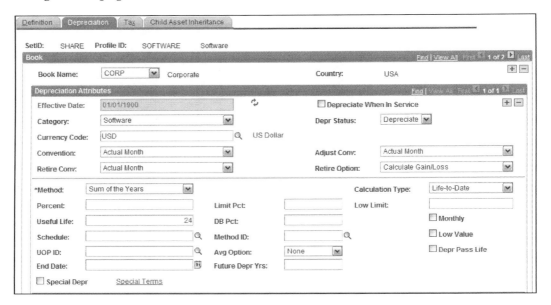

The remaining part of the asset profile page is shown in the following screenshot:

This is the tab where we need to select a book and define the rules for processing depreciation for assets with the given profile.

- **Book Name**: Select an asset book that we have defined earlier. To assign more asset books, click the + button at the right hand side of the page.

- **Category**: Select the asset category that we defined earlier.

- **Depr Status**: Specify if assets belonging to this profile should be depreciated or not. Available options are **Depreciate** and **Non Depr**.

- **Convention, Retire Conv, Adjust Conv**: These fields specify the conventions used for depreciation, retirements, and asset adjustments respectively. A convention essentially determines the timing and calendars for processing the depreciation.

- **Method**: PeopleSoft delivers close to 20 different methods for depreciation. These take care of commonly used depreciation methods (such as straight line and declining balance), country-specific methods (such as those used in Japan and Germany), or user-defined methods.

- **Useful Life**: This field specifies the number of periods for which the asset will be used.

- **End Date**: This date denotes the date when the system will stop depreciating the asset.

Although we can't discuss each field on this tab, you can appreciate the fact that we can specify different depreciation processing options for different books. As mentioned earlier, this gives a great flexibility in terms of following different rules for the same asset.

The next tab, **Tax**, is used to specify the tax-related attributes for the U.S., France, and India. We'll not discuss the fields on this tab due to page constraints.

In AM, we can establish parent-child relationships between assets. The **Child Asset Inheritance** tab is used to specify the attributes that a child asset can inherit from a parent asset.

The following screenshot shows the **Child Asset Inheritance** tab:

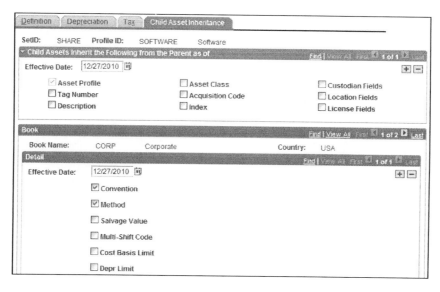

Configuring cost types

We can configure as many cost types as are necessary for recording various asset transactions. We'll see how cost types are used when we discuss the configuration of accounting templates.

Follow this navigation to set up a cost type:

Setup Financials/Supply Chain | Product Related | Asset Management | Financials | Cost Types

The following screenshot shows the **Cost Type** configuration page:

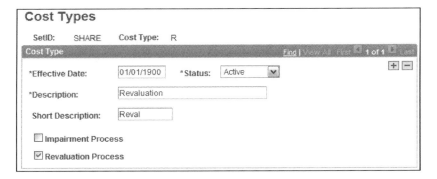

Configuring transaction codes

Transaction codes are primarily used for categorizing asset retirements.

PeopleSoft delivers a set of transaction codes that encompass possible methods of retirements. These can be used as they are or modified if necessary. The delivered values are A (Abandoned), C (Cannibalized), I (Inventory), IP (Investment Property), N (Donated), R (Scrap), RV (Revaluation), S (Sale), T (Trade-in), and Y (Casualty).

Follow this navigation to create or review transaction codes:

Setup Financials/Supply Chain | Product Related | Asset Management | Financials | Transaction Codes

Configuring accounting entry templates

An accounting entry template performs the critical function of providing the account values for creating accounting entries. It is based on the asset category, cost type, and transaction type combination that we provide. The system automatically populates the relevant accounting entry types for the specified inputs.

This is where we specify which account values should be used when we perform a specific transaction for a particular asset category.

Follow this navigation to create an accounting entry template:

Setup Financials/Supply Chain | Product Related | Asset Management | Accounting | Accounting Entry Templates

The following screenshot shows the **Definition** tab of the asset profile configuration page:

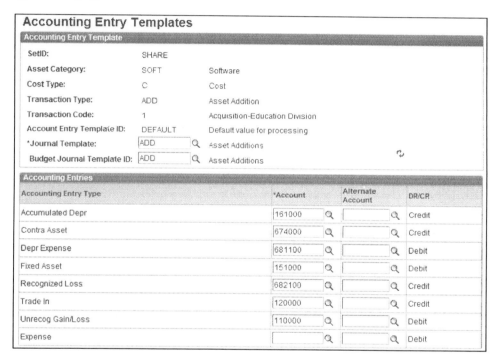

In this example, we have created a template for software asset category additions. We provide the following input parameters to create the accounting template: **SetID, Asset Category, Cost Type, Transaction Type, Transaction Code and Account Entry Template ID**.

The accounting entry types (such as Accumulated Depreciation, Expense, and so on) are automatically populated by the system based on the input parameters. Provide the account values for retrieved accounting entry types in the Account field. Thus, when we add an asset belonging to this category, the system will know which values to use while creating the appropriate accounting entries.

Accounting entry templates need to be set up for all of the following transaction types: ADD (Addition), ADJ (Adjustment), TRF (Transfer), RCT (Recategorization), DPR (Depreciation expense), PDP (Prior period depreciation), RET (Retirement), LPY (Lease payment), and INF (Inflation adjustment).

Configuring depreciation conventions

Depreciation conventions specify when the depreciation for an asset should begin. It evaluates the asset's in-service date to determine a date when depreciation will begin. For example, the convention Actual Day can be defined to instruct the system to start asset depreciation from the day it was put into service. Another convention (Following Month) means that depreciation should begin from the first day of the following month after the asset is put into service.

This is a two-step process where we need to configure a Depreciation convention first and then configure Convention builder.

Depreciation convention

Follow this navigation to review or configure depreciation conventions:

Setup Financials/Supply Chain | Product Related | Asset Management | Depreciation | Convention Definition

PeopleSoft provides various delivered conventions which can serve most requirements. However, if needed, we can configure new conventions as well.

The following screenshot shows a sample of a user-defined depreciation convention:

- **System Maintained**: This checkbox is selected for all system-delivered conventions. For conventions with this checkbox selected, the system does not allow the date entry for the From Date, To Date, and Begin Depreciation Date fields.

- **Begin Depreciation Date**: This section is used to specify the date ranges and corresponding depreciation beginning date. In the example shown previously, any asset that is put in service between January 1 and March 31 2011 will have its depreciation start date as March 31 2011.

Convention Builder

Convention builder helps in generating the depreciation timelines for each period for the convention defined earlier. Here we need to build a convention for a specific calendar. Calendars are defined separately and represent how many periods a year can have.

Follow this navigation to access depreciation convention builder:

Setup Financials/Supply Chain | Product Related | Asset Management | Depreciation | Convention Builder

The following screenshot shows a sample user-defined depreciation convention:

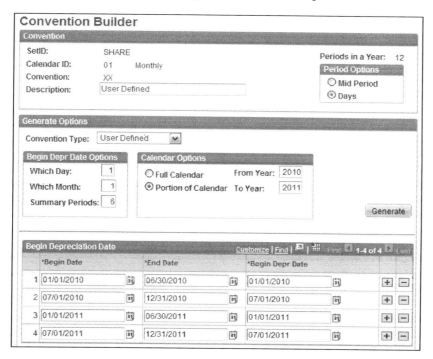

- **Convention Type**: This dropdown field determines the depreciation date for each date range in the grid at the bottom of the page. For example, if we select the value End of Month, the Begin Depr Date automatically is defaulted to the last date of the month. If User Defined is selected, we can specify when depreciation should begin in the Begin Depr Date Options section.

  Other options provided by PeopleSoft are End of quarter, End of year, Following month, Full year, Half year, Mid month, and Mid quarter.

- **Calendar Options**: Specify if we need to build the convention for the entire range of the calendar or just a part of it. In the previous example, we have specified 2010 and 2011 as the years.

- **Begin Depr Date Options**
    - **Summary Periods**: If we need to group calendar periods, specify the number of periods in one group. Here we need to group six periods (months) together.
    - **Which Day, Which Month**: Specify the month and day in a group when depreciation should begin.

Once these options are entered, click the Generate button. This generates the entries in the Begin Depreciation Date section. As you can see, for each six-month period the depreciation will begin from the first day of the first month in that group.

Configuring depreciation schedules

PeopleSoft delivers various tables that specify the depreciation percentage allowed for each period. These schedules are based on IRS depreciation methods.

Follow this navigation to review or modify the delivered schedules:

Setup Financials/Supply Chain | Product Related | Asset Management | Depreciation | Schedules

The following screenshot shows a part of the depreciation schedule for one sample method, **Declining balance with straight line switch**:

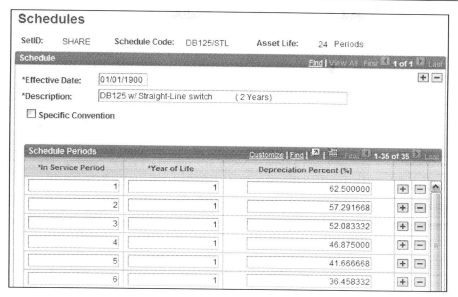

As you can see, for an asset in its first period of first year of useful life, 62.5% of its cost can be depreciated as an expense. In the second period, 57.29% can be depreciated, and so on.

We usually don't need to make any changes to the delivered depreciation schedules.

Configuring depreciation limits

Depreciation limits are used to specify the maximum amount that can be claimed as depreciation expense for a particular year. This limit can be set as an absolute amount or as a percentage of asset cost. The depreciation limit can be linked to the asset profile, thus applying it to all the assets with that profile.

Follow this navigation to configure depreciation limits:

Setup Financials/Supply Chain | Product Related | Asset Management | Depreciation | Limits

The following screenshot shows a sample depreciation limit definition:

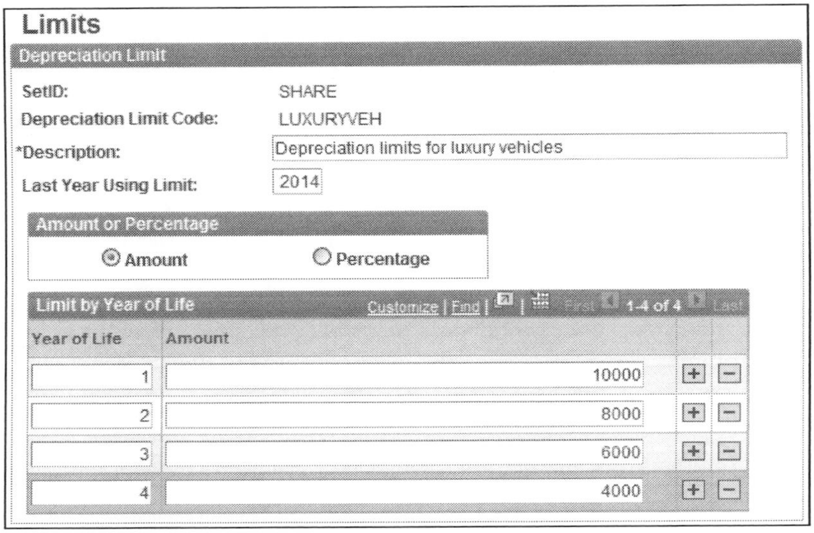

Limits

Depreciation Limit

SetID: SHARE
Depreciation Limit Code: LUXURYVEH
*Description: Depreciation limits for luxury vehicles
Last Year Using Limit: 2014

Amount or Percentage

◉ Amount   ○ Percentage

Limit by Year of Life   Customize | Find | 🔲 | 🔳   First ◄ 1-4 of 4 ► Last

Year of Life	Amount		
1	10000	+	−
2	8000	+	−
3	6000	+	−
4	4000	+	−

As you can see, based on this limit definition, there is a maximum amount defined for first four years of asset life. Even if an asset's cost is high and its depreciation amounts exceed the defined limits, the system doesn't allow that.

Now that we have familiarized ourselves with basic asset management configurations, let us discuss some of the important business processes.

Capital acquisition plans

As we briefly discussed earlier, capital acquisition plans are important to plan future asset acquisitions. We link them to assets once they are acquired to track the planned asset costs with the actuals. PeopleSoft allows us to create individual capital acquisition plans as well as high-level plans with multiple subsidiary plans for complex acquisitions.

Follow this navigation to create a new capital acquisition plan:

Asset Management | Asset Transactions | Capital Acquisition Planning | Create (CAP) Plan

The following screenshot shows the **Details** tab of the page:

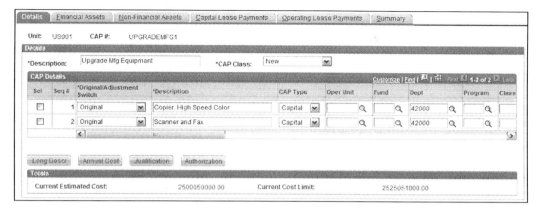

- **CAP Class**: This field shows the PeopleSoft delivered options **New, Necessity, Cost Reduction,** and **Expansion**. When we create a new plan, the status has to be **New**.
- **CAP Details**: As you can see, the given plan has more than one entry, as we need to purchase two assets.
  - **Original/Adjustment Switch**: When a new plan is created, the value in this field must be **Original**. If we modify the existing plan, it will need to be changed to **Adjustment**.

  Scroll to the right to see additional information fields.
  - **Estimated Cost**: Specify the approximate cost that we anticipate for an asset purchase.
  - **Cost Limit**: This field specifies the upper limit for the purchase cost. This is necessary as the asset costs can change by the time we purchase it.
  - **% Over Allowed**: Instead of specifying the cost limit, we can also specify the permissible % increase for the asset purchase cost.

The next four tabs (**Financial Assets, Non- Financial Assets, Capital Lease Payments,** and **Operating Lease Payments)** show any assets belonging to these categories that are linked to this plan.

Adding new assets

Recording an asset in the Asset Management system can be done in three different ways:

- Using online asset additions (manual)
- Uploading assets details using Excel spreadsheets
- Interfacing assets from external sources using Transaction Loader

Asset Management records two types of asset details:

- **Financial information**: These details include all the elements needed for accounting transactions of an asset, such as asset cost, books, depreciation method, useful life, and so on.
- **Physical information**: These details include all the physical attributes such as tag (serial) number, manufacturer, and so on.

An important feature offered by the AM module is the **capitalization threshold**. Some organizations may need to capitalize their purchases as capital or non-capital depending on the asset cost. We can specify an amount threshold beyond which the system can automatically categorize the assets as capital. PeopleSoft offers the following categories for the assets:

- **Capital assets**: These are also known as financial assets. AM records the financial as well as the physical information for these assets. All financial details are stored in the COST table.
- **Non-capital assets**: These are also known as non-financial or trackable assets. For these, only physical information is recorded in the COST table.
- **Expense assets**: These are not tracked in AM system, as their cost is less than the capitalization threshold. Such low-cost items are immediately expensed rather than gradually depreciated like capital assets.

Online asset entry

PeopleSoft offers two different methods for online asset entry: Basic Add and Express Add. Let's take a look at the basic asset add pages first.

Adding asset basic details

Follow this navigation to add or modify an existing asset:

Asset Management | Asset Transactions | Owned Assets | Basic Add | General Information

The asset entry component consists of various tabs that capture various asset details. We'll discuss some of the important tabs now.

The following screenshot shows the **General Information** tab of the basic add component:

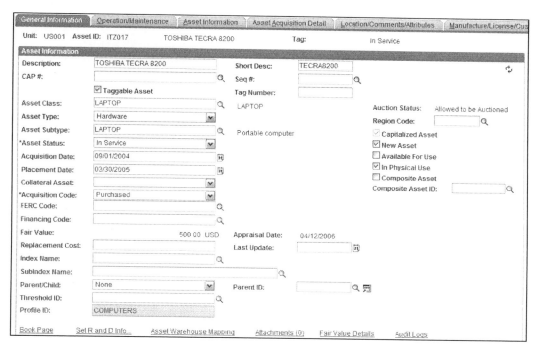

- **CAP # and Seq #**: These fields record the capital acquisition plan details. Once we link an asset to the CAP, these details are automatically updated for the CAP.

- **Asset Status**: Choose the value **In Service** to indicate that the asset has been put in use. If the asset is recorded now but is going to enter service later, we can use the value **Received**.

- **Fair Value**: We update the fair value of an asset on the Fair Value page. This value is automatically displayed in this field. Click the **Fair Value Details** hyperlink to update the details.

- **Parent/Child**: This field determines the nature of this asset. Available options are **None, Child, and Parent**. If the value **None** is selected, it means that this asset is neither a parent nor a child. If we designate this asset as a **Child**, we need to specify its parent asset in the **Parent ID** field.

- **Threshold ID**: We discussed the concept of a capitalization threshold earlier. If we define the threshold amounts, we can choose the threshold ID, so that the system can automatically categorize the asset once it is capitalized.

- **Profile ID**: Assign an asset profile to the asset so that it inherits the profile attributes.

The asset can be capitalized by clicking the **Capitalize** button on the **Asset Acquisition Detail** tab. We can record an asset and capitalize it at a later point of in time if required.

- **Book Page**: This hyperlink transfers the control to a new page that shows the asset books to which this asset is assigned. Remember that we attach books to the asset profile, from where they are inherited by the asset. The page shows the same books and field values that we specified on the **Asset Profile – Depreciation** tab. However, if we wish to make any changes to the field values at the asset level, we can. For example, if the useful life was specified as 24 months for the asset profile, it is defaulted for the newly added asset as well, but we can change it to, say, 36 months for this asset.

Operation / Maintenance, **Asset Information**, and **Location/Comments/Attributes** tabs are used to record physical information details such as manufacturer information, maintenance information, asset location, custodian information, and so on.

Asset Acquisition Detail tab is used to record all the components of asset's cost that need to be capitalized. Note that when an asset is capitalized, it is customary to include freight charges, insurance charges, and so on to the asset cost.

When we enter the basic asset information on the **General Information** tab and navigate to this tab for the first time, the asset is not yet capitalized. The fields on the **Asset Acquisition Detail** tab for a non-capitalized asset look like the following screenshot:

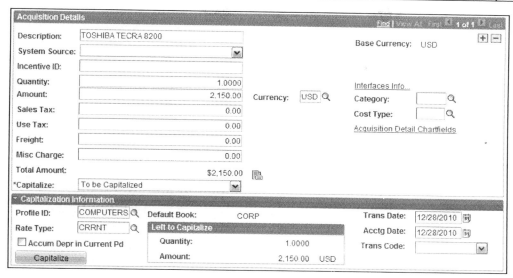

As you can see in the screenshot, the Amount field shows the asset cost, while other fields such as Sales Tax, Use Tax, and so on show other cost components that need to be added for capitalization.

Capitalize: This dropdown menu shows the current asset status as **To Be Capitalized**. If the asset should not be capitalized, we can choose the value **To Capitalize Later** or **Never Capitalize**.

Once all the cost rows are added, click the **Capitalize** button to capitalize the asset. This makes the cost rows unavailable for modification and changes the **Capitalize** field value to **Already Capitalized**. The following screenshot shows the changes to the Asset Acquisition Detail tab after the asset is capitalized:

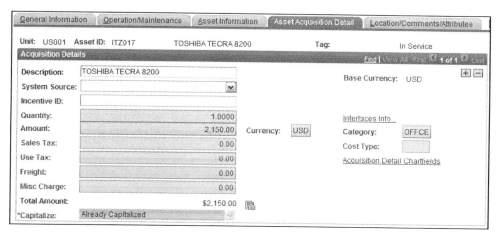

Adding express assets

Another way of quickly adding assets manually is by using the **Express Add** feature. This feature allows the asset entry along with the accumulated depreciation.

Follow this navigation to access the Express Add component to add assets:

Asset Management | Asset Transactions | Owned Assets | Express Add

The component consists of three distinct tabs for data entry. The following screenshot shows the **Cost/Asset Information** tab:

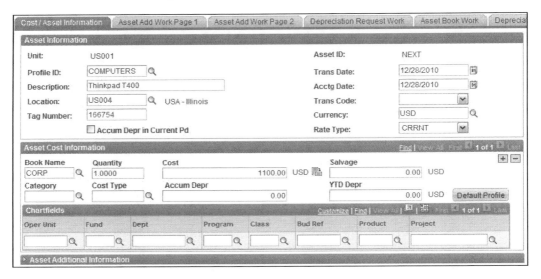

- **Accum Depr in Current Pd**: It is possible that the asset has already been in use and was being tracked in some other system. As a result, it would have already accumulated some amount of depreciation. This checkbox controls how the accumulated depreciation of the asset being added is treated. If this checkbox is selected, the accumulated depreciation is posted to the current period, otherwise the system posts it to the previous period.

- **Asset Cost Information**: This section is used to record the cost details. We can add as many rows here to enter costs as needed. Click the **Default Profile** button to automatically insert the lines based on the books attached to the asset profile.

The following screenshot shows the changes to the page after clicking the **Default Profile** button:

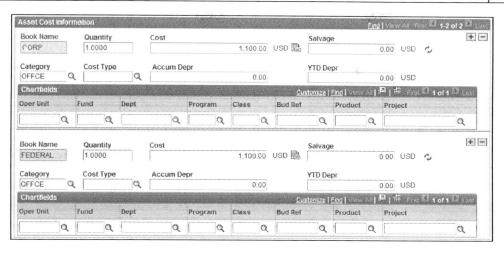

As you can see, the system populates the books which were assigned to the COMPUTER asset profile. Enter the cost type and chartfield details.

The **Depreciation Information** tab shows the depreciation parameters for each of the books associated with this asset. These are exactly the same as those on the Depreciation tab for asset profile. If required, we can change any parameter for this specific asset.

Tax Information tab is again similar to the Tax tab for the asset profile. The values are inherited from the profile set-up and can be changed for this asset if needed.

Data entry on these three tabs is all we need as most of the details are automatically defaulted from the asset profile.

Loading assets through interface

As a part of the Asset Management implementation, in most cases, we need to bring in assets from an existing non-PeopleSoft system. Considering the huge volume of assets involved, manual methods we saw previously are certainly not feasible. Also, after the implementation, new asset details are regularly sent by non-PeopleSoft systems as well as PeopleSoft Purchasing and Project Costing modules. PeopleSoft offers a group of staging tables and a delivered interface program to load asset data from these staging tables into the system.

The AM staging tables are as follows:

- INTFC_FIN: This table stores the financial asset data
- INTFC_PHY_A: This table stores the physical asset data
- INTFC_PHY_B: This table stores the physical asset data.

Loading the data into staging tables

If the source of asset information is a non-PeopleSoft system, we need to create a customized program that can load the data into the given staging tables. If it is the PeopleSoft module that sends the asset data, PeopleSoft delivers the program that loads the staging tables.

Previewing/approving the staged data

PeopleSoft offers three pages where we can preview the data in each of the three staging tables. The navigation for these pages is given in the following table:

Preview data in	Navigation
INTFC_FIN	**Asset Management	Send/Receive Information	Approve Financial Information	Review**
INTFC_PHY_A	**Asset Management	Send/Receive Information	Approve Physical Information	Review - A**
INTFC_PHY_B	**Asset Management	Send/Receive Information	Approve Physical Information	Review - B**

When the asset data is loaded into staging tables, we can decide to have the data to be auto-approved, meaning it is loaded with its status as **Approved**. In case it needs to be manually approved, transactions can be loaded with the **Auto-Approved** flag set to **No**. In this case, each transaction needs to be manually approved so that it can be loaded into AM.

The navigation for the approval pages is given in the following table:

Approve data in	Navigation
INTFC_FIN	**Asset Management	Send/Receive Information	Approve Financial Information	Approve**
INTFC_PHY_A	**Asset Management	Send/Receive Information	Approve Physical Information	Approve – A**
INTFC_PHY_B	**Asset Management	Send/Receive Information	Approve Physical Information	Approve – B**

Validating the staged data

Once the asset data is loaded into the staging tables, we need to validate it and identify if there are any data errors.

Follow this navigation to run the **Transaction loader edit** (AMIFEDIT) program:

**Asset Management | Send/Receive Information | Load Transactions |
Edit Transactions**

The following screenshot shows the run control page for this process:

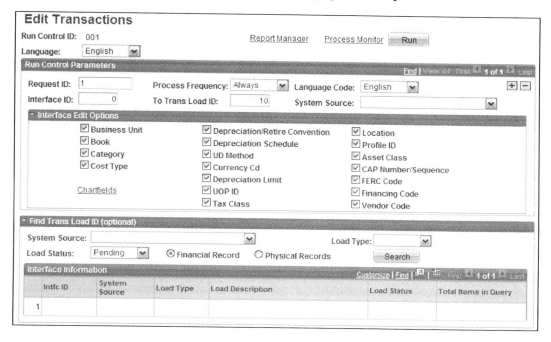

The **Run Control Parameters** section on this page specifies the criteria to select the data rows in the interface tables that need to be edited.

- **Interface ID, To Trans Load ID**: Each time asset data is loaded into staging tables all the transactions get a unique interface ID. This is helpful in identifying each interface batch. Specify the interface IDs that should be validated by the process.

- **System Source**: Each data row in the staging table also carries the system source information. Another way of filtering the data is by specifying the system source that sent the asset data.

- **Interface Edit Options**: This section lists the fields that need to be validated by the edit process. If we don't use any of these fields, we can skip the validation. Selecting the checkbox next to a field ensures that the system validates the values in that field and logs error messages for any invalid values. Uncheck the checkbox to prevent the validation of a field.

- **Find Trans Load ID**: This section is used to search the interface IDs of transactions so that we can use them in the **Interface ID** and **To Trans Load ID** fields to specify the range of desired data.

Specify a value in the **System Source** and **Load Type** fields to search the records in staging tables. Leave these fields blank to retrieve data rows belonging to all system sources. Click the **Search** button to see staged data with specified **Load Status**.

The following screenshot shows the results of a search:

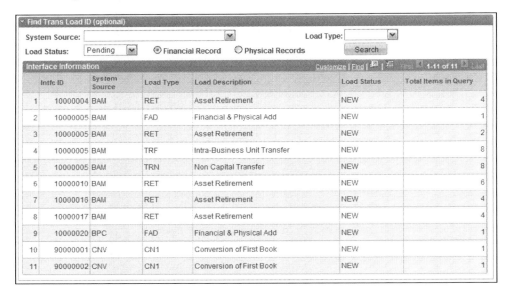

Click the **Run** button to initiate the process.

Loading the staged data into AM

The **Transaction Loader** (AMIF1000) process loads the validated data from staging tables into AM and automatically creates new assets.

Follow this navigation to execute the Transaction Loader process:

Asset Management | Send/Receive Information | Load Transactions | Load Transactions into AM

The following screenshot shows the run control page for **Transaction Loader** process:

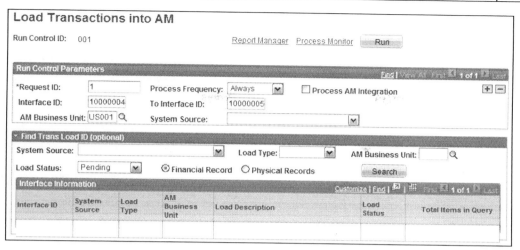

As you can see, the run control parameters are similar to those for the Transaction Edit process.

- **AM Business Unit**: Specify a value in this field so that assets for a specific BU are processed. Leave this field blank to load assets for all units that may be in the staging table.

- **Process AM Integration**: This option is used only for integrating data from PeopleSoft Maintenance Management module.

Processing depreciation

So far we have seen the basic configurations for performing depreciation and basic depreciation concepts. Now let's see how PeopleSoft AM performs the depreciation processing. PeopleSoft delivers the batch process **Depreciation Calculation** (AM_DEPR_CALC). This selects the assets based on the input parameters, refers to the depreciation attributes specified for the asset, and calculates depreciation amounts.

 This process only populates values in the depreciation table. It does not create any accounting entries.

Running Depreciation Calculation process

Follow this navigation to execute the **Depreciation Calculation** process:

Asset Management | Depreciation | Processing | Calculate

The following screenshot shows the run control page where we can specify the parameters for the process:

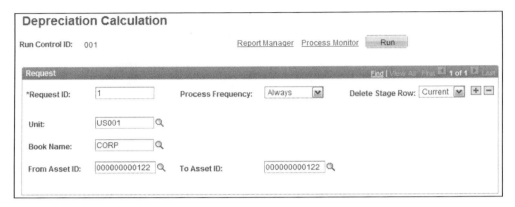

As you can see, we can specify the values for Business Unit, Book, and Asset ID to narrow down the processing or leave these fields blank so that all assets are processed.

Click **Run** to initiate the process.

It is important to run the Depreciation Calculation process before the accounting entries are created for assets. We will discuss the accounting entries creation process in a later section.

Previewing depreciation information for assets

PeopleSoft provides a set of pages where we can review the depreciation-related information for assets.

Follow this navigation to preview depreciation details:

Asset Management | Depreciation | Review Depreciation Info | Asset Depreciation

The following screenshot shows the **Asset** tab of the page:

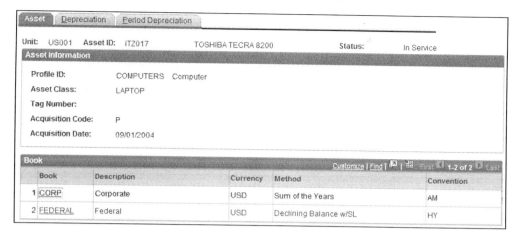

As you can see, this tab essentially gives a snapshot of different books to which this asset is linked, along with the depreciation methods and conventions followed.

The next screenshot shows the next tab, **Depreciation**:

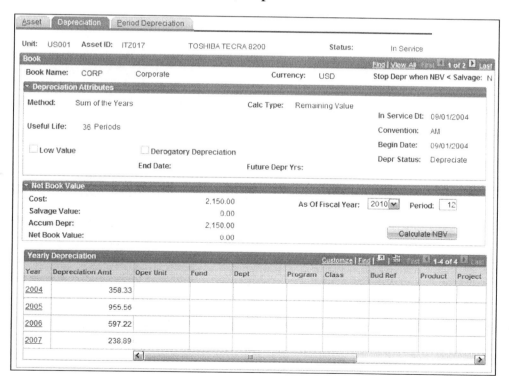

This tab shows the year-wise depreciation amounts for the asset.

The Net Book Value section shows the break up of cost and accumulated depreciation for the CORP book as of a specific date. Net book value (NBV) is essentially the difference between asset cost and accumulated depreciation so far. It indicates the remaining worth of an asset. In the given example, you can see that the asset has been fully depreciated and its net book value is zero.

Click the hyperlink for a year under the **Year** column to see detailed period-wise depreciation amounts. The system automatically opens the **Period Depreciation** tab and displays the depreciation amount for each period.

We can see the depreciation amounts for each of the books on this tab.

The next tab, **Period Depreciation**, contains the link **Depr Accum Adjustment**. This can be used adjust the accumulated depreciation for this asset.

Clicking this link opens a new page where we can change the accumulated depreciation amount. Let's say we find out that the total depreciation was incorrectly calculated and we need to reduce the accumulated depreciation by $100.

 After performing any such adjustments, we must run the Depreciation Calculation process.

The following screenshot shows the adjustment made to the total depreciation:

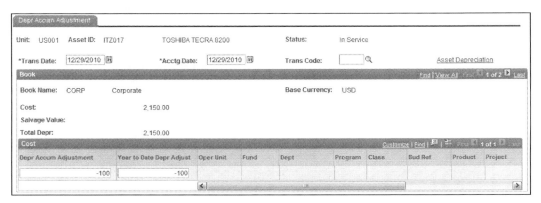

We need to enter the adjustment amounts in the fields as shown and save the page.

This results in changes in the year-wise depreciation amounts and, as a result, the NBV of the asset. The following screenshot shows these changes:

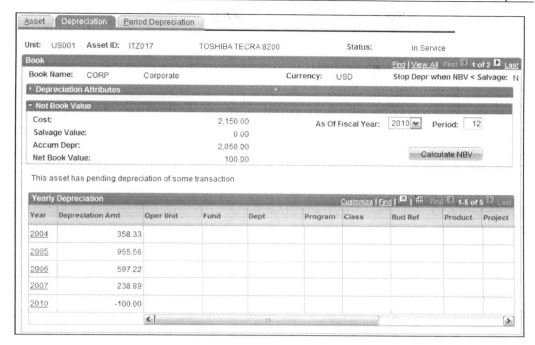

Understanding asset adjustments

An organization encounters various situations where changes need to be made to the asset details. These changes can be related to the physical or financial data. Physical asset details changes are limited to physical attributes such as color, weight, and so on, and they don't affect the asset value or depreciation. On the other hand, changes to financial data such as asset cost, category, depreciation convention, and so on impact the depreciation calculations and have tax implications.

PeopleSoft offers the following options for asset adjustments:

- **Addition**: This option is used to make any additions to the asset cost. The COST table in asset management tracks all transactions for an asset. This option results in an additional cost line with the ADD transaction type in the COST table.

- **Adjustment**: This option is used when a change (positive or negative) needs to be made to the asset cost. Positive adjustment is similar to the addition option given previously. However, the system adds a line to the COST table with the ADJ transaction type.

- **Fixed price markup**: This option is used while performing asset transfers to apply a markup to the asset cost.

- **InterUnit transfer**: This option is used to transfer assets from one BU to another, where these BUs represent different legal entities. For example, an organization decides to transfer a mainframe computer from its Chicago office (business unit US001) to Paris operations (business unit FRA01). Note that we can perform partial or complete asset transfers.

- **Recategorize**: This option is used place an asset in a different category or change its cost type. For example, we were using an asset category called COMPUTERS. Now we decide to create a new category called LAPTOPS and need to recategorize existing laptops and put them in this new category.

- **Revaluate**: We discussed earlier the index for revaluing assets. According to regulatory guidelines, assets need to be carried on company books at fair value and need to be revaluated regularly.

- **Transfer**: This option is used for chartfield transfers within the same business unit. For example, a truck that was being used by the Manufacturing department needs to be assigned to the Field Service department. In this case, the business unit remains the same, but we have to change the Department chartfield value.

Follow this navigation to access the cost adjustment and transfer feature:

Asset Management | Asset Transactions | Financial Transactions | Cost Adjust/ Transfer Asset

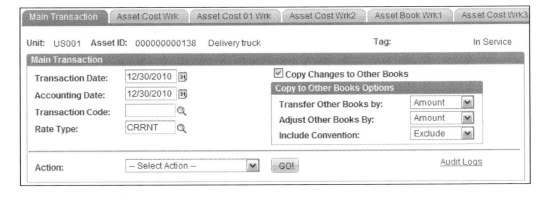

- **Copy Changes to Other Books**: Select this checkbox to carry over these asset changes to all the asset books to which it is assigned.

- **Transfer Other Books By, Adjust Other Books By**: As we are aware, assets can be linked to multiple books. Thus, when we transfer or adjust an asset in one book, the same needs to be performed in other books as well. These fields offer the options **Amount** and **Percent**.

Let's say that an asset is assigned to two books with costs as $1,000 and $800 and we adjust (increase) its cost by $100 in the first book, making it $1,100. If the **Adjust Other Books By** field contains the value **Amount**, the cost in other book also increases by $100, making it $900. On the other hand, if the **Percent** option is selected, the cost in second book increases by 10%, making it $880.

- **Action**: Select one of the options discussed previously from the dropdown menu and click the **GO!** button.

The system opens the **Cost Information** tab where we can specify the changes to the asset details.

The following screenshot shows the **Cost Information** tab when we select the value Addition:

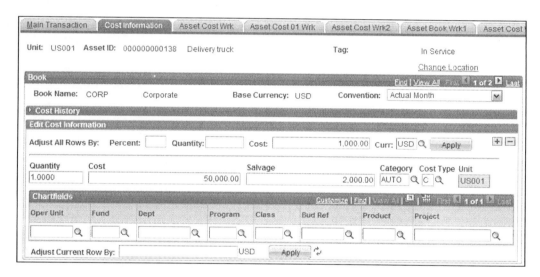

- **Adjust All Rows By Percent, Quantity,** or **Cost**: Use these fields to enter the percent or amount by which the asset cost needs to be adjusted.

Let's say that we wish to increase the cost for the asset shown previously by $1,000. So we need to specify the amount in the **Cost** field as shown next. Click the **Apply** button to apply these changes.

This automatically changes the asset cost from $50,000 to $51,000. Note that, even if we see only one chartfield row in the previous example, there can be multiple chartfield rows for an asset cost. For example, if the asset cost is being shared by two different departments in a 60:40 ratio, there will be two cost rows.

One cost row will show $30,000 with department one and another with $20,000 with department two. In this case, if we decide to adjust all rows by $1,000, the system prorates the amount and adds $600 and $400 to these two rows respectively.

If we select the **InterUnit Transfer** option in the **Main Transaction** tab, the **Cost Information** tab shows the following fields:

All other sections, such as **Cost History** and **Edit Cost Information,** are the same as given previously. In this case we need to specify the BU where this asset needs to be transferred. Enter a specific asset ID in the **New Asset ID** field or leave the default value **NEXT** as shown. The system will assign the next asset ID automatically. This option is needed when we have to remove an asset from a BU and assign to another BU.

Understanding asset retirements

Every asset needs to be retired at some point of its useful life. It can either serve its entire useful life and then retire or retire before completing its useful life. Consider two scenarios to understand this. A laptop may be retired at the end of its (hypothetical) useful life of five years. It is quite obsolete now and doesn't serve any useful purpose. On the other hand, a truck (with a hypothetical life of 10 years) can meet an accident just a year after its purchase and get completely damaged without any chance of repair. Thus it needs to be retired prematurely. We'll later see various methods by which we can dispose off the assets after retirement.

Just like asset transfers, we can retire assets fully or partially.

On the other hand, sometimes retired assets are brought back into service. This is known as **reinstatement**.

Manual asset retirement

Follow this navigation to access asset retirement page:

Asset Management | Asset Transactions | Asset Disposal | Retire/Reinstate Assets

The following screenshot shows the **Retire Assets** tab of the retirement page:

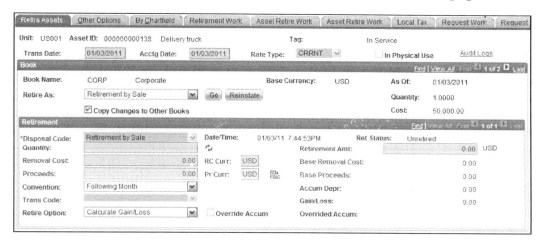

Retire As: This dropdown menu lists various options by which an asset can be retired. The available values are **Abandonment, Auto-Retire Fully Depr Asset, Cannibalize for Other Assets, Casualty Loss , Disappeared Assets, Disposal Due to Theft, Donated to External Group, Expensed, Like Kind Exchange, Missing Asset, Retirement by Sale, Returned to Inventory, Scrapped Assets,** or **Traded In for Another Asset.**

Based on the selected value, the page displays different fields.

- **Removal Costs and Proceeds**: These fields record the cost involved in disposal of the asset and the income from the disposal respectively.

- **Convention**: This option determines the date till which depreciation is calculated for retired asset. **Actual Day** results in depreciation calculated till the retirement date, **Actual Month** means depreciation is calculated till the last day of the previous month, and **Following Month** results in depreciation being calculated till the last day of the retirement month.

- **Accum Depr**: This field shows the accumulated depreciation for the asset that has been calculated so far.

To proceed with the retirement, select an option in the **Retire As** field and click the **Go** button.

As you can see, the same page is used to reinstate a retired asset.

Auto-retirement of fully depreciated assets

PeopleSoft offers a batch process known as **Auto-Retire** (AMRETFDA) to retire multiple assets together. Note that this process picks up only those assets that are fully depreciated.

Follow this navigation to execute the Auto-Retire process:

Asset Management | Asset Transactions | Asset Disposal | Auto-Retire Fully Depr Assets

The following screenshot shows the run control page to specify parameters the for Auto-Retire process:

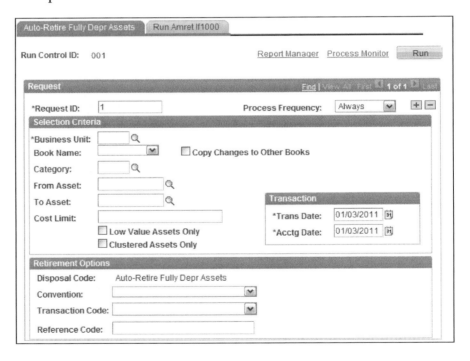

- **Business Unit**: Specify the BU value for the assets that have to be retired. Note that an AM BU needs to be enabled for the auto-retire feature to appear on this page.

- **Cost Limit**: We can specify a threshold for asset cost, so that the process can retire only those assets with a cost of less than a specified amount.

Creating accounting entries

Because Asset Management is a part of financial applications, one of its important functions is to maintain accounting entries for various asset transactions. We saw that PeopleSoft offers the following delivered transaction types: ADD, ADJ, TRF, RCT, DPR, PDP, RET, LPY, and INF. These represent various transactions for which accounting entries are created.

In PeopleSoft AM, there are two different processes that create accounting entries:

- **Accounting Entry Creation** (AM_AMAEDIST), which creates accounting entries for all non-depreciation transactions
- **Depreciation Close** (AM_DPCLOSE), which creates accounting entries only for depreciation in an accounting period

 Every time a transaction such as asset addition, adjustment, transfer, and so on is performed, the system creates an open transaction. This transaction remains open till it is processed by one of the previous processes.

Accounting entry creation (AM_AMAEDIST) process

When the Accounting Entry Creation process runs, it looks at the combination of asset category, cost type, transaction type, and transaction code for each transaction. Recall our discussion about the accounting entry template setup. Based on the given combination, it selects the appropriate template and uses that information to create accounting entries. This process can be executed as many times as needed.

Follow this navigation to execute the Accounting Entry Creation process:

Asset Management | Accounting Entries | Create Accounting Entries

The following screenshot shows the run control page for the process:

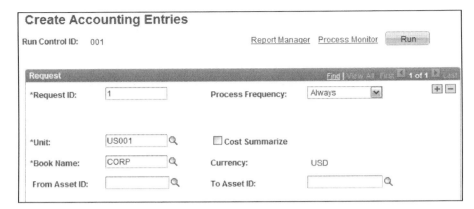

The **Business Unit** and **Book Name** parameters (indicated by an asterisk) are mandatory. Enter a range of asset IDs in the **From Asset ID** and **To Asset ID** fields or leave them blank so that the process creates accounting entries for all assets for a given BU and book.

If assets in a BU are tagged to multiple books (which most probably will be the case), the process needs to be run for each BU and Book combination. In order to do that, add a new section by clicking the **+** button and specify all required BU and Book combinations.

We can review the asset's accounting entries after the accounting entry creation process completes successfully.

Follow this navigation to review accounting entries:

Asset Management | Accounting Entries | Review Financial Entries

The following screenshot shows the accounting entries generated for an asset:

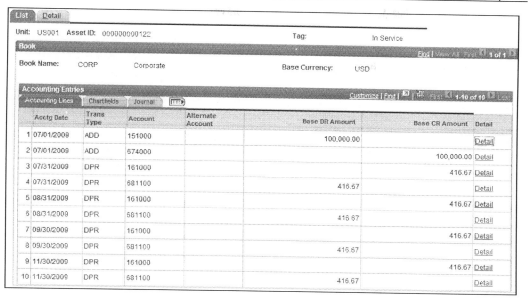

As you can see, this asset has five accounting entries with two lines each. The transaction type ADD means that the entry was created during asset addition. The remaining entries with DPR transaction type denote depreciation accounting entries created at the end of each month.

Depreciation Close (AM_DPCLOSE) process

The Depreciation Close process creates the accounting entries for depreciation for an open accounting period. It uses the **DPR** (Depreciation) and **PDP** (Prior depreciation period) accounting templates.

 The Depreciation Close process should be run only once for each accounting period. No transaction activity should be performed after this process is run.

The process creates accounting entries as follows:

- **DR   Depreciation Expense**
- **CR   Accumulated Depreciation**

The Depreciation Close process offers two run options:

- **Rerun Deprecation Close**: When this option is selected and no accounting entries exist, the process creates the depreciation accounting entries. If the entries are already created, no action takes place.
- **Reverse Posted Entries**: When this option is selected and journal entries are already created, the process reverses these entries.

Running the process with both of the previous options selected results in old accounting entries being reversed and new depreciation accounting entries created with new depreciation amounts.

Follow this navigation to execute the Depreciation Close process:

Asset Management | Accounting Entries | Close Depreciation

The following screenshot shows the run control page for the process:

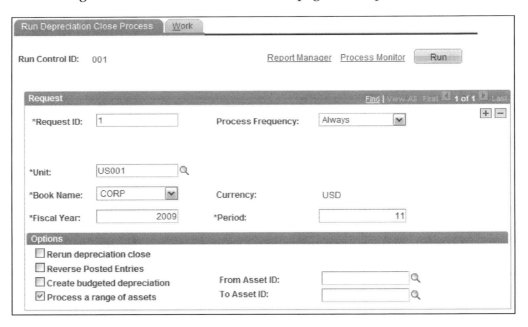

At the end of the accounting period when the period needs to be closed, run the process with both the **Rerun depreciation close** and **Reverse posted entries** options selected.

Loading reporting tables

We already discussed how PeopleSoft calculates depreciation using the Depreciation Calculation batch process. The AM module offers various delivered depreciation reports such as Depreciation by Period, Depreciation by Fiscal Period, and Depreciation Activity. In order to use these depreciation reports, we first need to execute a batch process known as Load Reporting Table (AMDPREPT).

Follow this navigation to run this process:

Asset Management | Financial Reports | Load Reporting Tables | Depr Reporting Table

The following screenshot shows the run control page used to specify the process parameters:

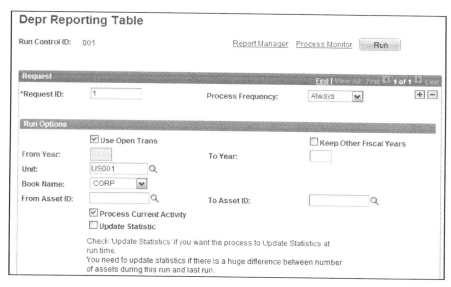

This process loads the depreciation details for assets in the **Depreciation Reporting table** (DEPR_RPT). All of the depreciation reports derive their data from this table, so it is important to load it using the batch process regularly.

- **Use Open Trans:** When this checkbox is selected, it instructs the system to process only the new open transactions. Recall that we saw that open transactions are created after any asset additions or adjustments. Leave this checkbox blank to specify the **From Year** and **To Year** values for asset depreciation.

- **Keep Other Fiscal Years:** This option instructs the system to retain the depreciation data for earlier years, which is loaded in the table.

Reviewing open transactions

As we briefly saw earlier, open transactions are created when we perform asset additions or adjustments. Each asset open transaction can have multiple transaction types, such as addition, retirement, reinstatement, and so on, associated with it.

Open transaction review is important because it allows us to know the asset processing status.

Follow this navigation to review open transactions for an asset:

Asset Management | Depreciation | Open Transactions | Review

The following screenshot shows the open transaction details for an asset for the ADD (Asset addition) transaction type:

- **Depreciation Calc Status:** This field shows the status of depreciation performed for this asset. A status of **Complete** means that the depreciation has been calculated.

- **Acctg Entry Creation Status:** This field tell us if accounting entries have been created and sent to General Ledger.

- **Reporting Process Status:** This field indicates if depreciation details for this asset have been loaded into the reporting table. A status of **Pending** explains that this asset has not been processed by the Load Reporting Table process.

The `OPEN_TRANS` table in PeopleSoft Asset Management is crucial in maintaining the asset transaction history. All operations performed on an asset are recorded in this table. For example, an asset is added, its value may be adjusted, it may be re-categorized, or it may be transferred to another business unit. The system inserts a row in the `OPEN_TRANS` table for each transaction with one of the types that we discussed earlier.

Summary

The Asset Management module is used to maintain an organization's fixed assets. These assets are characterized by the need to capitalize and depreciate them. New assets can be added using online pages or loaded automatically using the delivered interface program known as Transaction Loader.

Assets can be linked to multiple asset books to ensure that they can be processed differently according to different accounting regulations. An asset profile sets the default rules for asset processing, such as the depreciation method to be used, which are inherited by assets using that profile. This significantly reduces the new asset data entry efforts. If needed, these default rules can be overridden for an individual asset.

PeopleSoft delivers a set of transaction types that describe all possible actions (such as addition, adjustment, retirement, and so on) that we can perform. Accounting templates define the accounts to be used for each combination of asset category, cost type, transaction type, and transaction code.

Asset Depreciation is calculated for each accounting period. It indicates the amount of total asset cost that is recognized as expense in a period. The Depreciation Calculation process is used to calculate depreciation amounts for assets based on the rules defined for asset profile or asset.

Assets need to be retired when they reach the end of their useful life or even earlier. Retired assets can also be reinstated into service if required.

The accounting entry creation process is used to generate accounting entries for all non-depreciation transactions. The depreciation close process creates entries for depreciation transactions. This is run once at the end of every accounting period. The load reporting table process is used to load the depreciation reporting table. PeopleSoft's depreciation reports are based on this reporting table.

6
PeopleSoft Accounts Payable Module

PeopleSoft Accounts Payable module is one of the critical modules in the 'Procure to Pay' business process. In accounting terms, accounts payable means the amount that we are liable to pay to others. Usually, it is the next piece of the procurement activities after the PeopleSoft Purchasing module. A typical organization purchases a large number of goods and services from many vendors. Handling payments for these purchases in a timely manner is a critical task for the organizations. Accounts Payable (or AP as it is commonly known) module records invoices sent by vendors and tracks them to see when the payments for them are becoming due. It then issues the payments for eligible vendor invoices at the appropriate time. It also creates accounting entries for the vendor invoices and payments. In brief, AP is responsible for tracking and managing vendor invoices and payments.

In this chapter, we'll discuss the following topics:

- Accounts Payable process flow
- Understanding Accounts Payable concepts
- Common configurations (such as accounting templates, voucher origins, miscellaneous charge codes, and payment terms)
- Voucher entry (Manual voucher entry and voucher creation through automated interface)
- Matching
- Posting vouchers
- Voucher maintenance (such as deleting, closing, and unposting vouchers)
- Processing payments
- Withholding

Understanding Accounts Payable process flow

In PeopleSoft parlance, a vendor invoice is known as a **voucher**. We'll use this term throughout the chapter. You may recall from our discussion of Billing and Accounts Receivable modules, that an organization sells to its customers, sends an invoice and then receives the payments at a later point of time. Similarly, when it purchases something from a vendor, it usually receives the invoice along with the goods. The invoice amount needs to be paid later depending on the purchase terms.

The following schematic shows the basic Accounts Payable process flow:

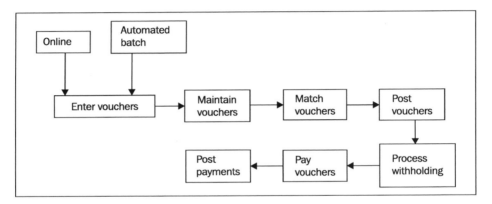

The Accounts Payable business process begins with the recording of a vendor invoice as a voucher. PeopleSoft offers manual as well as automated methods to create vouchers. For automated voucher creation, a group of staging tables is used. A batch process known as **Voucher Build** loads the data from these staging tables into AP to create vouchers. We can also upload voucher information from a pre-configured spreadsheet template. Another way to create vouchers is from the invoice details entered in PeopleSoft eSettlements module.

Once vouchers are created in AP system, there are various operations that may have to be performed. A voucher may have to be approved before a payment is made to the vendor; it may need to be deleted (say, due to incorrect entry) or closed (when we need not pay it anymore). These activities are known as **voucher maintenance**.

Organizations need to have very strict controls in place before any vendor payments are issued. It is critical to ensure that we don't simply rely on the vendor invoice and pay the invoice amount. PeopleSoft offers four different methods where a voucher can be matched against the purchase order, goods receipt, or inspection of received goods. A batch process known as **Voucher Matching** performs the validation based on pre-defined match rules. This ensures that we pay for only those things that we ordered and actually received.

Similar to other PeopleSoft financial modules, Accounts Payable module too creates accounting entries for various transactions. **Voucher Post** process generates accounting entries for vouchers that recognize the liability to the vendor.

Vendor payment processing is one of the most important aspects of AP module. PeopleSoft offers various payment methods by which we can create payments for purchased goods or services. A batch process known as **Pay Cycle** automates the selection of eligible vouchers and creation of payments through check printing, EFT, ACH, drafts, and so on. It can also calculate any applicable discounts.

Payment Post process creates accounting entries for the payments. Once a voucher is paid, it is closed in the system and the vendor liability is nullified.

Withholding is a process by which appropriate taxes are calculated for vouchers and the tax amount is automatically deducted from the payment made to the vendor. Depending on the requirements, system can generate a withholding payment to the tax authority while creating vendor payment. On the other hand, if required, it can just record the liability for the tax authority and track the net withholding amount payable.

Understanding Accounts Payable concepts

When organizations need to purchase something, they typically create a **purchase order** (referred as PO) and send it to the vendor. For example, to purchase 10 file cabinets from Furniture Inc. at the price of $500 each, an organization can create a PO that specifies the required dimensions, delivery terms, payment terms, quantity, price , and so on. When it receives this shipment, a goods receipt is created to document how many of the ordered cabinets were actually received. These activities are performed in PeopleSoft Purchasing module.

Now by this time Furniture Inc. would have sent the invoice for this purchase. This invoice amount can include not only the purchase price for ten cabinets but probably other expenses such as shipping costs, insurance charges, taxes, and so on. The invoice also typically carries applicable payment terms (that specify by which date we need to pay). It also may include any discounts if the payment is made before a certain date. Most of the business transactions take place on credit basis. Therefore, when we receive the file cabinets, we still haven't paid Furniture Inc. In accounting terms, we have a **liability** to pay the seller (or to put it simply, we owe Furniture Inc.). When we receive the vendor invoice, a voucher (which records the invoice details) needs to be created in PeopleSoft.

When this voucher is posted, the system typically creates an accounting entry as follows:

DR	**Expense (Storage equipment)**	**$5000**
CR	**Accounts Payable**	**-$5000**

Before we issue a check to Furniture Inc., it is important to verify that we are paying for the right quantity. For example, we ordered 10 cabinets, but if the vendor sent an invoice for 11, we should not end up paying $5500. Thus we need to carefully cross check the invoice against the goods receipt and pay only $5000. Also, it is possible that one of the 10 cabinets was completely damaged in transit or the vendor shipped only 9 cabinets. In such cases, it is obvious that we should pay only $4500. This is where we need to perform matching of the voucher with the original purchase order and goods receipt before it is paid.

Let's assume that voucher passes the matching validations and can be paid. The pay cycle process can evaluate the payment due date and checks if we can get any early payment discount. When the payment is created (let's say by a check) and posted, the system creates the following accounting entry:

DR	**Accounts Payable**	$5000
CR	**Cash**	-$5000

Thus, now the liability is eliminated and the voucher is closed.

Note that this was a highly simplified example. In reality, the accounting entries may include discounts, taxes, and so on.

Understanding common configurations

We will discuss some of the important configurations in respective sections such as matching, payment processing, and so on. In this section, we'll take a look at some of the common configurations that are applicable for the entire module.

These configurations include the following:

- Configuring accounting templates
- Configuring voucher origins
- Configuring miscellaneous charges
- Configuring payment terms

Configuring accounting templates

In the given sample accounting entries, we saw that the system needs the chartfield values for cash, accounts payable, and expense accounts. While the expense account is provided by the purchase order or manually specified on the voucher, values for cash, and accounts payable are derived from accounting templates.

Follow this navigation to configure accounting templates:

Set Up Financials/Supply Chain | Common Definitions | Accounting Entry Templates | Templates

The following screenshot shows a part of the accounting template page:

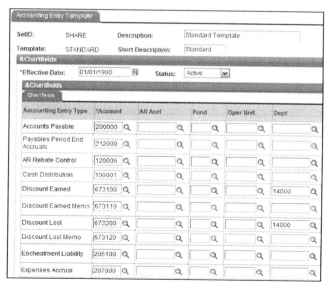

The system lists various accounting entry types for which we can specify the default chartfield values.

 Organizations typically use multiple accounts for **Accounts Payable**, **Discount** , and so on. To address this requirement, we can configure multiple accounting templates. As we'll see next, different templates can be specified for different voucher origins. If needed, we can also manually specify a template on the voucher as well.

We'll see how an accounting template is assigned to a voucher origin in the next topic.

Configuring voucher origins

Voucher origins identify the source of vouchers entering AP system. Vouchers can be entered online manually or may be loaded from various external sources. Various configuration options associated with origin help in specifying the ways in which vouchers should be processed. Each voucher must have an origin.

In Accounts Payable system, the hierarchy for defaulting the processing options is as follows:

- Business Unit (at the top)
- Voucher origin
- Control group
- Vendor
- Voucher (at the bottom)

Any processing option at any level automatically defaults to all the levels below (if no value is specified at the lower level). However a processing option value at a lower level overrides the default value from level above.

For example, let's assume that we specify USD as the default currency for the AP business unit. If no currency is specified at any other level, system automatically uses USD from the level above. However, if GBP is specified for a voucher origin, all vouchers with that origin will inherit GBP and not USD as their currency (assuming that no currency is specified for control group and vendor).

Follow this navigation to configure voucher origin:

Set Up Financials/Supply Chain | Product Related | Procurement Options | Vouchers | Voucher Origin

The following screenshot shows the **Accounting and Pay Options** tab of a sample voucher origin:

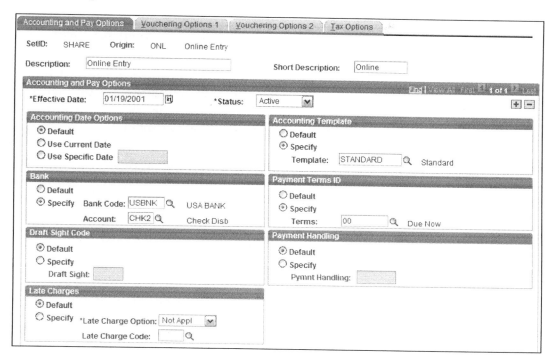

Voucher origins are important to establish different processing rules for different groups of vouchers. Even if all vouchers are processed similarly, we can still define different origins to logically segregate vouchers. For example, if we enter vouchers online, as well as receive through interface from two external systems, we can define three origins to identify where vouchers came from.

 It is mandatory that at least one voucher origin be configured.

- **Accounting Date Options**: This section specifies the accounting date for vouchers with this origin. Choose **Default** to use the option specified for AP business unit. Choose **Current Date** option so that system automatically uses the voucher entry date as accounting date.

- **Accounting Template**: Specify a template that we discussed earlier. Vouchers with this origin will use the default chartfield values defined in the specified template.

- **Bank**: This section specifies the organization's bank account that is used to issue payments for vouchers with this origin.

- **Late Charges**: This section is used to specify if late charges are calculated for vouchers paid after their due dates.

The following screenshot shows the **Vouchering Options 1** tab of voucher origin:

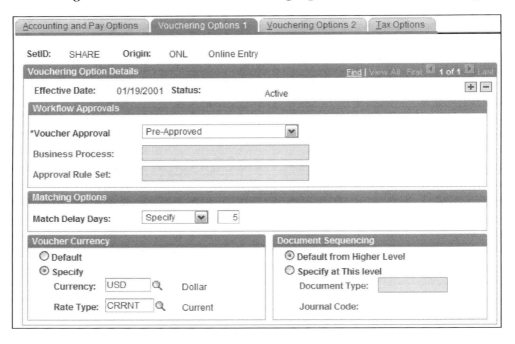

- **Voucher Approval**: This field specifies if vouchers need to be approved after they are entered. Available options are:

  ○ **Default from higher level**: This option instructs the system to use the approval option specified at the AP business unit.

  ○ **Pre-approved:** This option ensures that vouchers with this origin are approved as soon as they are created. There is no additional approval process needed.

  ○ **Approval framework**: System uses business rules configured using approval framework feature. These are pre-configured rules, which can be modified if required.

  ○ **Virtual Approver**: This approval mechanism requires configuring the approval rules using application designer by technical team members. Selecting this option enable Business Process and Approval Rule Set fields.

- **Match Delay Days**: This field specifies the number of days for which matching process is delayed for EDI and XML vouchers.

The following screenshot shows the **Vouchering Options 2** tab:

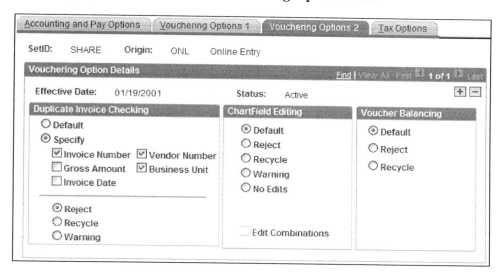

- **Duplicate Invoice Checking**: This section specifies the options for ensuring that duplicate vouchers are not entered. From the given set of five parameters, we can decide which parameters need to be considered. In the previous example, the system checks the combination of invoice number, vendor number and business unit to see if a voucher with this combination already exists. If such a combination is found, we can instruct the system to take appropriate action: **Reject** (which prevents the error voucher from being saved), **Recycle** (which allows the voucher to be saved but not processed any further) or **Warning** (which just shows a warning message but allows the voucher to be saved and processed).

- **Chartfield Editing**: This section is used to specify the action to be taken if a voucher has an invalid chartfield combination. Selecting the **No Edits** option prevents the system from performing chartfield combination validation.

- **Voucher Balancing**: This section specifies how the system should handle out of balance vouchers (where sum of line amounts does not match total voucher amount).

- **Tax Options**: This tab specifies the sales tax and VAT options for this origin.

Note that similar configuration options exist for all the levels of hierarchy.

Configuring miscellaneous charges

When we receive an invoice from the vendor, there may be various costs and charges that need to be recorded apart from the actual item cost (which is known as **merchandise amount**). The invoice may include freight expenses (shipping cost), insurance cost, various taxes , and so on. These are known as **miscellaneous charges**. If we wish to record all these elements separately, we need to configure miscellaneous charge codes.

Follow this navigation to setup miscellaneous charge codes:

Set Up Financials/Supply Chain | Product Related | Procurement Options | Charges/Costs | Misc Charge/Landed Cost Defn

The following screenshot shows a sample code defined for insurance costs:

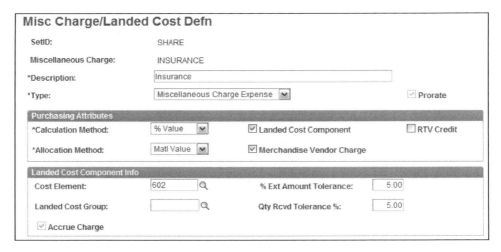

We can define as many miscellaneous charge codes as required depending on organization's requirements:

- **Type**: Each code needs to be given a category from the following available options: **Freight Expense, Miscellaneous Charge Expense, Sales Tax Expense, Use Tax Expense, and VAT Input Non-Recoverable**.

- **Prorate**: This checkbox if selected, results in miscellaneous charges to be prorated (proportionately divided) among all voucher lines. Otherwise, the charge amount is recorded separately on the voucher.

- **Calculation Method**: This field specifies how the miscellaneous charge needs to be calculated. For example, insurance cost can be a percentage of total invoice amount (as shown) whereas the freight cost can be calculated on the weight of the item.

- **Landed Cost Component**: PeopleSoft Cost Management module calculates the landed cost of purchased item. This checkbox (if selected) indicates that the miscellaneous charge needs to be included in the inventory cost. Selecting this option enables the **Landed Cost Component** Info section, where additional options for Cost Management module can be specified.

- **Merchandise Vendor Charge**: If selected, this field denotes that the vendor is charging this particular cost. If it is not checked, it means that another 3rd party vendor is charging for these services.

Configuring payment terms

Each credit sale transaction is accompanied by payment terms. The purchaser agrees to pay the seller after a certain number of days. In addition, some times the seller accepts to give a discount if the payment is made within a specific time limit.

Follow this navigation to set up payment terms:

Set Up Financials/Supply Chain | Product Related | Procurement Options | Payments | Payment Terms-Single Payment

The following screenshot shows a sample payment term, according to which, the payment needs to be made in 30 days (from the purchase) and a 2% discount is given if the payment is made within 10 days.

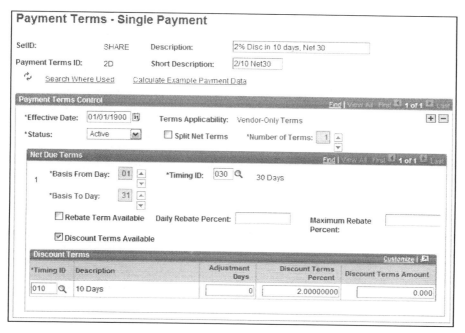

In industry terms, Net 30, Net 60 , and so on, means that last day for the payment is 30 days, 60 days , and so on respectively.

- **Net Due Terms**: This section specifies the last day of the payment. **Timing ID** field indicates the number of days available for an organization to make the payment.

- **Discount Terms Available**: Select this checkbox if vendor has agreed for any discount for the early payment. This enables the **Discount Terms** section.

- **Discount Terms - Timing ID**: Specify the number of days within which discount can be availed.

- **Discount Terms Percent / Discount Terms Amount**: Specify the discount as % of invoice amount or a flat amount in these fields.

Entering vouchers

PeopleSoft offers various methods of entering vouchers such as: manual entry, spreadsheet upload and through automated voucher interface. As we have seen in case of other modules, manual voucher entry is suitable for low volume scenarios, while using the automated interface is ideally suited for bringing in vouchers from external systems in large numbers. Let's familiarize ourselves quickly with these different methods.

Manual voucher entry

PeopleSoft offers the following types of vouchers:

- **Regular vouchers**: These are the most widely used standard vouchers.

- **Adjustment vouchers**: These are used to make debit or credit adjustments to an existing voucher.

- **Journal vouchers**: These vouchers are used to modify accounting entries of an already posted voucher.

- **Prepaid vouchers**: If we have made any advance payments to a vendor, these vouchers are used to record the same.

- **Register vouchers**: In certain situations (such as VAT applicable purchases), we may need to create and post vouchers without knowing the accounting details. Register vouchers are used to record such transactions against suspense (temporary) accounts. Once the chartfield details are known, register vouchers are unposted and correct details are recorded.

- **Reversal vouchers**: These are used to reverse accounting entries of an already posted voucher.

- **Single payment vouchers**: These vouchers are used to make a one-time payment to a vendor, without defining that vendor in the system.

- **Template vouchers**: In order to reduce data entry efforts, we can create templates to be used for entering regular vouchers.

- **Third party vouchers**: These are used to record non-merchandise costs such as shipping, insurance , and so on.

The fields on the voucher entry pages are different for these different voucher types. However, we will discuss only the regular voucher entry.

Follow this navigation to enter a voucher:

Accounts Payable | Vouchers | Add/Update | Regular Entry

The following screenshot shows a part of the **Invoice Information** tab of voucher entry page:

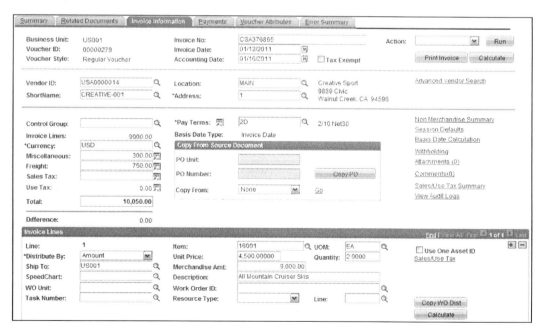

Invoice Information tab consists of three sections: **Voucher header**, **Voucher lines**, and **Distribution** (accounting) lines. A voucher can have multiple voucher lines, while each voucher line may have multiple distribution lines.

In the previous example, let's say that we purchased two mountain skis from a vendor. They were priced $4500 each, while the insurance and freight costs came to $300 and $750 respectively.

As you can see, we record the invoice number, vendor ID, payment terms, miscellaneous charges, and freight charges in the appropriate fields. We can click the currency selector icon next to the Miscellaneous, Freight, Sales Tax, Use Tax fields to enter the miscellaneous charge codes (that we configured earlier) and amounts.

Voucher line details can be entered by adding multiple lines in the **Invoice Lines** section. In our example, we have a single invoice line where we have recorded the item ID (product number in our database), unit price, quantity and total merchandise cost.

Copy From Source Document: In the previous example, we manually entered all the voucher details. We can also create it by copying the data on an existing voucher, a voucher template, purchase order or a goods receipt, so that all voucher details are automatically populated by the system. We can select the appropriate value from the **Copy From** dropdown menu and click **GO** hyperlink to select a source document.

The following screenshot shows the **Distribution Lines** section where we enter the accounting information for given invoice line.

 The account value in this section is used for the Expense line of the voucher's accounting entry.

The following screenshot shows the **Payment** tab of voucher.

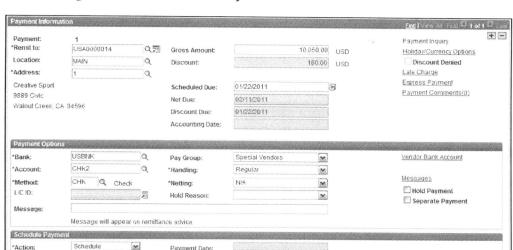

- **Scheduled Due**: This field shows the date when the voucher will be picked up for payment.

- **Net Due, Discount Due**: These fields show the date when the voucher is due for payment and the day before which discount can be availed. As can be seen, the last date for paying the given voucher is 11th February, although discount for this voucher is available if it is paid before 22nd January.

- **Payment Options**: This section contains fields such as the bank, bank account, payment method , and so on. If we select the **Hold Payment** checkbox, this voucher is not picked by the pay cycle process. This continues until the checkbox is unchecked.

> All these field values are automatically defaulted by the system based on the values specified at the business unit / voucher origin / vendor / control group. However they can be changed at the voucher level if necessary.

- **Schedule Payment**: This section controls the payment action for the voucher. When the **Action** dropdown menu contains the value **Schedule**, the pay cycle picks it up when it is due and automatically creates the payment. If we decide to manually write a check and issue it, select the value **Record** in this field. This enables other fields in this section where we can record the payment date and check number, and so on.

The following screenshot shows a part of the **Voucher Attributes** tab:

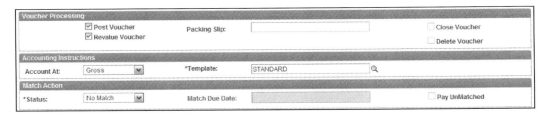

- **Post Voucher**: This flag controls whether the voucher can be posted or not. Deselect this checkbox to prevent the voucher from being posted.
- **Template**: This field shows the accounting template that will be used to derive appropriate chartfield values for this voucher's accounting entry.
- **Match Action – Status**: This field shows the matching status of the voucher. A value of **No Match** indicates that voucher is not to be matched.

Voucher creation through automated interface

As discussed earlier, AP vouchers can be created from various external sources. Other PeopleSoft modules (such as Order Management, Purchasing) as well as non-PeopleSoft systems can send the voucher data. PeopleSoft offers a group of staging tables (VCHR_HDR_STG, VCHR_LINE_STG, VCHR_DIST_STG, VCHR_PYMNT_STG, VCHR_MSCH_STG, VCHR_BANK_STG, VCHR_IBANK_STG, and VCHR_VNDR_STG) that can store the interface data. In addition, an interface program known as **Voucher Build** (AP_VCHRBLD) loads the data from these staging tables into AP to create vouchers.

> Voucher Build process can create vouchers from data stored in locations other than the voucher staging tables. For example, ERS vouchers are created from the goods receipt and purchase order data.

Follow this navigation to execute the Voucher Build process:

Accounts Payable | Batch Processes | Vouchers | Voucher Build

The following screenshot shows the run control page where we can specify the process options.

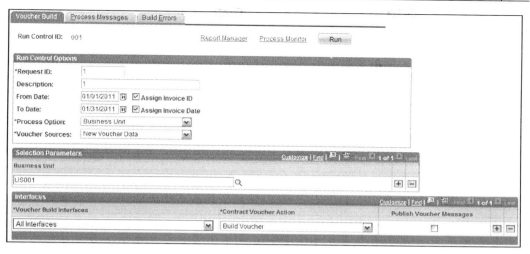

- **Assign Invoice ID**: When a source sends the voucher data, it may or may not send the invoice ID. If the invoice ID is not sent and we wish the system to automatically assign it to the newly created vouchers, select this checkbox.

- **Assign Invoice Date**: If the system source doesn't send the invoice date, select this checkbox, so that the process assigns current date as the invoice date.

- **Process Option**: This field offers the following options:
    - **Business Unit**: This option is used to process vouchers for a single business unit. Specify the value in Business Unit field.
    - **Process All Units**: This option processes vouchers for all business units.

- **Process Contract**: This option processes vouchers for a single contract ID. Selecting this value enables the Business Unit and Contract ID fields.

- **Process Group**: This option processes vouchers for a single control group ID. Selecting this value enables the Business Unit and Control Group ID fields.

- **Process Origin**: This option processes vouchers from a specific origin. Selecting this value enables the SetID and Origin fields.

- **Process Vendor**: This option processes vouchers for a specific vendor. Selecting this value enables the Business Unit and Vendor ID fields

- **Process Voucher**: This option processes a specific voucher.

- **Voucher Sources**: This field specifies the status of vouchers that need to be processed by Voucher Build. Available options are:

    ◦ **All (Unrestricted)**: The process selects new as well as recycled vouchers (these vouchers encountered errors and were flagged as 'Recycled').

    ◦ **Errors/Staged Vouchers**: This option selects those vouchers that encountered pre-edit errors in an earlier prior Voucher Build process run.

    ◦ **New Voucher Data**: The process selects only new transactions from a source.

    ◦ **Recycled Vouchers**: Only recycled vouchers in the online voucher tables.

    ◦ **Voucher Maintenance**: Vouchers that have been modified using the Voucher Maintenance feature.

    ◦ **Voucher Mass Maintenance:** Vouchers that have been modified using the Voucher Mass Maintenance feature (where changes are made to multiple vouchers in one go).

- **Voucher Build Interfaces**: This field is used to specify the source from which vouchers need to be created. Select a specific value or select **All Interfaces** so that the process selects transactions from all sources.

Understanding matching

As we discussed briefly previously, voucher matching is a critical feature for any Payables system. It serves as an important business process control for organizations to ensure that they pay only for those goods and services that they ordered and actually received. PeopleSoft offers the following matching methods:

- **Two-way matching**: Vouchers are compared against purchase orders (created in Purchasing module) to ensure that we pay for what we ordered.

- **Three-way matching**: Vouchers are compared against purchase orders and goods receipts (created in Purchasing module) to ensure that we pay for what we ordered and actually received. This is used when we order something and make it mandatory to create goods receipts.

- **Four-way matching**: This method is used where receiving as well inspecting the received goods is mandatory. Vouchers are compared against purchase orders, goods receipts and goods inspections (created in Purchasing module) to ensure that we pay only for what we ordered, actually received and passed our quality control.

- **Receipt-only matching**: This method is used when we receive goods without creating purchase orders. Vouchers are compared against non-PO goods receipts.

Each matching method is suitable for different scenarios and organizations choose the method that is best suited for their business conditions.

If a voucher fails the matching due to any inconsistency, it is flagged as an exception. We can either override the match exception or correct the inconsistency and rerun the matching process. If configured accordingly, a voucher with match exception cannot be paid.

Some of the important steps involved in the matching process are as follows:

- Configuring match rule types
- Configuring match rules
- Configuring match rule controls
- Running the matching process
- Clearing match exceptions on matching workbench

Configuring match rule types

PeopleSoft delivers a large number of match rules that can cover many diverse business requirements. These rules are categorized into the following types: System, Data entry, Merchandise – Quantity, Merchandise – Unit Price, Merchandise – Amount, and Summary/Global match only.

Follow this navigation to access match rule type page:

Set Up Financials/Supply Chain | Product Related | Procurement Options | Vouchers | Match Rule Type

The following screenshot shows Merchandise – Quantity **Match Rule Type**:

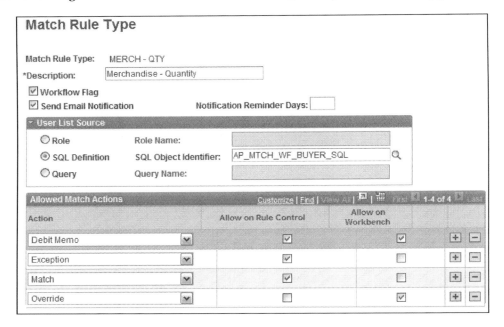

- **Workflow Flag**: Select this flag if the system needs to create automatic notifications to specified users if vouchers encounter match exceptions.

- **User List Source**: This section is available only if the workflow flag is selected. Here we specify which users should be notified in case of match exceptions. The user group can be specified as those with a specific role or through a SQL definition or a query.

- **Action**: This field determines which action should be taken by a match rule from this category. Available options are: **Match** (change the voucher line status to **Matched**), **Exception** (mark a voucher line as Exception), **Debit Memo** (create a debit memo for the difference amount where voucher amount doesn't match), **Override** (change the status of a voucher line to **Matched** without changing the underlying reason).

- **Allow on Rule Control**: This flag makes an action available on the match rule control.

- **Allow on Workbench**: This flag makes an action available on the matching workbench.

Each match rule needs to be assigned to a match rule type and inherits the options specified for its parent match rule type.

Configuring match rules

A match rule is essentially a condition against which the vouchers are tested. If the voucher fails that condition, it is marked as an exception.

Follow this navigation to access match rule page:

Set Up Financials/Supply Chain | Product Related | Procurement Options | Vouchers | Match Rules

The following screenshot shows a sample match rule RULE_R950:

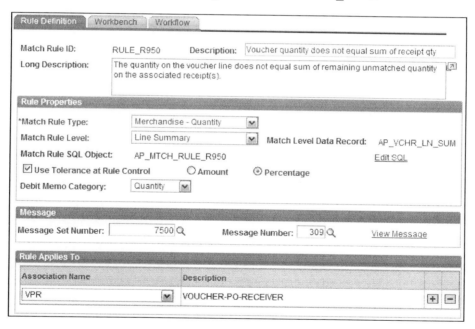

- **Match Rule Level**: Specify if the match rule should be applied at the line level of header level. Available options are: **Line Summary** and **Header Summary**.

- **Use Tolerance at Rule Control**: We can specify the tolerances for match rules. For example, we can specify that the system should accept any differences between voucher quantity and received quantity, as long as the difference is less than 5% of voucher quantity. Select this checkbox to allow such tolerances to be specified on match rule control (which we'll discuss in the next section).

Configuring match rule control

A match rule control is collection of match rules that need to be used during the matching process. An organization needs to use only some of the delivered match rules depending on its requirements. Also, if necessary, tolerances can be specified on the match control.

Follow this navigation to access match rule control page:

Set Up Financials/Supply Chain | Product Related | Procurement Options | Vouchers | Match Rule Control

The following screenshot shows a sample match rule control:

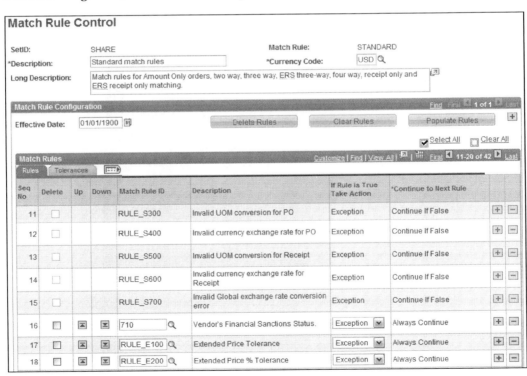

Note that this sample match rule control has a total of 42 match rules, of which the screenshot shows a few. When a new control is created, system automatically populates the system match rules at the beginning. These are denoted by the prefix 'S'. These cannot be deleted from the match rule control.

Add any additional rules by clicking the + button.

- **If Rule is True, Take Action**: This field specifies the action to be taken when a match condition comes true (for example, voucher quantity is not equal to receipt quantity). Available options are: **Match** (match the voucher line), **Exception** (mark the voucher line as Exception) and **Debit memo** (create a debit memo voucher).

- **Continue to Next Rule**: This field controls when the next match rule needs to be applied. Available options are **Always Continue**, **Continue if False** and **Continue if True**.

- **Tolerances**: This tab is used to specify any amount or % tolerances for match rules. As we saw earlier, this can be done only if tolerance option is enabled for the match rule definition.

Running the matching process

The matching process uses the match rules specified as part of match rule control and evaluates the vouchers against purchase orders / receipts / inspections.

Follow this navigation to execute the matching process:

Accounts Payable | Batch Processes | Vouchers | Matching

The following screenshot shows run control page for the matching process:

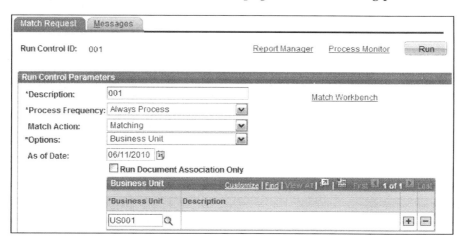

- **Process Frequency**: Select the value **Always Process**
- **Match Action**: Available options are **Matching** (matching process only), **Matching & Workflow/Email** and **Workflow/Email Notify**.
- **Options**: Select the appropriate option for the process from the following values: All Business Units, Business Unit, Control Group, Origin, and Voucher.

Click **Run** button to initiate the process.

Click **Match Workbench** hyperlink to access the page which shows the results of matching process. This is the place where we can perform various actions such as overriding the match exceptions.

Match workbench

Follow this navigation to access the matching workbench page:

Accounts Payable | Review Accounts Payable Info | Vouchers | Match Workbench

The following screenshot shows the options for searching vouchers:

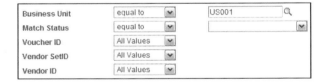

Match Status: This field shows various options for the matching status of vouchers that need to be retrieved. Available values are: Manually overridden, Match dispute, Match exceptions exist, Matched, Overridden – credit note, To be matched.

The actions we can perform on the retrieved vouchers depend on their status. The following table lists various actions that are possible from the matching workbench.

Action	Description
Matching	Runs the matching process on selected vouchers.
Undo matching	Changes the match status of a matched voucher to **To be matched**
Send notification	Sends a worklist or email notification for selected voucher with **Match dispute** or **Match exceptions exist** status
Match dispute	Puts the voucher on hold
Override	Changes the voucher status to **Manually Overridden**
Credit note	Changes the match status on the voucher to **Overridden - Credit Note**

Posting vouchers

Voucher posting process is used to create accounting entries for vouchers. We discussed the accounting entry templates in the common configurations section. The offset accounts that we specify on accounting entry templates are used by the voucher posting process to generate accounting entries.

Follow this navigation to access the voucher posting page:

Accounts Payable | Batch Processes | Vouchers | Voucher Posting

The following screenshot shows the run control page for the voucher posting process:

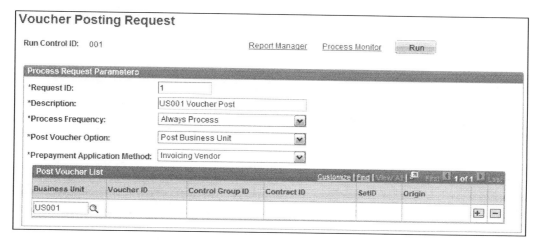

It is important that the **Post Voucher** flag on the Voucher – Attributes tab must be checked for the Voucher Post process to select a voucher and post it.

Post Voucher Option: This field determines how to specify the input parameters for selecting the vouchers to post. The input parameter fields displayed on this page depend on the selected option. Available values for this field are:

- **Post All Units**: The process posts all eligible vouchers from all the AP business units.
- **Post All Vchrs for Closed Pymt**: The process posts all eligible vouchers for closed payments from the specified business unit.
- **Post Business Unit**: The process posts all eligible vouchers from the specified AP business unit.
- **Post Contract**: The process posts all eligible vouchers associated with the specified contract.
- **Post Group**: The process posts all eligible vouchers from the specified AP business unit and control group. A control group is a mechanism to group vouchers. It is used to control data entry, validate control totals and approve vouchers.
- **Post Origin**: The process posts all eligible vouchers from the specified SetID and voucher origin.
- **Post Voucher**: The process posts the specified vouchers.

Maintaining vouchers

As part of regular business process, there are many situations where voucher processing flow needs to be stopped. It can be due to incorrect data entry, disputes with vendors, and so on. PeopleSoft AP module offers three different actions for maintaining vouchers: Deleting, Closing, and Unposting. We'll briefly discuss these actions.

Deleting vouchers

A voucher can be deleted only if all the following conditions are satisfied:

- It is not posted.
- It is not selected for payment.
- No part of the voucher has been paid.

When a voucher is deleted, it can't be accessed from any PeopleSoft page.

To understand the voucher deletion, consider a scenario: A voucher for a vendor is entered. Before it is posted, it is found out that item shipped by the vendor was defective and was returned with no return charges. As a result, we no longer need to pay the vendor and the voucher can be deleted.

Follow this navigation to delete a voucher:

Accounts Payable | Vouchers | Add/Update | Delete Voucher

Closing vouchers

A voucher can be closed only if all the following conditions are satisfied:

- It is posted.
- It is not selected for payment.
- It is not fully paid.

When a voucher is closed, the remaining liability amount is written off and the all voucher processing is considered complete. Closing a voucher automatically creates reverse accounting entries for the open liability amount (in other words, expense account is credited, while the liability account is debited). Once closed, no changes are allowed to the voucher.

Consider the earlier scenario once again where a purchased item was returned due to a defect. However, by the time we discover the product defect, the voucher is already posted. We have returned the item and decided not to pay the vendor. As the voucher is posted, it can't be deleted. However we can close it, so that there is no remaining vendor liability.

Follow this navigation to close a voucher:

Accounts Payable | Vouchers | Add/Update | Close Voucher

Unposting vouchers

Unposting a voucher simply reverses the accounting entries that are created during the voucher post process. Once unposted, we can change the chartfield information for the voucher.

Consider a scenario where we post a voucher and discover that a wrong value is used for the Department chartfield. Technically speaking, we can close the voucher, but then it'll need to be reentered with correct chartfield details. We can unpost the voucher instead, correct the Department value and post it again.

Follow this navigation to unpost a voucher:

Accounts Payable | Vouchers | Add/Update | UnPost Voucher

Processing payments

Creating payments for vendors and issuing them is one of the critical aspects of PeopleSoft AP module. PeopleSoft offers a wide range of payment methods that can be used to create payments: **ACH (Automated Clearing House)**, System Check, Wire Transfer, Electronic Funds Transfer, Drafts, Giro-EFT and Letter of Credit. A batch process known as Pay Cycle (AP_APY2015) is used to select the eligible vouchers and create payments for them.

We'll discuss the following important steps involved in payment processing using the Pay Cycle:

- Configuring pay cycle steps
- Configuring pay cycle step group
- Specifying payment selection criteria
- Executing pay cycle batch process

Configuring pay cycle steps

Pay cycle is a group of multiple steps, each responsible for a specific task. Each step is essentially a different program. For example, if we are processing check payments, it involves distinct steps such as Payment selection (where eligible vouchers with payment method of 'Check' are selected), Payment Creation (where actual payment records are created in the system), Printing checks (using pre-printed or blank check stock), Creating a positive payment file (to be sent to the bank as a confirmation for printed checks), and so on.

The steps involved in a pay cycle are different for different payment methods. To give another example, if we are processing EFT payments, it involves other steps such as EFT Format (which formats the electronic payment file in the appropriate format), Print EFT advices (which creates payment advices / records with details of EFT payments). PeopleSoft delivers a set of pay cycle steps (that is, programs) for handling all the required payment methods.

We may not need to use all the given pay cycle steps (if we don't use all the payment methods. On the other hand, depending on the organization's requirements, we may need to create our own customized steps.

Follow this navigation to access the pay cycle step page:

Accounts Payable | Payments | Pay Cycle Definition | Step

The following screenshot shows a step—**Payment Selection**:

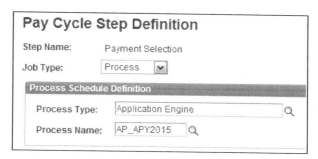

- **Job Type**: This field shows the nature of the process that is defined in this step. Available options are **Info** (which indicates that this step is not a process to be run on process scheduler) and **Process** (which means that this step is an independent background process that we can see on process scheduler for its completion).

- **Process Type**: This field shows the PeopleSoft technology (such as SQR, Application engine, and so on.) used to develop the process step.

- **Process Name**: This field shows the name of program used for the pay cycle step.

Configuring pay cycle step group

A step group is a collection of required pay cycle steps. As we saw earlier, each step has a unique objective. If an organization uses only **Check** as payment method, it is obvious that it doesn't need steps such as EFT Format.

A step group consists of relevant pay cycle steps along with their possible statuses and run levels. We can create as many step group as needed for different scenarios. The pay cycle process uses the specified step group and executes the steps in it.

Follow this navigation to configure a pay cycle step group:

Accounts Payable | Payments | Pay Cycle Definition | Step Table

The following screenshot shows a sample step group for check payments:

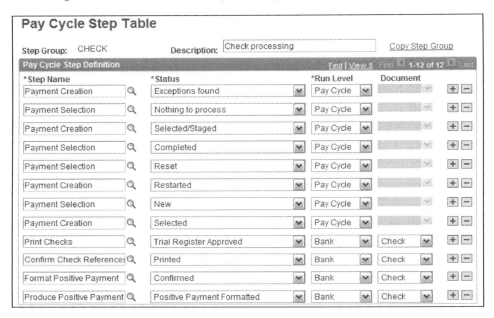

In the previous example, we have added the following required steps for check processing: **Payment selection, Payment creation, Print Checks, Confirm check references** (this step confirms the check numbers that will be used for the new checks), **Format positive payment** (this step formats the positive pay file to be sent to the bank as check confirmation) and **Produce positive payment file**.

- **Run Level Status**: This field indicates all the possible pay cycle statuses when a step can be started.

- **Run level**: This field specifies whether a step affects transactions for the entire pay cycle run or an individual bank. Available options are **Pay Cycle** and **Bank**.

- **Document**: This field is available only if the **Bank** option is selected in the field. In this example, as we are processing checks, we select **Check** as the Document value.

Specifying payment selection criteria

Now we have built the structure of the steps that need to be followed for cur pay cycle. In addition to this, we also need to specify the parameters used to select eligible vouchers for creating the payments.

Follow this navigation to specify the payment selection criteria:

Accounts Payable | Payments | Pay Cycle Processing | Payment Selection Criteria

The following screenshot shows the **Dates** tab of the page:

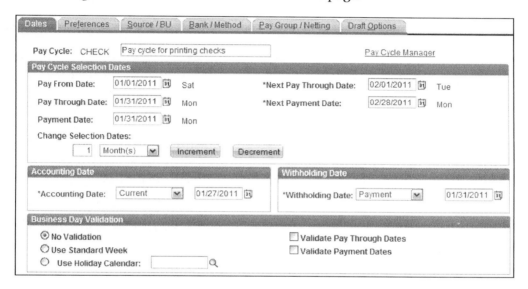

- **Pay From Date, Pay Through Date**: These fields specify the date range for vouchers to be selected. All eligible vouchers with scheduled pay date in this range are selected for payment.

- **Payment Date**: This is the date that is assigned to all the generated payments.

- **Change Selection Dates**: Select the appropriate option (Days/Weeks/ Months) and use the **Increment/Decrement** buttons to automatically change the date range. This is useful for reusing the pay cycle with only a change in date range.

The following screenshot shows the **Preferences** tab:

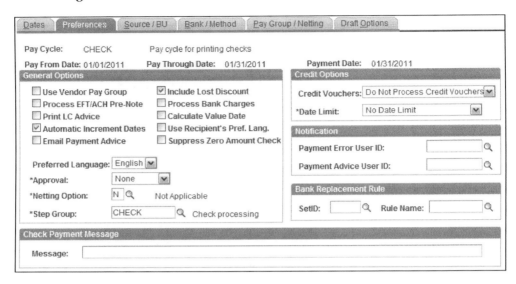

- **Approval**: This field specifies if the pay cycle run needs to be approved or not and if approval is required, by whom. Available options are **None** (no approval required), **User** and **Certifier**. If approval is required, the approver needs to access the pay cycle on the Pay Cycle Approval page.

- **Step Group**: Specify a step group to instruct the pay cycle which steps need to be executed. In this example, we are using the CHECK step group we configured earlier.

The following screenshot shows the **Source/BU** tab:

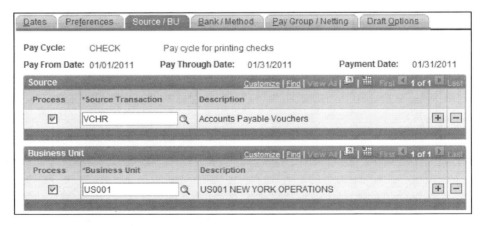

- **Source**: Specify the source for which the payments need to be created. Available values are EXAD (Employee cash advances created in Expense module), EXPN (Employee expense reports created in Expense module), TR (Treasury settlements from Treasury modules), TRET (Treasury EFT payments) and VCHR (AP vouchers).

- **Business Unit**: Specify vouchers from which business units need to be selected for paying.

The following screenshot shows the **Bank/Method** tab:

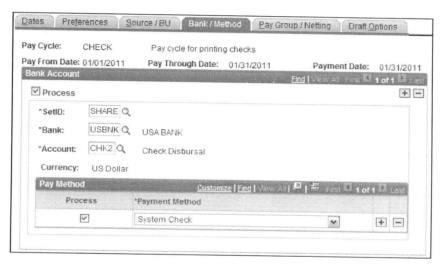

Specify the organization's bank account from which the payments should be created. This is the place where we also specify the payment method to be used for creating payments.

We'll not discuss the last two tabs as they are specific to draft payments and bilateral netting.

Thus, when the pay cycle is run, it selects only those vouchers that satisfy all the specified criteria.

Running pay cycle using pay cycle manager

Pay cycle manager is a utility that is used to process pay cycles as well as review any exceptions that occur during the execution of the process.

Follow this navigation to access Pay cycle manager:

Accounts Payable | Payments | Pay Cycle Processing | Pay Cycle Manager

The following screenshot shows the **Pay Cycle Manager** page:

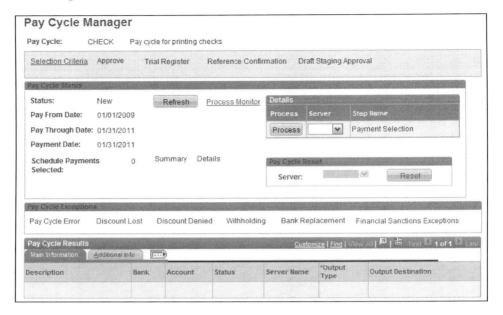

Details section: The following processes can be available in this section—Payment Selection, Payment Creation, Payment Selection &Creation, and Draft Staging (used only for draft payments).

 It is not necessary that all the given processes are available when the pay cycle is run. A process will be visible only if it is included in the step group.

Once a pay cycle is selected on the pay cycle manager, it can be started by clicking the **Process** button for **Payment Selection** or **Payment Selection & Creation**. We can run the selection and creation processes one after the other or together.

 Status of a pay cycle when it is started changes as follows: **New | Selected (Selection phase is successfully complete) | Created (Creation phase is successfully complete) | Approved (Approval is complete)**. If pay cycle approval is not required, the status changes as **New | Selected | Approved**.

The section at the top of the page shows various hyperlinks. These become active as the pay cycle goes through various steps.

Selection Criteria	Click to access the payment selection criteria page
Approve	Click to access the pay cycle approval page
Trial Register	Click to access the Trial register report run control page
Reference Confirmation	Click to access the page where we can confirm that reference information (check numbers) for pre-printed checks match with those of system created payments.
Draft Staging Approval	Used only for draft payments to accept or reject a staged draft.

After the payment selection and payment creation steps are completed, subsequent steps (such as Print Checks, Format Positive Payment File, and so on.) are listed in the **Pay Cycle Results** section. Each of these steps has a **Process** button next to it, to initiate it. When all the steps are executed successfully, pay cycle status changes to **Complete**.

Pay cycle exceptions section

This section contains hyperlinks for various exceptions after the selection and creation processes are complete.

Pay Cycle Error	Click to access the Pay cycle Errors page to review errors
Discount Lost	Click to access the Lost Discount Alert page. This page shows the vouchers that were not selected and (even though their due dates are not reached) early payment discounts for them can be lost.
Discount Denied	Click to access the Discounts Denied page. This page shows the vouchers that were not selected in the pay cycle run as it was determined by the system that it is better to let go the early payment discount and wait till the voucher due date.
Withholding	Click to access the Withholding Exception page
Bank Replacement	Click to access the Bank Replacement Exceptions page
Financial Sanctions Exceptions	Click to access the Pay Cycle Financial Sanction Warnings page. This page is used to create alerts for payments to vendors who may be on the financial sanctions list.

Resetting the pay cycle

Sometimes after the payments are selected (or created), we may find that the entire pay cycle run needs to be canceled. This can be done using the Pay Cycle Reset section. The steps involved in reset process are shown in the following table:

Reset performed after this stage	Steps
Payment Selection	Select the server name
	Click Reset button
Payment Creation	Open the pay cycle approval page
	Reject the pay cycle
	Open the pay cycle manager page
	Select the server name
	Click Reset button

To sum up, the following steps are typically executed while running the pay cycle:

- Run the Payment Selection step.
- Check the selected vouchers using the Summary or Detailed hyperlinks.
- Run the Payment Creation step.
- Run the Trial Register report to see the payments that are created in the system.
- Approve the pay cycle.
- Run subsequent steps in the Pay Cycle Results section.

Note that this sequence is a generic one and may be different from the way your organization processes pay cycles.

Posting payments

Payment posting process creates accounting entries for the payments (by debiting the liability account on the voucher and crediting the cash/bank account specified for the bank account). Of course this is the simplest form payment accounting entry, as it may involve additional lines for withholding, discounts, and so on.

Follow this navigation to access the payment posting page:

Accounts Payable | Batch Processes | Payment | Payment Posting

The following screenshot shows the run control page for the payment posting process:

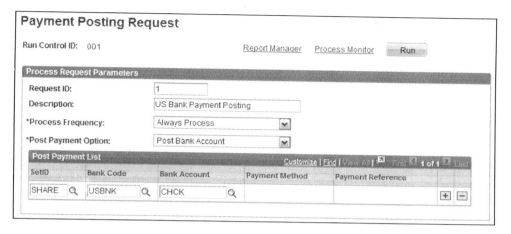

Post Payment Options: This field controls which payments are selected for the posting. Selected option determines which of the fields become available for data entry in the **Post Payment List** section. Available options are as follows:

- **Post All Banks:** This option selects payments issued from all bank accounts
- **Post Bank Account:** Use this option to post payments from a single bank account.
- **Post Payment:** This option is used to post an individual payment (or multiple payments if we know the payment reference numbers).
- **Post Payment Method:** Use this option to post payments with a specific method (such as Checks).

Cancelling payments

After payments are created, sometimes they need to be canceled due to various reasons. Let's understand how we can do that.

Follow this navigation to access payment cancelation page:

Accounts Payable | Payments | Cancel/Void Payments | Payment Cancelation

The following screenshot shows the **Cancel Payment** page:

The upper half of the page shows details of the payment that we wish to cancel. The lower half shows various options available for canceling the payment.

Payment Status: This field controls the how the payment needs to be canceled. The options and their description are given in the following table:

Payment Status	Description
Void	Void a payment if it is created but not yet released. For example, when checks are printed and it is found that one of them is incorrect, it can be voided.
Stop	Stop a payment when it is released. For example, after we print the check and mail to the vendor, we discover that it was sent to the wrong address. In such a case, stop the payment.
Undo Cancel	Use this option to reverse any cancelation that you already may have done for a payment. For example, we cancel a payment (by voiding or stopping) and then realize that it should not have been done. We can undo a cancelation only if the canceled payment was not posted.

Cancel Action: This field determines the corrective action after the current payment is canceled. The following table explains the options and their objectives:

Cancel Action	Description
Re-Open Voucher(s)/Re-Issue	This option makes the voucher (associated with the canceled payment) available for paying when the pay cycle runs next time. Thus, the payment can be reissued.
	Use this option when there is some problem (such as some of the checks were damaged during printing process) and the payment needs to be reissued.
Re-Open Voucher(s)/Put on Hold	This option puts the payment for associated voucher on hold by automatically selecting the Hold Payment flag on the voucher's Payment tab. The payment is not processed until this flag is not checked. In this case, the Hold Reason needs to be selected.
	Use this option where we cancel a payment and need a manual review (such as incorrect amount on the voucher) of the voucher before it is reissued.
Do Not Reissue/Close Liability	This option ensures that the canceled payment is no longer reissued. Any liability for the voucher is closed.

Escheating payments

Sometimes, the payments created by the pay cycle are not claimed by their intended vendors. For example, we create a payment but the vendor goes out of business and there is no one to claim the payment. Another commonly encountered situation is when mailed checks are returned due to incorrect addresses. In some countries, these payments need to be handed over to the government authorities. This process is known as escheating the payments.

Follow this navigation to access payment escheatment page:

Accounts Payable | Payments | Cancel/Void Payments | Escheat Payment

The following screenshot shows the Payment Escheatment page:

Payment Status: This field controls the escheatment action. The options and their description are given in the following table:

Payment Status	Description
Escheated	Use this option to mark the payment as escheated. This automatically selects the Cancel Action field value as **Escheated.**
Stale Dated Payment	Use this option to mark the payment as stale dated instead of escheated
Undo Escheatment	Use this option to cancel the escheatment that we may already have done for a payment. This removes the Escheated status of the payment.

Withholding

In many countries, organizations withhold (deduct) a percentage of the payment (as a tax to the government) while issuing payments to their vendors. For example, our organization purchases goods worth $10,000 from Computers Inc. Assume that this purchase attracts 30% tax for the vendor. In this case, Computers Inc. (seller) is liable to pay $300 on the sale of $1000. However, this tax amount is deducted by the buyer while issuing the payment itself and directly paid to the government. In other words, the purchasing organization will create a payment for only $700 for Computers Inc. Remaining amount of $300 is directly paid to the government.

PeopleSoft AP withholding feature can be used to address withholding requirements of various countries. Although it is not possible to discuss the entire process and related configurations, we'll take a quick glance at some of the important configurations.

Withholding configurations

Important withholding configurations are withholding rules (which specify the % of voucher amount that needs to be deducted), types and classes (country specific withholding needs), jurisdictions, and entities (organizations that govern taxation for a country, such as Internal Revenue Service for the USA). Withholding entity is a critical configuration, as this is where we specify the withholding remit vendor (to whom we need to pay the deducted tax amounts), applicable withholding classes and other controlling information.

Any vendor, for whom the tax amount needs to be withheld, needs to be designated as a withholding applicable vendor. This is done by selecting the Withholding checkbox for that vendor.

We also need to define the layout and contents for the withholding reports.

All the given configurations result in the withholding control details being populated on the voucher for a withholding vendor. If required, these details can be overridden and modified.

Processing withholding

Processing vendor withholding consists of the following important steps:

- **Ente ring withholding vouchers**: When a voucher is created for a vendor that is setup as a withholding vendor, is automatically considered eligible for withholding processing. However, a user can mark some or all voucher lines as not withholding applicable.

- **Calculation of withholding amounts**: Actual withholding tax amounts are calculated during voucher posting or payment posting process, depending on the setup.

- **Paying withholding vouchers**: There are two ways in which withholding payment can be created depending on the system setup. One possible way is creation of two separate payments (one for the vendor and the other for the withholding amount). The other way is creating only the vendor payment and recording a liability for the future withholding payment.

- **Posting withholding transactions**: PeopleSoft offers a batch process (AP_WTHD) to post the withholding transactions. This process loads the voucher and payment details into the withholding transaction tables. Subsequent withholding reports are created from these tables. Note that payment posting process must be run before this process.

- **Performing withholding adjustments**: After the withholding transactions are posted and reviewed, sometimes they may need to be adjusted. This can be done either manually or using a batch process (AP_WTHD_UPDT).

- **Generating withholding reports:** At the end of the accounting year, statutory withholding reports need to be sent to the relevant tax authorities. PeopleSoft can create withholding reports in various formats or a data file that can be electronically transmitted.

Summary

Accounts Payable module is an important part of the procure-to-pay process and is responsible for recording, tracking and processing of vouchers (vendor invoices). It also performs the critical task of creating vendor payments.

Vouchers can be manually entered or brought through an interface using the Voucher Build process. Vouchers maintenance process includes voucher deletion, voucher closing, and voucher unposting. Voucher Matching is an important process that validates the vouchers before they are paid. PeopleSoft offers four different methods of matching, where vouchers can be validated against purchase orders, goods receipts, or inspections. We need to configure match rule control that determines which match rules need to be used for the matching process.

Pay Cycle process is used to create vendor payments. PeopleSoft supports a large number of payment methods. A step group contains the payment steps required to process and create payments for a specific payment method. Pay cycle process is driven by the step group and executes the steps in it. Pay cycle manager is used to process a pay cycle.

Voucher posting creates accounting entries for vouchers, while Payment posting process creates accounting entries for the payments.

Withholding processing enables an organization to automatically deduct the applicable tax amount for vendor vouchers. We can address the withholding requirements of various countries in PeopleSoft Payables module.

7

PeopleSoft General Ledger Module

So far we have discussed the sub-modules in the PeopleSoft financial applications. As we previously saw, all these modules create accounting entries and send them to General Ledger. It would not be an exaggeration to say that General Ledger is the heart of the PeopleSoft financial applications. This module performs the critical function of consolidating the accounting information from various sources (PeopleSoft modules as well as non-PeopleSoft systems) and performing management reporting. We can generate important financial statements such as the Income Statement, Balance Sheet, and Cash Flow Statement from the data consolidated by the module. We discussed most of the important building blocks of General Ledger (such as chartfields, journals, and ledgers) in *Chapter 1, PeopleSoft Financials Fundamentals*.

In this chapter, we will discuss the following topics in greater detail:

- Understanding journal entry methods (such as manual journal entry, using the Journal Generator process, and flat file journal import)
- Journal processing (the Journal Edit process, and the Journal Post process)
- Understanding interim and year-end closing
- Understanding allocations

Understanding journal processing

Journal is a mechanism to record accounting entries in a summarized form. There are multiple ways in which journals are created in the General Ledger. In *Chapter 1, PeopleSoft Financials Fundamentals*, we saw how we can configure accounting entry definitions, accounting entry templates, and journal sources. Now we'll explore other aspects such as journal creation, editing, and posting.

Journal creation

There are four ways in which journals can be created:

1. Manually from journal entry pages
2. Using the Journal Generator process to create journals from other PeopleSoft modules as well as non-PeopleSoft systems
3. Spreadsheet journal upload
4. Flat file import

Let's discuss these methods in detail.

Using the Journal Generator process

Journal Generator is used to create journals from PeopleSoft sub-modules as well as accounting entries generated and sent by external non-PeopleSoft systems. As we have previously discussed, each sub-module such as Billing, Accounts Receivable, and so on, creates accounting entries for its transactions. Journal Generator uses various configurations to create journals from the accounting entries.

Follow this navigation to execute Journal Generator:

General Ledger | Journals | Subsystem Journals | Generate Journals

The following screenshot shows the run control page for the process:

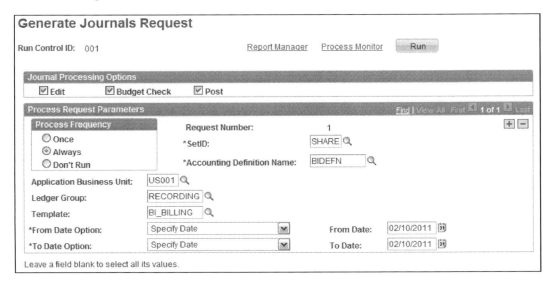

In order to generate journals for a PeopleSoft module, the following important inputs are needed:

Input	How it helps in creating journals
Ledger group	A ledger group specifies the various ledgers that are included in it. This specifies the ledger where these journals are ultimately recorded. Recall that a ledger group is linked with a Ledger Template, which specifies the database tables to store the journal and ledger data. Thus this field drives the destination for journals that will be created. In the previous example, we have specified that new journals should be posted to the ledgers in the RECORDING ledger group.
Accounting definition	An accounting definition specifies the source from which journals need to be created. You may recall that an accounting entry definition specifies the table that holds accounting entries for a module. It also drives how journal summarization needs to happen. In the example shown, we have specified that journals should be created for the Billing module and it should select the accounting entries from the BI_ACCT_ENTRY table as configured for the BIDEFN accounting definition.
Template	A journal generator template specifies the type of transactions in a module, for which journals should be created. It also determines any prefix to be used for newly created journal IDs. In our example, we are creating journals for billing invoice transactions. These journals will have IDs such as BIXXXXXX, as BI_BILLING template specifies that BI prefix be used for these journals.

- **Application Business Unit**: Depending on the accounting entry definition that we enter, this field shows the list of business units for that module. For example, if the value **BIDEFN** is used, this field prompt makes all Billing business units available for selection. Select a BU to create journals.

- **Journal Processing Options**: This section gives options to run additional processes apart from the Journal Generator. Selecting **Edit** automatically triggers the Journal Edit process which validates the new journals. Selecting **Budget Check** automatically triggers the Commitment Control Budget Processor which checks if sufficient budget is available for the new journals. Selecting **Post** automatically triggers the Journal Post process which posts the new journals to the ledger.

Assuming that all process options are selected, the processes are executed in this sequence: **Journal Generator | Journal Edit | Budget Processor (optional, used only with commitment control) | Journal Post**. Before running any process, all the previous processes must be executed.

The SetID, Accounting definition, and date parameters are mandatory. A value can be specified in the remaining fields, or they can be left blank.

Note that we can enter multiple sets of input parameters by using the + button to add more sections.

Click the **Run** button to initiate the Journal Generator process.

Manual journal entry

While most of the journals are created from other modules through Journal Generator, a significant number of situations need manual journal entry. A journal, like many other transactions such as a Billing invoice or AP voucher, consists of a header and one or more journal lines. Let's quickly see how it is done.

Follow this navigation to create a new journal:

General Ledger | Journals | Journal Entry | Create/Update Journal Entries

The following screenshot shows the **Header** section of a journal:

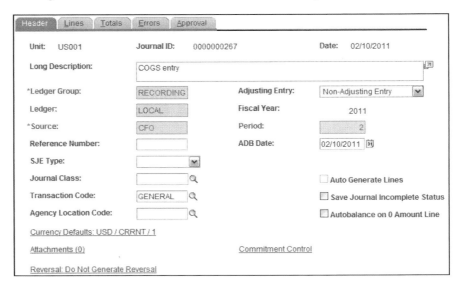

- **Ledger Group**: Select a ledger group where this journal needs to be posted.

- **Ledger**: Specify a ledger value within the ledger group where the journal needs to be posted. Note that a ledger group may contain multiple ledgers. We can post this journal to all those ledgers by leaving this field blank or only post it to a specific ledger by specifying it in this field.

- **Auto Generate Lines**: This checkbox is important if we need to post a journal to multiple ledgers simultaneously in a ledger group. You may recall that the **Keep Ledgers in Sync** option for a ledger group ensures that entries need to be posted to multiple ledgers. If this option was selected for the ledger group (specified on this page), then the **Auto Generate Lines** checkbox also needs to be selected. If the journal needs to be posted to a single ledger, this checkbox can be left unchecked.

- **Adjusting Entry**: Usually at the end of a period or a financial year, manual adjusting entries are passed to close the balances of revenue and expense accounts. This field identifies if the journal entry is adjusting or not. Select from the available options of **Adjusting Entry** or **Non-Adjusting Entry**.

Once the journal header details are entered, enter the journal line details on the **Lines** tab.

The following screenshot shows the **Lines** section of the journal:

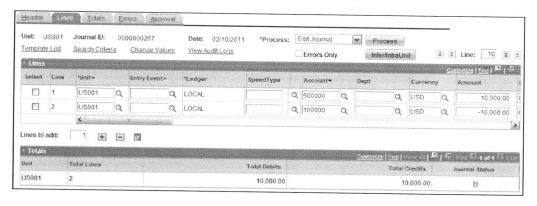

As you can see, this journal has two lines: a debit line for $10,000 to account 500000 and a credit line for the equal amount to account 100000. Once we scroll to the right, additional chartfields are visible. We record the amounts and chartfield details for the journal in this tab.

The **Totals** section at the bottom of the page shows a summary of journal lines for each business unit.

A journal may contain lines for multiple GL business units.

A hyperlink in the **Journal Status** column shows if the journal has any errors. A value of 'N' indicates that there are no errors. Clicking the status value opens the **Errors** tab, which shows errors in the journal header as well as lines.

- **Process:** We already briefly discussed some of the journal batch processes. We can initiate these processes from the journal entry page itself to process the current journal immediately. Select a value from the dropdown menu and click the **Process** button to perform an action. The available options are as follows:
    - **Budget Check Journal**: Runs the Commitment Control Budget Processor.
    - **Copy Journal**: This option opens the Journal copy page used to create a copy of the journal.
    - **Delete Journal**: The current journal is deleted.
    - **Edit Journal**: The Journal Edit process is triggered.
    - **Edit Chartfield**: This option initiates the Chartfield Edit process, which validates if chartfield values are correct. It also validates if the correct chartfield combinations are entered on the journal.
    - **Post Journal**: The Journal Post process is initiated.
    - **Print Journal (Crystal), Print Journal (XMLP)**: This option initiates the print process for the current journal using Crystal report or XML Publisher, which are different reporting technologies used by PeopleSoft.
    - **Refresh Journal**: All journal details are reloaded and refreshed.
    - **Submit Journal**: The journal is submitted for approval through the workflow.

- **Totals**: This tab is used to enter any control totals for debit and credit sides. This is useful to track any discrepancy between the sum of all entered line amounts and control amounts.

- **Approvals:** This tab is used if journal approval workflow is used. This tab shows the current approval status of the journal. An approver can select the appropriate approval action and submit the journal. Available approval options are **Approve, Deny,** and **Recycle** (send back to the previous user without approving or denying).

Understanding intraunit and interunit journals

Let's consider two different scenarios to understand the concept of interunit and intraunit transactions. We'll then discuss the creation of interunit and intraunit journals.

Scenario 1

Assume that an organization has two business units (US001 and UK001) for its U.S. and UK operations respectively. Now the US001 unit needs to purchase a critical part of machinery from a UK-based vendor. Let's say that, due to certain business reasons, the UK unit purchases this part and makes a payment on behalf the U.S. business unit. Of course, the U.S. unit will need to reimburse the UK unit for the purchase at a later point in time.

Thus, when UK001 receives the purchased item, it creates a liability to pay the vendor. At the same time, it creates another accounting entry to record a receivable amount from the US001 unit. Such a transaction involving two or more different business units is known as **Interunit transaction**.

Scenario 2

Assume that the U.S. operations of this organization (business unit US001) has two departments (MFG and SALES) representing Manufacturing and Sales respectively. Now a purchase of an item is made by the Sales department on behalf of the Manufacturing department. As each of these departments may have their own departmental spending budgets, they'd need to track such transactions for settling (reimbursing) later.

Similar to the previous scenario, the Sales department will create a receivable entry to record the amount due from the Manufacturing business unit. Such transactions between two different entities (represented by chartfields such as FUND / DEPARTMENT) from the same business unit are known as **Intraunit transactions**.

PeopleSoft automatically creates the balancing Receivable / Payable entries between the involved entities.

PeopleSoft sub-modules such as Purchasing, Accounts Payable, and so on automatically create interunit and intraunit accounting entries. We can also manually create interunit and intraunit journals in General Ledger.

Creating an interunit journal entry is quite straight-forward. Recall that the business unit value on the **Journal-Header** tab (called the **Anchor Business Unit**) is the same (US001) as that on the **Journal-Lines** tab in our given sample example. If we enter a BU value on the journal lines that is different from the anchor business unit, PeopleSoft recognizes that journal as an interunit journal. The Journal Edit process then creates the balancing journal lines.

In order to create intraunit journals, we first need to identify the chartfield that needs to be used as the balancing chartfield. Recall our discussion of the **Ledger Group – Balancing** tab from *Chapter 1, PeopleSoft Financials Fundamentals* where we do that. If we anticipate departments in an organization to create intraunit transactions, the **Department** chartfield will be designated as the balancing chartfield. Similar to creating interunit journals, if we enter multiple values for the balancing chartfield, the journal is recognized as the intraunit journal.

Understanding flat file journal entry

You may encounter many scenarios where PeopleSoft General Ledger needs to import journals created in external non-PeopleSoft systems. Note that this option is different from using Journal Generator for non-PeopleSoft systems.

 Journal Generator can be used to create journals only when external non-PeopleSoft systems send accounting entries to the interface table JGEN_ACCT_ENTRY. The flat file import feature is used when the non-PeopleSoft systems send the actual journal header and lines data.

PeopleSoft delivers a pre-defined layout for the journal data in a flat file format. There are five possible types of records in the data file depending on the first character in a data row. The following table lists those types:

Record type	Description
# (Comments)	This record type is used to record any comments. It should not be used to record any accounting data.
H (Journal header)	This record type includes all the header details (such as Business Unit, Journal ID, Journal date, and so on) similar to what we have seen on the Header tab of the manual journal entry page.
L (Journal line)	This record type includes all the journal line details (such as line number., chartfields, amounts, and so on) similar to the Line tab of the manual journal entry page.

Record type	Description
V (VAT line)	Includes the VAT details for the journal such as physical nature, VAT amount and so on.
C (Control totals)	Contains control details such as the number. of journal lines, debit, and credit control totals for each combination of Business Unit and applicable chartfields.

Note that the journal data files need not contain all the record types. However, it must have the Journal Header, Journal Line, and Control Totals records at minimum.

Once the data file containing journal header and line details is ready, a batch process named **Load Journals From a Flat File (GL_JRNL_IMP)** needs to be executed. This process reads the data from data file, loads them into PeopleSoft, and creates journals.

Follow this navigation to run the process:

General Ledger | Journals | Import Journals | External Flat Files

The following screenshot shows the run control page for the flat file journal import process:

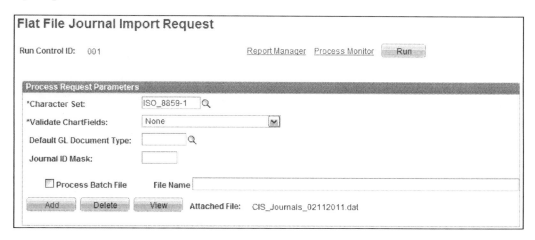

- **Validate Chartfields:** This field specifies the type of chartfield validation that the system performs on the journal data in the file. The available options are **Account & Alternate Account** (only these two chartfields are validated), **All Common Chartfields** (the system validates all chartfields except Project Costing related chartfields), and **None** (no chartfields are validated).

- **Journal ID mask:** This field is used to specify the prefix for the journals that are created from the flat file. This is used to identify journals from this source. Note that this prefix is needed only if the flat file does not contain the journal ID in the header record.

- **Add:** Use this button to upload a data file. The attached file name is shown on the page.

Click the **Run** button to initiate the process.

 It is important to run the Journal Edit process to validate the journals after they are created from flat file. This needs to be done before accessing these journals from the online journal pages.

Using the journal edit process

Once journals are created in General Ledger, they must be validated using the Journal Edit (GL_JEDIT) process. This process performs various validating actions to ensure that all chartfield values and their combinations are valid and that the journal debit and credit amounts are in balance. As we saw in the manual journal entry section, we can initiate the Journal Edit process from the journal entry page itself. However, this mode of running the process edits only a single journal. PeopleSoft offers another way of running the process in batch mode to process multiple journals.

Follow this navigation to initiate the Journal Edit process in batch mode:

General Ledger | Journals | Process Journals | Edit Journals

The following screenshot shows the run control page for the process:

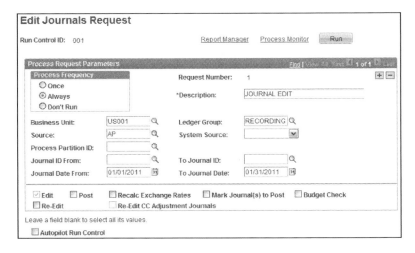

As you can see, we can use various input parameters to select journals to be edited. As the note on the page says, leaving a field blank results in the process selecting all the values for that field.

Various checkboxes at the bottom of the page are used to instruct the system to process additional steps such as Journal Post, Budget Check, and so on.

Note that **Edit** checkbox is always checked on the Journal Edit run control page.

Mark Journal(s) to Post: A journal must be marked for posting so that it can be picked up by the subsequent Journal Post process. If this checkbox is selected, the Journal Edit process marks the valid journals for posting. If this is not done, the journals need to be manually marked for posting using a page.

Click **Run** to initiate the process.

Using the journal post process

The final step in the journal processing is that of posting them to General Ledger. When we post a journal using the Journal Post (GLPPOST) process, its amounts update the final balances for appropriate chartfield combinations in the LEDGER table. A journal must be validated by the Journal Edit process and not have any errors to be posted.

Follow this navigation to initiate the Journal Post process in batch mode:

General Ledger | Journals | Process Journals | Post Journals

The following screenshot shows the run control page for the process:

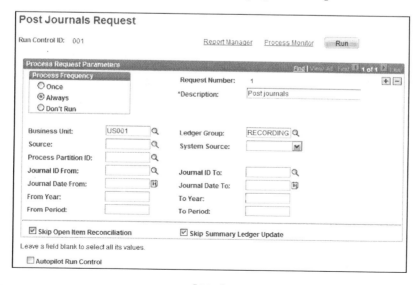

Again, as you can see, the page shows various fields to be used as the input parameters for deciding which journals to select for posting.

Click **Run** to initiate the process.

Understanding interim and year-end closing

Closing is an important process in the accounting calendar of an organization. Before discussing how PeopleSoft handles this function, we'll spend some time in understanding this important accounting concept.

All accounts are categorized based on the financial statement they appear on. Thus all Revenue and Expense accounts are called **Profit and Loss Accounts,** as they appear on the Profit and Loss statement, while Asset, Liability, and Equity accounts are known as **Balance Sheet Accounts**.

While the profit and loss statement, also known as the Income Statement, shows an organization's revenue and expense status at a particular moment in time, the balance sheet shows the accumulated balance of its assets, liabilities, and owners' equity. At the end of the financial year, all profit and loss accounts need to be closed and their balances transferred to the balance sheet in the form of net profit or loss. This net balance is transferred to a special purpose account known as **Retained Earnings**. This process is known as **Closing**.

Although closing needs to be performed at the end of each financial year, many organizations also do it at the end of every accounting period as well. This is known as **Interim Closing**.

Let's consider an example to help us understand this process further:

Assume that an organization uses two revenue accounts and two expense accounts for its operations. Let's say that it follows a financial calendar from January 1 through December 31, with 12 accounting periods (corresponding to each month). The accounts details are as follows:

Account ID	Type	Description
100000	Revenue	Software revenue
150000	Revenue	Hardware revenue
200000	Expense	Manufacturing expenses
250000	Expense	Advertising expenses
900000	Equity	Retained earnings

Of course, this is a highly simplified example, as a typical organization uses hundreds of different accounts. Now assume that these accounts have the following balances on the last day of the financial year:

Account ID	Debit Balance	Credit balance
100000		- 20,000
150000		- 30,000
200000	25,000	
250000	15,000	

> Revenue accounts always have a credit balance, while the Expense accounts always have a debit balance. Asset accounts also always have a debit balance, while Liability and Equity accounts always have credit balance.

Now the profit and loss accounts are closed by passing an accounting entry and transferring the balance to the retained earnings account (900000) as follows:

Debit/Credit	Account	Description	Amount
Accounting Entry 1			
DR	100000	Software revenue	20,000
CR	900000	Retained earnings	-20,000
Accounting Entry 2			
DR	150000	Hardware revenue	30,000
CR	900000	Retained earnings	-30,000
Accounting Entry 3			
DR	900000	Retained earnings	25,000
CR	200000	Manufacturing expenses	-25,000
Accounting Entry 4			
DR	900000	Retained earnings	15,000
CR	250000	Advertising expenses	-15,000

As a result of these accounting entries, the balances of all the revenue and expense accounts become zero, while the balance of the retained earnings account is as shown next:

Retained Earnings Account (900000)	
Debit	**Credit**
	-$20,000
	-$30,000
$25,000	
$15,000	
Total debit: $40,000	Total credit: $50,000
Net balance: $10,000 credit (profit)	

Unlike the revenue and expense accounts, which are closed every year, balance sheet accounts carry over their balance from one year to the next. They are never closed. Thus, the retained earnings account, belonging to the Equity category, carries over its balance. When an organization makes a profit, a credit balance is transferred to the retained earnings. If it incurs a loss, a debit balance is transferred to retrained earnings.

> The retained earnings account balance appears on the balance sheet on the credit side.

System defined adjustment periods:

An accounting year consists of various accounting periods. If an organization follows a 12-period accounting year, each period corresponds to a calendar month. On the other hand, if it uses a four-period year, then each accounting period corresponds to a quarter (three months). In most of the cases you'll encounter a 12-period calendar with periods ranging from one to 12. Each accounting entry must be recorded in an accounting period.

However, there are additional periods that are used to record adjustments to the previous accounting periods. We can define additional adjustment periods (such as 901, 902, and so on, for actual accounting periods one, two and so on). These are the user-defined periods. In addition, the PeopleSoft system uses three adjustment periods for the closing process. These periods are described in the following table:

Period	Purpose
0	As we discussed earlier, balance sheet accounts carry forward their balances from one year to the next. Period 0 is used to store the account balances from previous year. For example, if the cash account contains a balance of $10,000 at the end of period 12 (the last period) of 2010, it is carried over to period zero of 2011.
998	This is the default adjustment period for recording manual adjustment entries. For example, at the end of the year, we may need to adjust the accumulated depreciation of a particular asset. If no other user-defined adjusting period is specified, the system records it to the period 998.
	Recall the 'Adjusting entry' option on the journal header tab. It is used while creating manual adjustment entries.
999	This period is used to record the accounting entries for the year-end closing. In the previous example, when we transfer the balances from the revenue and expense accounts to the retained earnings account, the entries use period 999.

Offset accounts:

In the previous example, the profit and loss accounts were closed directly into the retained earnings account. This can be done for the interim as well as year-end closing process. However, PeopleSoft offers another option for interim closing.

In this case, profit and loss accounts are closed to an offset account instead of retained earnings account.

Now that we are familiar with the concepts, let's see the relevant PeopleSoft configurations and processes for the same. Let's assume that account 950000 is defined as the Retained Earnings Offset. Thus when we want to close the revenue account 100000, we close it as follows:

DR	A/C 100000 (S/W Revenue)	20,000
CR	A/C 950000 (Ret. Earnings Offset)	-20,000

As a result, it is the offset account that holds the final account balances, and each interim close process posts the balance to this account rather than the retained earnings account. At the end of the financial year, another entry is passed to close the offset account as follows:

DR	A/C 950000 (Ret. Earnings Offset)	20,000
CR	A/C 900000 (Ret. Earnings)	-20,000

Understanding the PeopleSoft configurations for closing process

The following configurations are necessary to perform the closing process:

- **ChartField value sets**: A value set identifies the chartfields that need to be used for the closing process
- **Closing rules**: These rules define various processing options that control the interim as well as year-end closing processes

Creating chartfield value sets

A chartfield value set is nothing but a group of chartfields. As we saw earlier, revenue and expense accounts need to be processed in the closing process. As there are hundreds of accounts that need to be closed, using a value set greatly simplifies the process.

Follow this navigation to create a chartfield value set:

Set Up Financial/Supply Chain | Common Definitions | Design Chartfields | ChartField Value Sets | Setup ChartField Value Sets

The following screenshot shows a sample value set for specifying various expense accounts related to manufacturing costs:

In the previous example, we assume that an organization uses many accounts, from 100001 to 110000, to record various manufacturing costs. Rather than specifying all these accounts individually for closing, it is much easier to create a value set and specify it.

- **Values by Chartfields – Field Name**: We can specify as many chartfields as needed. In the previous example we have used Account, which will usually be the chartfield that must be specified.

- **How Specified**: This field determines how the chartfield values are specified. The available options are **Selected Detail Values** (where we can specify individual chartfield values), **Range of Values** (where we can specify 'from' and 'to' values, and all values between them), and **Detail-Selected Parents** (where we can use trees to specify required values).

Configuring closing rules

This is an important configuration that sets the rules to be used in the closing process.

Follow this navigation to create a closing rule:

General Ledger | Close Ledgers | Closing Rules

The following screenshot shows a sample closing rule for interim closing:

 Closing rules for year-end closing and interim closing need to be defined separately. Some of the configuration options for interim closing rules are not seen on the year-end closing rules.

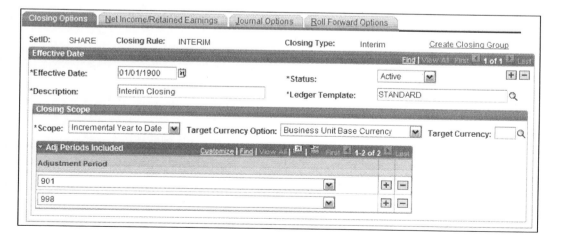

- **Ledger Template**: A closing rule needs to be associated with a ledger template that we define for an organization's ledgers. It determines that the chartfields are available for the closing process.

- **Closing Scope**: This section is available only for interim closing rules. Options in this section are used to define the scope of balance amounts that need to be closed.

- **Scope**: Available options are **Incremental Current Period** (account balances for the entire current period are closed), **Incremental Year to Date** (account balances entered since the last closing process till the close process run date are closed), and **Incremental Year to Curr Period** (account balances created from period one till the end of current period are closed).

- **Adj Periods Included**: This field specifies the adjustment periods to be closed during the interim closing.

The following screenshot shows the **Net Income/Retained Earnings** tab. This tab specifies the source for closing process and the destination retained earnings account(s):

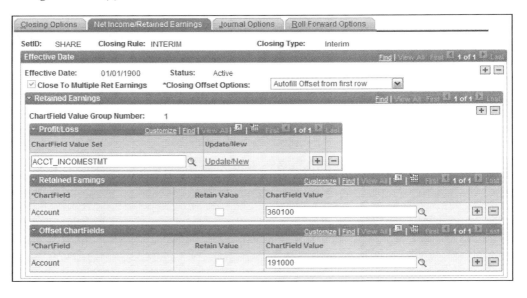

- **Close To Multiple Ret Earnings**: We can decide to close the expense and revenue account balances to a single retained earnings account or multiple accounts. In other words, we can specify different retained earnings accounts for different sets of source accounts. Selecting this checkbox allows the system to use multiple retained earnings accounts. If it is unchecked, the system uses the default account specified on the **Closing Options** tab.

- **Chartfield Value Set**: Select a set of chartfields, as discussed in the previous section, to close account balances from these accounts.

- **Retained Earnings**: Specify the target retained earnings account where the account balances need to be transferred.

- **Offset Chartfields**: This option is available for interim closing only. Specify the account to offset retained earnings accounting entries.

- **Journal Options**: This tab, shown in the following screenshot, is used to specify parameters for creation of journals containing the closing entries.

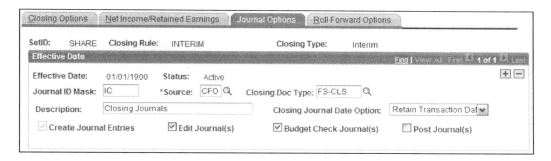

- **Journal ID Mask**: This field specifies if the closing journals need to have a prefix to identify them. If no prefix is needed, the value **NEXT** is used so that the system automatically assigns the next journal ID.

- **Create Journal Entries**: If selected, this checkbox instructs the system to create journal entries for the closing process. This is optional for year-end close, while interim close always creates journal entries.

- **Edit Journals, Budget Check Journals, Post Journals**: These options are available only for interim closing. Select these checkboxes so that the system automatically runs the corresponding process for the newly created closing journals.

- **Roll Forward Options**: This tab shows options for carrying forward the profit and loss accounts.

Configuring a closing process group

A closing group is a collection of closing rules that we wish to execute. We can have one or multiple closing rules in a closing group.

Follow this navigation to create a closing process group:

General Ledger | Close Ledgers | Closing Process Group

The following screenshot shows a sample close group created for interim closing:

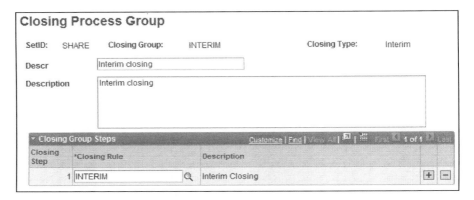

As you can see, the closing process group contains only one interim closing rule. However, if needed, additional closing rules can be added by using the + button.

The Close process does not have an option to specify whether we wish to run interim close or year end close. In order to do that, define separate closing process groups containing interim and year end close rules respectively. Whenever we wish to perform an interim close, simply use a process group containing interim close rules. To perform year-end close, use a process group containing year-end close rules.

Running closing process

Follow this navigation to run the Ledger Close (GLPCLOSE) process:

General Ledger | Close Ledgers | Request Ledger Close

The following screenshot shows the run control page for the close process:

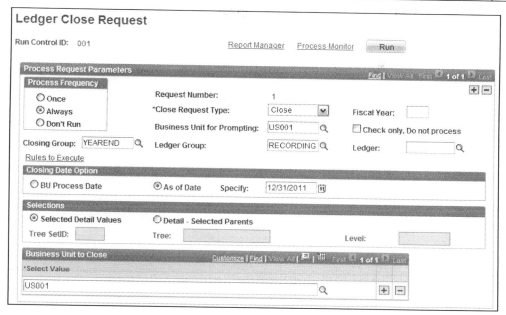

- **Close Request Type**: PeopleSoft offers the option of reversing the close process in case of an error. Select a value in this field, either: **Close** to perform the close process or **Undo** to reverse an already-performed close process.

- **Closing Group**: Select an appropriate closing group in this field, depending on whether we need to perform interim or year-end close.

> The Interim close process is not mandatory, but most of the organizations perform it at the end of each accounting period. This helps in keeping the retained earnings account updated regularly. Interim close is similar to the year-end close except for the fact that it does not carry forward balance sheet accounts to period zero of the next year.

- **Check Only, Do Not Process**: The Close process during its execution performs various validations such as checking if all chartfields, chartfield values, and retained earnings accounts are valid. Select this checkbox and run the process to perform only these validations.

Click on the **Run** button to initiate the process.

Understanding allocations

Processing allocations is an integral part of accounting processes. An organization incurs various expenses that later need to be allocated (distributed) among various units using certain parameters. These expenses typically include, but are not limited to, rent expenses, utility expenses, salaries for support functions such as human resources and IT support, general expenses such as advertising, and so on.

Let's consider a simple example to understand this concept. Assume that an organization has 400 employees working in its two departments—hardware sales and software services. This organization also has an administration support department. For the sake of simplicity, we'll assume that it uses only two chartfields: Account and Department. Let's say the chartfield values are as follows:

Account		Department	
Value	Description	Value	Description
900000	Salary expenses	A300	Hardware sales
		A400	Software services
		A500	Administration

The salary for the administration staff is $100,000 for the year 2011. This would be posted to the ledger as follows:

Account	Department	Debit	Credit
900000	A500	$100,000	

As administration staff salary expense was incurred for the entire organization, it needs to be allocated to the departments A300 and A400 based on some parameter(s). We can use any parameter or multiple parameters to decide how this can be done. It can be divided between the departments simply equally or based on their revenues, headcount, and so on. Let's say that the headcount of these departments is used as basis for allocation. Thus, if the number of employees in departments A300 and A400 are 100 and 300 respectively, then $25,000 of the administration salary expenses will be allocated to A300, while $75,000 will be allocated to department A400.

There are three important terms related to PeopleSoft allocation process that we need to remember:

- **Pool**: This is the amount that needs to be allocated. In our example, the administration salary expense is the pool.

- **Basis**: This is the parameter that determines how the pool amount needs to be allocated. In our example, the department headcount is the basis.
- **Target:** This is the destination to which the pool amount needs to be allocated. In our example, both departments A300 and A400 are the targets.

Note that there could be different instances of allocation basis. For example, we may use staff headcount, area (for allocating rent expenses), number of months, and or others so on. Such non-accounting entities are recorded using what is known as **statistical accounts**. These accounts, although similar to regular accounts such as revenue, expense, and so on, are not used to store financial data.

Allocation configurations

There are two configurations we need to perform for an allocation process:

- Allocation step
- Allocation process group

The allocation process for an organization may contain only a single allocation step or multiple steps for a complex scenario. An allocation process group contains one or more allocation steps to be followed by the allocation process.

Configuring an allocation step

An allocation step specifies the rules for allocation such as defining the pool, basis, target, and so on.

Implementation challenge

An organization wishes to allocate its rent expenses, paid by its administration department, to all other departments. The allocation should be done by floor space occupied by each of the departments.

Solution

Assume that this organization uses the same department values as shown previously. It uses account 100000 to record rent expenses and statistical account 350000 to record the floor space of each department.

Thus, the ledger will have following entry for the rent expense:

Account	Department	Debit	Credit
100000	A500	$100,000	

This will be the pool amount.

The ledger will have following entries for the statistical account (floor space):

Account	Department	Floor Space (sq. ft.)
350000	A500	5,000
350000	A300	5,000
350000	A400	15,000

Note that statistical account entries do not have debit or credit balances. This will serve as the basis.

Now, if we distribute the total rent expense in proportion of the floor area, A500 and A300 should get 1/5 of total rent each, while A400 should be allocated three-fifths of the rent expense. Thus the accounting entry would be as follows:

Account	Department	Debit	Credit
100000	A500		- $100,000
100000	A500	$20,000	
100000	A300	$20,000	
100000	A400	$60,000	

Here the first line is known as the **Offset**, while the last three lines are the **Target**.

Follow this navigation to define an allocation step:

Allocations | Define and Perform Allocations | Define Allocation Step

We will discuss only the first five important tabs for this configuration.

The following screenshot shows the **Type** tab of an allocation step.

Note that the chartfield values used in our illustrative example and those in the given screenshot may not match.

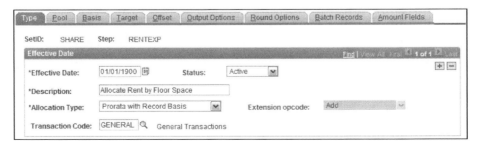

In this example, we have to allocate the rent (pool) with floor area as the basis.

- **Allocation Type**: This field decides how the pool amount is allocated. The available options are **Spread Evenly** (the pool amount is divided equally among the target values), **Prorata with Record Basis** (the pool amount is divided on the values in the basis amount), **Allocate on Fixed Basis** (the pool amount is divided among target values based on fixed percentage values that we specify), **Copy** (the pool amount is copied to the target with or without percentage changes), and **Arithmetic Operation** (we can specify a mathematical formula between the pool and basis to derive the allocation amount).

- **Extension Opcode**: This field is enabled when we select **Arithmetic Operation** as the Allocation Type. It has following values to define the formula: **Add, Subtract, Multiply,** and **Divide**.

  The following screenshot shows the **Pool** tab of the allocation step:

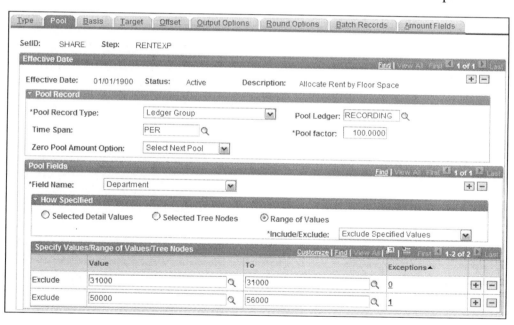

- **Pool Record Type**: This field is used to decide how pool amounts are specified. The available values are **Ledger Group** (which indicates that the pool amount is stored in chartfields in a ledger group), **Fixed Amount** (used if we wish to directly specify an amount to be allocated) and **Any Table** (where we can specify a table where the pool amount is stored). Note that the last option is used for the Project Costing module.

- **Time Span**: This field determines the year and accounting periods for which the pool amount should be considered. For example, if we wish to allocate administration salary expenses for the entire year 2011, we need to specify so. If this field is left blank, the system allocates the pool amount for all fiscal years and periods.

 When we specify the pool record type as Ledger Group, the system automatically uses the calendar used by the specified ledger group.

- **Pool Factor**: We can specify what percent of the pool amount needs to allocated, by using this field. A value less than or greater than 100% can be used.
- **Zero Pool Amount Option**: This field is used to decide what should happen if the pool amount retrieved by the system is zero. Available values are **Calculate This Pool, Select Next Pool, Stop Processing,** and **Calc No Rows as Zero**.
- **Pool Fields**: This section is used to specify one or more pools.
- **Field Name**: This field specifies the chartfield parameters for selecting the records for pool amount. For example, if we wish to allocate the rent expenses of a particular department, we need to specify two parameters: the accounts that hold rent expense amounts and the department that incurred the expense.

Once we specify a chartfield, its values are specified using one of the following methods: **Selected Detail Values** (where we list each individual chartfield value), **Selected Tree Node** (where we specify a tree node and all the values below it), and **Range of Values** (where we specify from and to values).

The following screenshot shows the **Basis** tab of the allocation step.

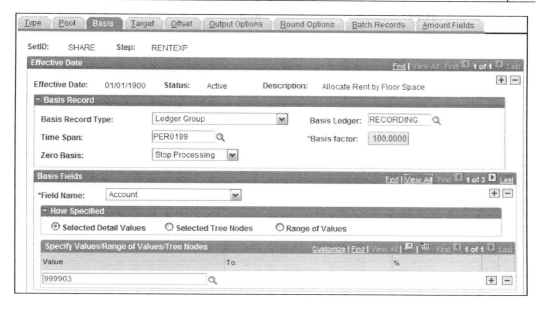

Fields in the **Basis Record** section are again similar to those on the previous tab.

The **Basis Fields** section specifies the parameters for deriving the basis amounts. In the previous example, the floor space is used as the basis. Thus, the system needs to know the area of all the departments to which rent has to be allocated. In other words, we need to specify two parameters as the basis fields: Account, which is the statistical account that records the floor area, and the Department(s), whose area needs to be retrieved.

The following screenshot shows the **Target** tab of the allocation step:

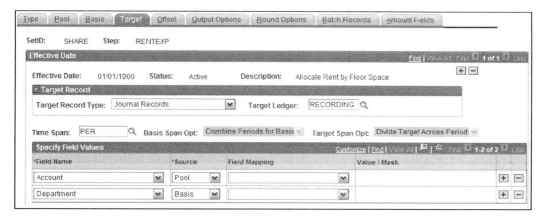

The Target tab is used to specify the chartfields and their sources to create the target entries.

As we know, the target in our example is a group of departments among which the rent expense is to be allocated. The Account values came from the Pool, while the Department values came from the Basis.

In this tab, we specify all the chartfields to be used for the target (Account and Department) in the **Field Name** column. Also, we need to specify where the values for these chartfields can be derived from in the **Source** column.

Target Record Type: This field specifies the database table that needs to store the accounting entries for the Target. Available values are **Journal Records** (the system uses the journal table for given ledger group) and **Any Table** (if we wish to specify a different table).

The following screenshot shows the **Offset** tab for the allocation step:

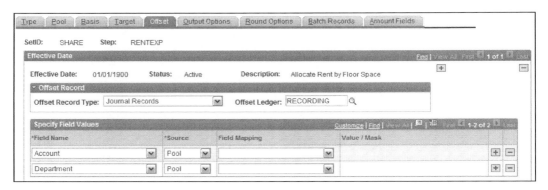

This tab specifies the chartfields and the source for their values to create the offset for the pool entry. In our example, both the Account and Department values were derived from the Pool, so that is what we specify in the **Field Name** and **Source** columns.

Configuring an allocation group

An allocation group contains all the allocation steps (one or multiple) that need to be executed.

Follow this navigation to define an allocation group:

Allocations | Define and Perform Allocations | Define Allocation Group

The page need not be explained, as it is quite straightforward.

Running the allocation process

The Allocation (FS_ALLC) batch process executes the allocation steps within an allocation group. It uses the setup options in these allocation step(s) to create the allocation journals.

Follow this navigation to execute the Allocation process:

Allocations | Define and Perform Allocations | Request Allocation

The following screenshot shows the run control page for the Allocation process:

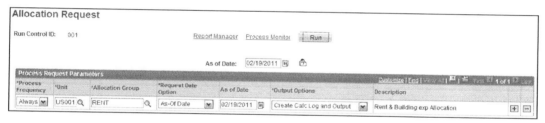

Output Options: This field has the following options:

- **Create Calc Log - No Output**: This option results in creating a log of all allocation calculations without creating any journals or ledger entries. PeopleSoft recommends using this option to run the process before performing the actual allocation.
- **Create Calc Log and Output**: The process creates a calculation log and generates journals and ledger entries.
- **No Calc Log - Create Output**: The process creates journals and ledger entries, but no calculation log.

Summary

PeopleSoft General Ledger is the central repository of all accounting information created by accounting transactions. All other modules (such as Billing, AR, AP, and so on) send their accounting details to the General Ledger in the form of journals. Journals can be created manually using online pages, imported from non-PeopleSoft systems as flat files, or uploaded using Microsoft Excel spreadsheets. Journal Generator is an important batch process used to create journals from accounting entries from other PeopleSoft modules. Journal Edit and Journal Post are other important components of journal processing.

Once journals are posted, they update the account balances in the LEDGER table.

At the end of an accounting year, the balances of revenue and expense accounts need to be transferred to the retained earnings account in the balance sheet. This process is known as Closing. Organizations can perform interim closing (optional) apart from the year-end closing. PeopleSoft uses the closing rules and the Ledger Close batch process to perform closing.

The Allocations process distributes expenses incurred by an entity, such as a Department, to multiple entities. The Allocation batch process uses the rules set up in allocation steps to perform allocations.

The General Ledger module acts as a source from which various management reports can be generated. GL account balances are used to create financial statements such as income statements, balance sheets, and cash flow statements.

8
PeopleSoft Expenses Module

In a large organization, the task of tracking and managing expense claims for employees is quite effort-intensive. The PeopleSoft Expenses module is an important self-service application used to automate and streamline the employee travel and expense transactions. The PeopleSoft Expenses system features can be categorized into four broad areas: cash advances, expense reports, timesheet data, and travel authorizations. Usually cash advances are given to employees before going on business travel. Expense reports are used to claim the reimbursement for business expenses incurred by the employees. Travel authorizations are used to pre-approve the estimated travel costs. The Expenses module can integrate with an external travel reservation application to perform travel reservations. Timesheets are used to record employees' working hours.

In this chapter, we will discuss following topics related to the most commonly used system features: the processing of cash advances and expense reports. We will look at:

- Understanding expenses processes
- Understanding cash advances and expense report configurations
- Understanding workflow approvals
- Importing external data (Credit card data and Benchmark data) into the Expenses module
- Processing cash advances
- Processing expenses reports

Understanding expenses processes

The following schematic describes the high-level processes in the PeopleSoft Expenses module:

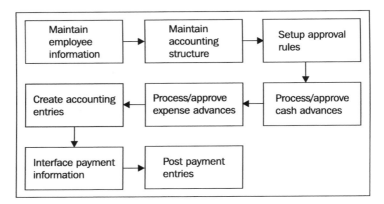

As this module is intended to be used as a tool by the employees in an organization, it needs to maintain their employee profiles. PeopleSoft offers two different methods to do this. Employee information stored in the Expenses module includes elements such as address, bank account information, credit card details, default accounting information, and so on. We can load all the necessary employee details from the PeopleSoft Human Resources Management System (HRMS) using a delivered batch process or we can create the employee profiles manually using the online pages.

The PeopleSoft Expenses module needs to create accounting entries for expense reports and cash advances. The default chartfield information for creating these accounting entries comes from the business units, employee profiles, cash advance sources, and expense types.

The Expenses module provides a flexible approval workflow to route the Expenses expense transactions through multiple levels of hierarchy. The number of levels of approval and the roles involved can be configured depending on the organization's requirements. We can design approval rules by specifying parameters such as which transactions need to be routed through approval, which users can be approvers, which transactions can be approved by an approver, and so on. PeopleSoft delivers various pre-configured roles and transaction types, that can be used as needed, significantly simplifying the approval rules design.

Cash advances are paid to employees to cover their business travel expenses. An employee can submit a request for cash advance which, when approved by all necessary approvers, can result in a payment. On the other hand, an employee can withdraw cash from an ATM using his/her company credit card and the details can be automatically loaded into PeopleSoft to create a cash advance transaction. A cash advance can be then applied to one or more expense reports submitted by that employee. This is helpful to ensure that an employee is not paid twice.

Expense reports are used to record the business expenses incurred by an employee. It can record each expense item and its relevant details. If these expenses were paid with a company credit card, the expense details can be automatically imported on the expense report, thus saving the data entry effort. Once submitted, the expense report is routed through the approval hierarchy. As mentioned earlier, a report can be linked with a cash advance. Once approved, the expense report is ready to be paid. The payment to the employee can be made through the Accounts Payable pay cycle or through the PeopleSoft Payroll module.

The Expenses module can create accounting entries for the cash advance and expense reports before and after the report is paid. These entries can be passed to the General Ledger module for creating journals.

Understanding cash advance and expense report configurations

In order to use the cash advance and expense report features, we need to perform various setups. In this section, we'll familiarize ourselves with some of the most important configurations.

- Maintaining employee profiles
- Cash advance sources
- Expense types
- Location amounts
- Per diem ranges
- Per diem amounts

Maintaining employee profiles

The PeopleSoft Expenses module is intended to be used by an organization's employees to create expense reports and get their business expenses reimbursed. Therefore, it is important that the system maintains detailed information about all valid employees. We'll quickly look at two different methods of maintaining employee details in the Expenses module.

Manually updating employee data

This method is recommended when an organization does not use PeopleSoft HRMS applications.

Follow this navigation to maintain employee information:

Travel & Expenses | Manage Employee Information | Update Profile

The Employee Data tab is used to record the name and address details of the employee and is not shown.

The following screenshot shows the Organization Data tab of the employee profile:

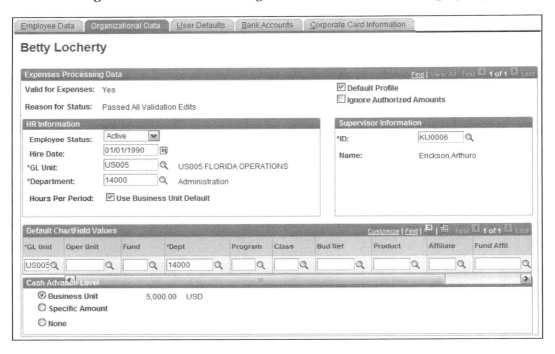

This tab stores some of the most important employee details needed for Expenses Processing. The GL Unit and Department fields are important to create appropriate accounting entries for this employee's expense transactions.

The Supervisor Information section contains important details for routing the expense transactions for approval.

Details entered in the Default Chartfield Values section are automatically populated on this employee's expense reports and cash advances. However, they can be changed on these transactions if needed.

The Cash Advance Level option determines the maximum cash advance amount that can be given to an employee. The possible options are Business Unit (the same amount as is specified for Expenses business unit), Specific Amount (which can be manually specified), or None (meaning this employee is not eligible for any cash advances).

The User Defaults tab is used to specify various default values that can be automatically populated on this employee's expense reports and cash advances. This significantly reduces the data entry efforts.

The following screenshot shows the Bank Accounts tab:

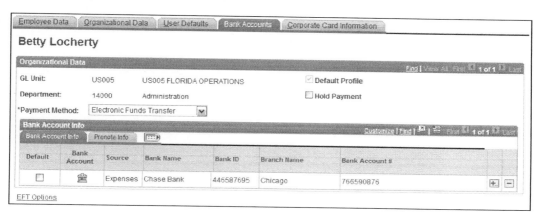

This tab records the employee's bank account information used for expense reimbursement. It is needed primarily for the electronic deposit of the expense reimbursement amount directly into the employee's account. If an organization issues checks for expense reimbursement, it may not be needed.

We can add multiple bank accounts for an employee by using the + button. Account details can be added by clicking the symbol in the Bank Account column.

- Hold Payment: If this checkbox is selected, no expense reimbursement can take place for this employee.

- Corporate Card Information: This tab is used to record any official credit, debit or ATM cards that the employee may be using. Some organizations issue corporate cards to employees for business expenses and directly reimburse the amounts to card vendors. In such cases, it is important to link expense report items to the card vendor payments using the card numbers.

Apart from recording basic details such as card number, expiry date, and so on, we can control the card usage by the employee by specifying various details such as a maximum credit limit, a maximum amount that can be spent in a billing cycle, a maximum amount for a transaction, and so on.

Loading employee data from PeopleSoft HRMS

If an organization is using the PeopleSoft Human Resources Management System, it is the primary source for storing employee information. The Expenses module can simply subscribe to the information from HRMS. This can be done using a combination of PeopleSoft-delivered application messages and an interface batch program.

A group of application messages load the Expenses staging tables with various details such as an employee's personal information, e-mail addresses, phone numbers, departments, and so on. A batch process known as Expenses Employee Update (EX_EE_UPDATE) then loads these details automatically from staging tables into the Expense module.

Follow this navigation to execute the Expenses Employee Update batch process:

Travel & Expenses | Manage Employee Information | Load Employee Data

The following screenshot shows the run control page for the process:

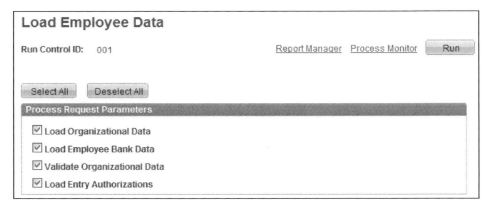

There are four different process parameters that can be specified:

1. **Load Organizational Data**: This option is used to load employee information such as hire date, business unit, department, supervisor information, and the amount of cash advance that can be paid. Note that these are the same details that we manually enter on the Organizational Data tab on the employee profile page.

2. **Load Employee Bank Data**: This option is used to load employee bank account data. Note that these are the same details that we manually enter on the Bank Accounts tab on the employee profile page.

3. **Validate Organizational Data**: As the employee information is coming from an external source, it is important to validate it before being used. This option verifies if the departments and business units assigned to employees are valid and defined in PeopleSoft Expenses.

4. **Load Entry Authorizations**: Each employee needs to have a user ID to access and use Expenses module features. This option loads user IDs assigned to the employees.

Configuring cash advance sources

A cash advance source essentially determines how the advance amount is paid to the employee.

Follow this navigation to setup a cash advance source:

Set Up Financials/Supply Chain | Product Related | Expenses | Management | Cash Advance Source

The following screenshot shows a sample cash advance source:

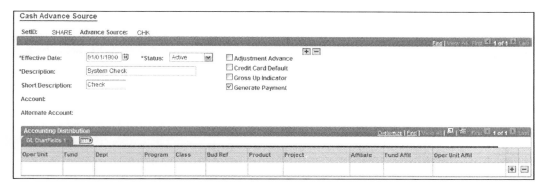

Note that we can have two different types of cash advances, depending on whether a system needs to generate a payment or not. For example, in an organization, an employee can withdraw an amount from an ATM using his/her corporate credit card and use it as an advance for a travel expense. In this case, the system doesn't need to issue a payment, it simply needs to record the fact that cash advance was paid through ATM. Another example of this type of cash advance is through traveller's checks. On the other hand, an organization may issue a check or deposit the amount directly in an employee's bank account after the cash advance request is approved. In these cases, the PeopleSoft system needs to create a payment.

- **Generate Payment**: As discussed previously, if a source, such as checks or Electronic Fund Transfer, needs to create a payment through the Accounts Payable or Payroll system, select this checkbox. Unchecking this checkbox enables the Account field and Accounting Distribution section.

- **Account, Alternate Account, Accounting Distribution section**: These fields are used to enter chartfield information to be used for those sources that need not create a system payment.

When a cash advance source generates system payment, its accounting entry is as follows:

DR   **Cash advance account** (specified on the accounting entry template in Accounts Payable)

CR   **Cash account**

If a source does not create a payment, the accounting entry is as follows:

DR   **Cash advance account** (specified on the accounting entry template in Accounts Payable)

CR   **Chartfields specified on this page** (Account field and Accounting Distribution section)

Click the Reimbursement hyperlink to specify who gets the advance amount. The new page shows two options: Employee and Vendor. If we select the Vendor option, additional details such as Vendor ID need to be specified.

While it's easy to imagine that an employee is paid the cash advance, you may be wondering why we need to pay the cash advance amount to a vendor. In a situation like ATM cash withdrawal, the employee will get a statement from the credit card company that needs to be paid. If the organization pays that employee's corporate card dues, the payment will need to be made to the vendor (that is, the credit card company).

Configuring expense types

This is one of the most important configurations for processing expense reports. An expense type provides valid categories of business expenses that can be reimbursed. It also drives the chartfield details for creating accounting entries. A typical organization may have various expense types such as airfare, hotel expenses, Visa fees, taxi expenses, per diem (daily allowance), and so on. It should be noted that actual expense types to be configured entirely depend on an organization's requirements.

Follow this navigation to set up an expense type:

Set Up Financials/Supply Chain | Product Related | Expenses | Purchase |
Expense Type

The following screenshot shows the sample expense type Airfare:

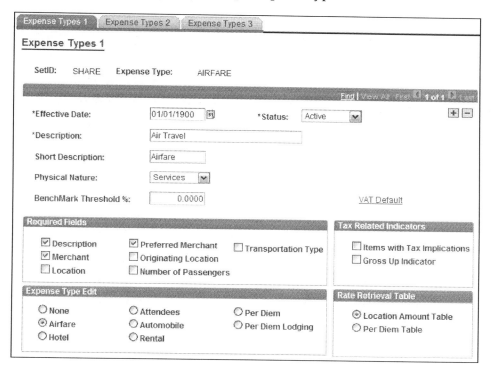

- **Benchmark Threshold** %: Some organizations use benchmark data for
  expenses. We will discuss loading the benchmark data in a later section. This
  field instructs the system how much an employee can exceed the expense
  benchmark data. Let's consider an example to understand this. We may use
  a benchmark that says the average hotel room cost in New York is $400 per
  night. If we specify a threshold of 10% in this field, the system will allow
  hotel expense claims by employees up to $440 per night. Any amount higher
  than this will be flagged for review.

- **Required Fields**: This section specifies various details that must be provided
  by the employee while using a particular expense type. In the given example,
  when an employee claims airfare expense, the system forces him/her to
  provide a text description, the merchant (airline used for the travel) and a
  preferred merchant. If these details are not provided, the expense report
  cannot be saved.

- **Expense Type Edit**: These are additional mandatory information elements that must be provided by the employee. In the given example, we have selected the Airfare option, which results in the system forcing the employee to enter the air ticket number. If we configure an expense type for hotel expense, select the Hotel option, which will result in the system forcing the employee to enter number of nights spent at the hotel.

- **Items with Tax Implications**: Certain expense reimbursements, such as club membership expenses, are treated as taxable income by the tax authorities. If an expense type is taxable, select this checkbox.

- **Gross Up Indicator**: If the expense amount reimbursed to the employee is taxable, an organization may decide to pay the tax amount in addition to the expense amount. For example, an employee is paid an amount of $ 500, taxed at the rate of 10%. In that case, he/she will receive only $ 450. To avoid this, the organization may pay the employee the expense amount as well as its tax amount (USD 550). Select this checkbox to enable this feature.

The following screenshot shows the Expense Types 2 tab:

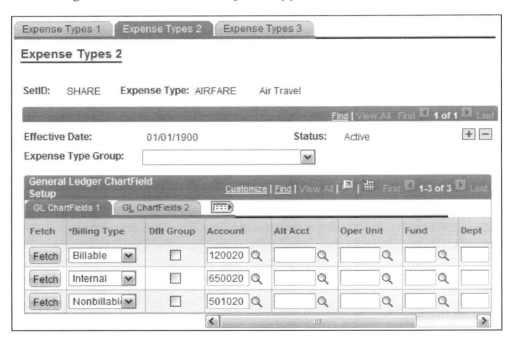

This tab is used to specify accounting information for the expense type.

- **Expense Type Group**: If desired, we can associate an expense type with an expense type group, which we would need to configure before the expense type. This helps in automatically populating some of the information for the expense type. It is not a mandatory step.

- **GL Chartfield Setup**: This section records the chartfields to be used for creating accounting entries for this expense type. PeopleSoft offers three billing types: Billable (this expense was incurred for a project and can be billed to a client), Internal (this expense was incurred for an organization's own work) and Nonbillable (this expense was incurred for a project but cannot be billed to a client). If we wish to record expense accounting entries for billable and non-billable purposes to different accounts, we can do so.

The following screenshot shows the Expense Types 3 tab:

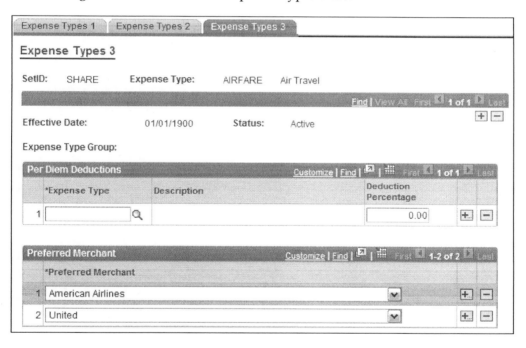

This tab is used to specify the preferred merchants for an expense type, although the actual list of preferred merchants is defined on a different page. If an employee uses a merchant other than these preferred merchants, the system flags that transaction and forces him/her to provide a reason for non-compliance. In the given example, we have specified two airlines as preferred merchants for air travel. This is an important mechanism to enforce organization's expense policies.

Configuring expense location amounts

This is another important expense report configuration. An organization needs to have some benchmark amounts for various locations depending on average level of expenses that are typically incurred. For example, when an employee submits a hotel expense with a rate of $400 per night in New York, there should be a mechanism to decide if this is a reasonable amount. As you can imagine, the average hotel room rate in New York will certainly be different from one in Houston. At the same time, these rates may change due to seasonal factors. For example, a hotel room in Orlando will cost much more during the holiday season compared to other times of the year.

The parameters that need to be considered to make this decision are location, expense type, and time of the year.

Follow this navigation to set up expense location amounts:

Set Up Financials/Supply Chain | Product Related | Expenses | Location | Expense Location Amount

The following screenshot shows benchmark data for lodging expenses for various locations:

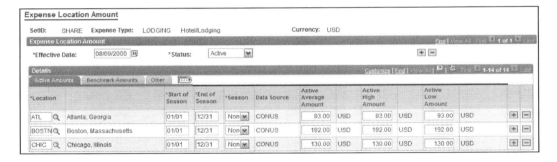

 Note that we need to define locations and location groups before defining the expense location amounts.

Using this page, we can define benchmark amounts for an expense type and a currency. We can also specify amounts for various times of the year for a particular location.

- Location: This field is used to select a location defined on a separate page
- Start of Season, End of Season: These fields are used to specify the dates of a period

- Data Source: As mentioned earlier, these amounts can be entered manually or loaded from the external sources CONUS or Runzheimer
- Active Average Amount, Active High Amount, Active Low Amount: These amounts specify the average, maximum, and minimum amounts

If we wish to set up different rates for the same location, add multiple rows with different season ranges and rates.

Configuring per diem ranges

Employees travelling to a different location for business get daily allowances by organizations. In some cases, the per diem rates have different slabs. Thus, per diem amounts depend on the location as well as date ranges (number of days of travel).

Follow this navigation to set up per diem ranges:

Set Up Financials/Supply Chain | Product Related | Expenses | Location | Per Diem Range

The following screenshot shows date ranges for per diem:

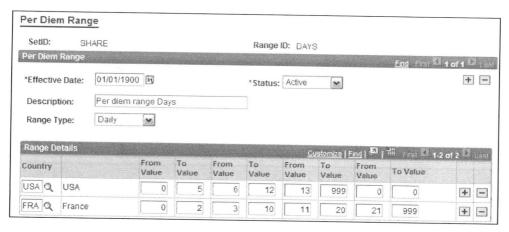

- Range Type: This field determines the unit for the ranges. The available values are Daily and Hourly.
- From Value, To Value: We can specify up to four ranges. The To Value for the last range always must be 999.

Configuring per diem amounts

Based on the per diem ranges defined previously, we can specify the actual per diem amounts for various locations in a country.

Follow this navigation to set up per diem amounts:

Set Up Financials/Supply Chain | Product Related | Expenses | Location | Per Diem Amounts

The following screenshot shows per diem amounts for France based on the ranges defined previously:

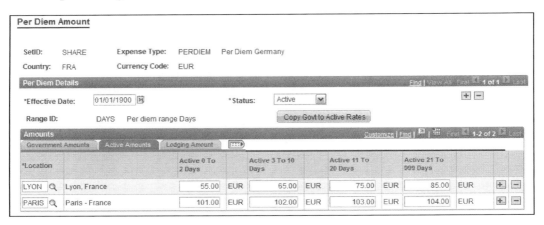

The given screenshot shows the Active Amounts tab. These rates are used by the expense reports to calculate the per diem amount depending on the number of days that an employee stays in a location.

Understanding expenses approvals

For any organization that processes cash advances and expense reports, it is extremely important that strict financial controls are in place to ensure that fraudulent expenses are not claimed and paid. This is where the PeopleSoft Expense module's flexible approval feature comes into picture. PeopleSoft delivers various pre-configured approval rules and roles as part of the Approval Workflow Engine (AWE). We can configure various approval and audit rules for expense transactions by modifying these pre-configured objects.

In this section, we'll discuss some of the important configurations for expense approvals:

- Approver types
- Transaction definitions
- Refinement templates
- Privilege templates
- Approver profiles
- Approver assignments
- Approver routing lists

Defining approver types

The expenses approval hierarchy in an organization consists of various roles, that perform different actions. For example, an expense report may go to the accounts supervisor first, who checks if the accounting chartfields are appropriate for that expense (that is, is the expense being charged to the correct department?). When it passes that check, it may be routed to the department manager who will verify the validity of that particular expense (that is, was this business expense justified?). It may further be reviewed by an auditor to see if appropriate organization policies are being followed (that is, has the employee submitted expense receipts, and are there any violations of preferred merchant policies?).

The following table lists the pre-defined approval roles delivered by PeopleSoft:

Approver type	Description
EXAPPROVER (Expense approver)	This role can be used by a department manager.
POSTPAYAUD (Post Pay Auditor)	This role can be used by an auditor who reviews payments that are already made.
PREPAYAUD (Pre Pay Auditor)	This role can be used by an auditor who reviews payments before they are made.
PROJAPPRVR (Project approver)	This role can be used by a project manager approving project-specific expenses. This also needs to be set up in Project Costing module.
PROJSUPP (Project supplemental approver)	This role can be used by a conditional approver for project-specific expenses.

Approver type	Description
REVIEWER (Reviewer)	This role can be used by a reviewer to identify the policy compliance of expenses.
SUPERVISOR (Supervisor)	This role is used to denote the reporting manager of an employee. If you are using the PeopleSoft HRMS modules, the employee-supervisor details are recorded in it.

Note that we need not use all the approver types mentioned here. Also there could be following scenarios which are quite straightforward:

- Scenario 1: An expense approval needs an approval from the reporting manger only. In this case, we need to use only the SUPERVISOR approver type.
- Scenario 2: An expense approval needs an approval from the project manger only. In this case, we need to use only the PROJAPPRVR approver type.

Follow this navigation to create or modify an approver type:

Set Up Financials/Supply Chain | Product Related | Expenses | Management | Approval Setup | Approver Types

The following screenshot shows a sample approver type:

- Approver Category: This field defines the role of an approver type in the approval process. The available values are Expense Approver, Post Pay Audit, Pre Pay Audit, Project Supplemental, Project Manager, Reviewer, and HR Supervisor. Even if we create a new role, it still needs to be assigned to one of the previous categories.

- Routing Chartfield: This important field determines how the expense transactions are routed to a given approver type. Assume that we need an approval role that is responsible for approving expense reports on the basis of Operating Units (that is, expense reports need to be routed to different approvers based on the Operating Unit). In this case, we need to select the Operating Unit chartfield in this field. We'll shortly see how this option affects further configurations.

Defining transaction definitions

PeopleSoft delivers five transaction definitions that can be processed through the approval hierarchy: cash advance, expense report, travel authorization, time report, and time adjustment. We can decide to activate any transaction so that the Approval Framework Engine can process it. Let's say that an organization uses cash advances and expense reports. If it decides that all cash advances need to be automatically approved but the expense reports need to be routed through necessary approvals, we can simply deactivate the cash advance transaction and activate the expense report transaction for workflow.

A transaction definition determines which approver types need to approve a transaction along with the approval actions they can perform.

Follow this navigation to configure a transaction definition:

Set Up Financials/Supply Chain | Product Related | Expenses | Management | Approval Setup | Transaction Definition

The following screenshot shows a sample transaction definition for expense report:

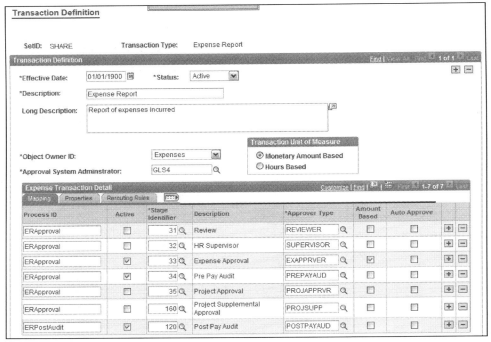

- **Transaction Unit of Measure:** For cash advances, travel authorizations, and expense reports, the unit of measure is Monetary Amount Based, while for time reports and time adjustments, it is Hours Based.

- **Mapping:** This tab shows the approver types that must approve this transaction.

- **Active:** Select this checkbox for an approver type if that role needs to approve the transaction. In the previous example, we have configured it in such a way that all expense reports must be approved by an Expense Approver, Pre Pay Auditor, and Post Pay Auditor. If we have defined our own approver types, we can add them by clicking the + button.

- **Amount Based:** An organization may have a policy that transactions have to be routed to different approvers depending on its amount. If this checkbox is selected, it instructs the system that amount-based routing rules are to be used. In the given example, we are mandating that Pre Pay Auditor and Post Pay Auditor approver types will not be covered by amount-based routing. In other words, all transactions will be routed to them irrespective of their amounts. We'll see how to configure these rules in a short while.

The following screenshot shows the options on Properties tab for expense report:

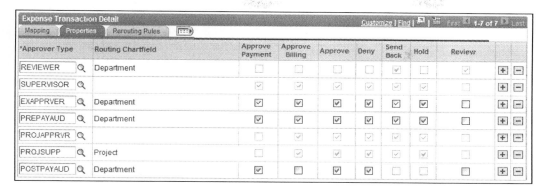

This tab shows which actions, such as Approve payment, Approve billing (of an expense to the client), and so on, can be performed by a selected approver type. Note that rows for only 'Active' approver types are enabled.

The following screenshot shows the Routing Rules tab:

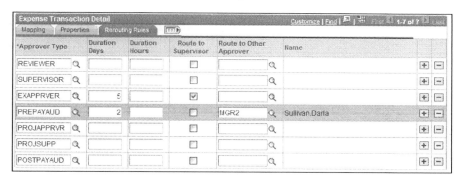

This tab specifies the action to take if the transaction is not acted upon by an approver within a specified time.

- Duration Days and Duration Hours: These fields specify the maximum time allowed for a transaction to remain in queue for an approver type.

- Route to Supervisor: If this option is selected, the transaction is routed to the reporting manager of the employee after the time threshold. In the given example, if an Expense Approver (the Department Manager in our example) does not take any action for five days, the expense report will be automatically routed to the employee's supervisor.

- Route to Other Approver: If transactions need to be routed to a specific person, specify that employee name in this field. For example, if the auditor does not process the expense report in two days, we can route it to the manager of the audit group—Darla Sullivan.

As you can see, transaction definitions can offer a lot of flexibility in terms of setting up the approval rules to suit an organization's needs.

Defining refining templates

In some cases, an organization may not want each transaction to be audited and approved, since it can result in huge overheads. A refinement template essentially decides which of the transactions need to be routed through an approval process. We can decide to create refinement templates for all or some of the approver types that we use.

Follow this navigation to configure a refinement template:

Set Up Financials/Supply Chain | Product Related | Expenses | Management | Approval Setup | Refinement Template

The following screenshot shows part of a refinement template for Pre Pay Auditors:

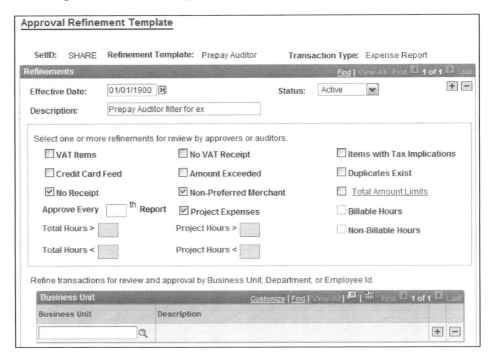

The upper part of the page shows various conditions that we can select so that only transactions satisfying any one of these conditions are routed for approval. In the previous example, we are specifying that expense reports will be selected for approval only they are not accompanied by valid receipts, or have not used a preferred merchant, or are related to a project expense.

The bottom portion of the page contains options to filter transactions on the basis of Business Unit, Department, User, Expense Type, or Time Code. Thus, if we wish to force transactions from specific business units or users through approval, we can do so.

We can assign this refinement template to any approver type. If we assign the given template to the Pre Pay Auditor approver type, only the selected transactions will be audited.

Defining privilege templates

When an approver accesses a transaction, he/she may or may not need the rights to review or modify some of the details of that transaction. For example, a Department manager may find out that a chartfield value on an expense report submitted by an employee is incorrect. Now, instead of rejecting that report and asking the employee to resubmit it with the right value, it may be easier if the manager himself modifies that value and approves it. Whether an approver should have these rights is of course determined by an organization's policies. A privilege template specifies various attributes that an approver can view or modify on a transaction.

Follow this navigation to configure a privilege template:

Set Up Financials/Supply Chain | Product Related | Expenses | Management | Approval Setup | Privilege Template

The following screenshot shows a privilege template:

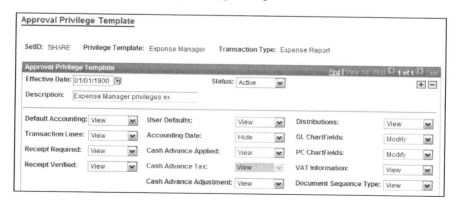

As you can see, we can specify the privileges for various attributes (such as chartfield details, transaction lines, and so on) for a transaction. PeopleSoft offers the following privilege values (actions that an approver can perform):

- View: Approver can only see the attribute on the transaction without the ability to modify or delete it
- Modify: Approver can modify the attribute on the transaction
- Add: Approver can add this attribute on the transaction
- Delete: Approver can delete this attribute from the transaction
- Full: Approver can modify, add, or delete the attribute on the transaction
- Hide: This attribute is hidden on the transaction when the approver opens it

Not all the privilege values are available for all attributes. For example, for the **Receipt Required** flag, only the **Hide** and **View** options are available.

Similarly to a refinement template, we can assign a privilege template to an approver type.

Configuring an approver profile

Each approver in the Expenses system needs to have an approver profile. It determines the expense transactions that can be processed by an approver as well as specifying applicable refinement and privilege templates.

Follow this navigation to modify or create an approver profile:

Set Up Financials/Supply Chain | Product Related | Expenses | Management | Approval Setup | Approver Profile

The following screenshot shows a delivered approver profile for an expense approver:

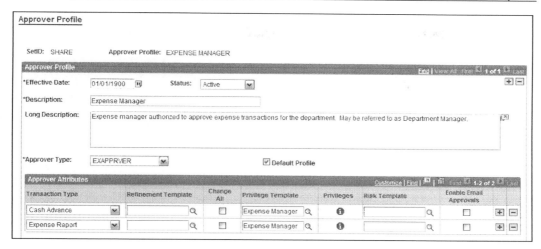

In the given example, we have defined a profile for an expense manager, a department manager who is the first approver for cash advances and expense reports.

- Approver Type: Select the appropriate approver type from the available options. We have already seen the approver types delivered by PeopleSoft.

- Transaction Type: Select the transaction types that we set up as Active. In the given example, we are assuming that that organization is using approvals for only cash advances and expense reports.

- Refinement Template: Attach a refinement template if we wish to filter the transactions that are routed to this approver profile. If we need to force all transactions to be approved, leave this field blank.

- Privilege Template: Attach a privilege template to determine the details that an approver can see and modify.

- Risk Template: Attach a risk template in this field. A risk template defines the financial risk levels for expense transactions. We will not discuss this configuration, as it is not mandatory.

> To continue with our hypothetical requirement of using Department Manager, Pre Pay Auditor, and Post Pay Auditor for approvals, we will need to have three approver profiles. It does not matter what a profile is named. We can modify existing profiles or create new ones if needed.

Assigning approvers to approver profiles

After all the given configurations are complete, we need to specify the actual approvers to populate each approver profile. Once a user is assigned to a profile, he/she automatically inherits the approval rules that we have configured so far.

> If an organization uses approvals by only HR Supervisor or the Project Manager, it is not necessary to assign these approvers to a profile. The system can find out the supervisor or project manager for an employee from the HRMS / Project Costing module and route the transaction directly to an appropriate approver.

Follow this navigation to assign users to an approver profile:

Set Up Financials/Supply Chain | Product Related | Expenses | Management | Approval Setup | Approver Assignment

The following screenshot shows the approver assignments for an approver profile:

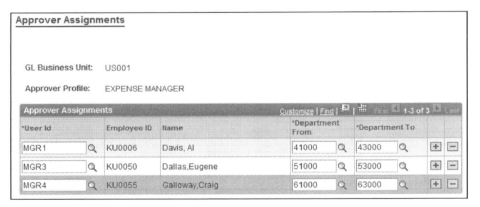

As you can see, we are specifying three approvers to function as Expense Manager (Department Managers) depending upon the department value on the submitted expense transaction.

Note that the Department From and Department To columns are visible because we specified Department as the routing chartfield for the EXAPPROVER approver type. If we had used a different chartfield there, it would have been reflected here.

In other words, all expense transactions submitted by employees belonging to department ID 41000 to 43000 will be routed to Al Davis for first-level approval, while those from employees from department IDs 51000 to 53000 will be sent to Eugene Dallas.

Let's say there are only two Pre Pay Auditors in this organization. We can specify the approver assignment and routing for this role as shown in the following screenshot:

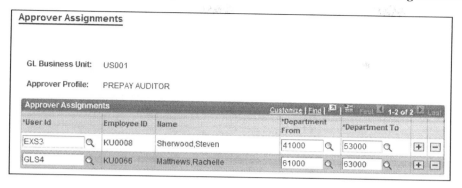

Thus, after Al Davis approves any expense transaction, it will then move to Steven Sherwood to be audited.

Configuring approver routing lists

As we briefly mentioned earlier, an organization may have rules that need additional approvals when expense transactions exceed a certain threshold. In our sample example, all transactions need an approval from the Department Manager before they go to an auditor. Let's say that a new policy change makes it mandatory that all transactions above $5,000 need to have an additional approval from the General Manager as well. In this case, this is said to be a supplemental approval.

We saw that project-related transactions can be approved by the Project Manager. If needed, we can have supplemental approval for project expenses as well.

Approver routing lists are created for one approver type and expense transaction.

Note that amount-based routing rules are needed only if the approver type for a transaction is set up for amount-based routing. Recall the Mapping tab for the transaction definition set up.

Let's say we have three levels of amount based approvals: the Department Manager for amounts up to $5,000, the General Manager for amounts up to $5,000, and the Vice President for amounts more than $10,000. Thus, depending upon the transaction amount, it'll move through one, two, or three different approvers.

Follow this navigation to modify or create an approver routing list:

Set Up Financials/Supply Chain | Product Related | Expenses | Management | Approval Setup | Approver List

The following screenshot shows the approver routing list for expense reports and expense approver role for the given scenario:

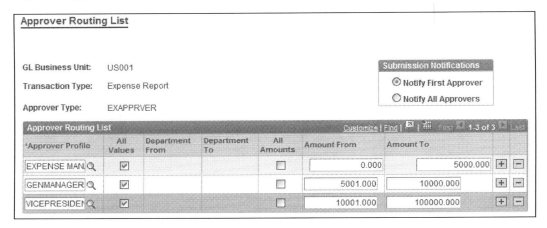

- **Submission Notifications:** This field controls how the system notifications are sent to these approvers:
  - **Notify First Approver:** This option results in the system notifying the first level approver first. After he/she approves the transaction, the higher level approvers are sequentially notified. Thus approvals take place in linear order.
  - **Notify All Approvers:** This option results in the system notifying and routing transactions to all approvers in the list. Any approver can access and approve the transaction at any time.
- **Approver Profile:** Select the approver profiles in the order of the desired routing.
- **All Values:** If this checkbox is selected, the From and To fields for the chartfield values are disabled and all values are automatically selected by the system.
- **Amount From, Amount To:** Specify the amount ranges for each level of approver profile.

Putting it all together

By this time you may feel a little overwhelmed by the various steps you need to complete to enable the approval framework. Let's summarize these steps to look at the complete picture.

Configuration	How it relates to organization's requirements
Approver types	Identify different roles in organization's approval process. Identify if the organization needs simple approvals by Project Manager or Supervisor (Reporting manager). Map required roles to delivered approver types or create new approver types. Typical approval roles are Expense Approver, Pre Pay Auditor, and so on. Identify the chartfield (Department, Operating Unit, and so on by which transactions need to be routed.
Transaction definitions	Identify the expense transactions that need to be routed through approval. Activate those transactions. Identify which roles need to be involved in approval process for that transaction and activate them. Identify the order in which the transaction needs to be routed for these roles. Specify any parameters to reroute transactions in case no action is taken.
Refinement templates (Optional)	Find out if all the expense transactions need to be approved. If not, identify the conditions based on which transactions are selected for approval.
Privilege Templates	Decide on the information that approvers can access and/or modify an expense transaction they need to approve.
Approver profiles	Identify how many approver levels are needed for an approver type. For example, Department Manager, General Manager, and Vice President are the required approver profiles, all belonging to EXAPPROVER type. Similarly there may be two levels of auditors, needing two separate profiles belonging to PREPAYAUD type. Thus, each approver level needs a profile. Assign the privilege and refinement templates to the approver profile.
Approver assignments	Decide which employees need to be assigned to an approver profile.
Approver routing lists	Identify any business policies that dictate additional approvals based on amounts or hours. Configure the routing lists by specifying the profiles in the order of increasing amount limits.
	Create routing list for each transaction and approver type.

Interfacing external data with expenses

Now that we have familiarized ourselves with some of the important Expenses configurations, we'll now move to another important area. The Expenses module is capable of integrating with various external non-PeopleSoft entities to import data using delivered interface batch processes. In this section, we'll discuss two of the most widely used integrations: with credit card vendors and benchmark data organizations.

Importing credit card data

As we discussed earlier, organizations can utilize corporate cards to be used by employees. When the card vendor sends the statement for expense transactions, PeopleSoft can automatically load them into the Expenses module. Once loaded, employees can be notified of the pending charges. They can copy these transactions onto their expense reports. Finally, if so desired, the payment can be directly made to the card vendor.

PeopleSoft offers delivered integration with five different credit card vendors: American Express, Diners Club, MasterCard, US Bank, and Visa. These vendors provide credit card data in pre-defined formats specified by PeopleSoft, which can be readily imported into the Expenses system.

Follow this navigation to execute the Expense Data Source Load (EX_DATA_LOAD) process:

Travel & Expenses | Corporate Credit Cards | Load External Data Sources

The following screenshot shows the run control page for the process;

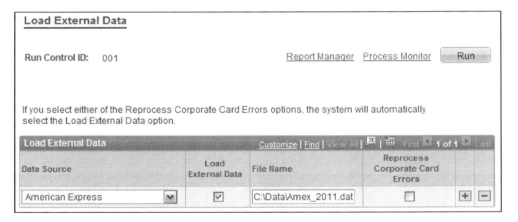

- Data Source: This field specifies the source of credit card data. We can select one of the five card data sources as discussed previously.
- File Name: Specify the file path and file name containing the data that need to be loaded.
- Load External Data: This checkbox must be selected if we wish to load the data from the input data file specified in File Name field.

- Reload Corporate Card Errors: If the process finds any data errors (such as incorrect card number, invalid expense code, and so on) in the data file, it loads those error transactions into vendor specific error tables. We can review them from online pages and make necessary corrections. This checkbox needs to be selected to load the corrected transactions from the staging area rather than the new data from input data file.

Select the **Reprocess Corporate Card Errors** option alone if you wish to reload only the corrected transactions. Select the **Load External Data** option alone if you wish to load only the new card data from the input file. Select both the checkboxes if new transactions as well as corrected transactions from previous run need to be loaded.

Importing benchmark data

In the configurations section, we discussed setting up of expense location amounts which determine minimum and maximum expense ranges for different expense types at different locations. If the number of expense locations is small, maintaining them manually is not a problem. However, when we need to deal with a large number of locations, it can become quite a challenge.

PeopleSoft delivers three pre-configured integrations to automatically load the benchmark expense data:

- Expense data from Runzheimer International
- Expense data from U.S. federal government for the continental U.S. (CONUS)
- Expense data from U.S. federal government for foreign countries (OCONUS)

Importing benchmark data consists of two steps:

- Specify the pre-configured file layout and application message
- Execute the inbound file publish processing

Follow this navigation to specify file layout parameters:

Enterprise Components | Integration Definitions | Inbound File Rule

The following screenshot shows the layout parameters for Runzheimer data load for USA:

Note that PeopleSoft delivers the following pre-configured layouts with Inactive status:

Data load	File identifier
Runzheimer USA data	BENCHMARK_RNZ_USA_LOAD
Runzheimer non-USA data	BENCHMARK_RNZ_NONUSA_LOAD
CONUS	CONUS_LOAD
OCONUS	OCONUS_LOAD

 We need not change any parameters for the file identifiers. Simply change the status to **Active** to use a file identifier.

In order to load data into Expenses module using the pre-defined layout, we need to execute the EOP_PUBLISHF process.

Follow this navigation to access the run control page for this process:

Enterprise Components | Integration Definitions | Initiate Processes | Inbound File Publish

The following screenshot shows the run control page for the process:

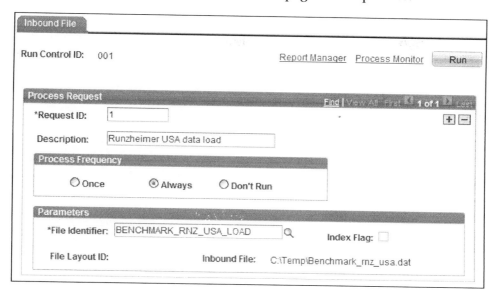

In the previous example, we are importing the Runzheimer data for USA, using the file identifier shown earlier.

File Identifier: Select the previously activated file identifier in this field and click Run to execute the process.

This process loads the expense location amount page that we saw in the configurations section with the appropriate source name in the Data Source column.

Creating cash advances

PeopleSoft Expenses offers a capability where an employee can create a cash advance request, which can be routed through various levels of hierarchy before it is approved. Depending on an organization's policy, an approved cash advance may or may not result in a system-generated payment. Irrespective of payment creation, a cash advance must be created and approved to maintain an audit trail.

Follow this navigation to enter a cash advance request:

Travel and Expenses | Travel and Expense Center | Cash Advance | Create

The following screenshot shows a sample cash advance:

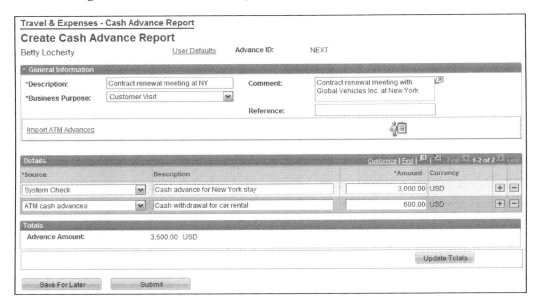

- **Business Purpose**: This is a mandatory field where we can select a business purpose (defined on a configuration page) for the cash advance.
- **Details section**: This area is used to enter individual cash advance lines. Select an appropriate cash advance source in the Source column along with its description and advance amount.
- **Import ATM Advances**: This hyperlink is used to automatically populate the ATM advance amounts withdrawn using the employee's corporate card. When this hyperlink is clicked, the system opens a new page which shows the employee's ATM transactions. Note that the integration between PeopleSoft and the credit card vendor needs to be enabled first to be able to use this feature.

Click the Submit button to submit it for approval or the Save For Later button to save it for later modifications.

Once it is submitted for approval, the system shows a confirmation message as shown in the following screenshot:

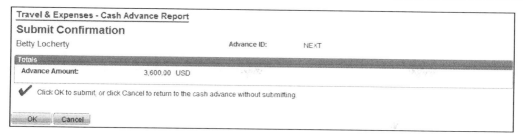

Once a cash advance is successfully submitted, the system generates a cash advance ID.

Reconciling cash advances

As we briefly discussed earlier, a cash advance can be applied to an employee's expense reports. Let's assume that an employee gets a cash advance of $2,000 for a business travel. During the business trip, the employee incurs expenses totalling $1,800. When he/she returns from the trip and submits an expense report, a link on the expense report page allows the employee to associate the cash advance with the expense report. In this case, as the employee spent only a part of the advance amount, he/she needs to return the remaining amount to the organization. On the other hand, if the expense report amount exceeds the cash advance, the employee needs to be paid the excess amount.

The cash advance reconciliation page is used to view the expense reports associated with an advance and record any payments from employee for the unused advance amount.

Follow this navigation to perform cash advance reconciliation:

Travel and Expenses | Manage Accounting | Reconcile Cash Advance

Cash advance actions

The following actions can be taken on a cash advance:

Cash advance deletion

A cash advance can be deleted as long it is not active in the approval process (that is, if it is not submitted for approval or if it has been denied by an approver). Once it is deleted, it is no longer available on any of the cash advance search pages. No accounting entries are created for a deletion.

Follow this navigation to delete a cash advance:

Travel and Expenses | Travel and Expense Center | Cash Advance | Delete

Cash advance closing

Some times, a cash advance may be already approved when we need to cancel it. This is possible using the Cash Advance Close Feature, as long as it is not being processed for payment. Closing can be done after accounting entries are created for the cash advance.

Follow this navigation to mark a cash advance for closing:

Travel and Expenses | Process Expenses | Close Expenses | Mark Cash Advance for Close

After marking a cash advance for close, the Close Liability process needs to be run to create reverse accounting entries.

Processing expense reports

A typical expense report processing cycle consists of the following steps:

1. The employee creates an expense report to record all the expense transactions, such as hotel, taxi, airfare, meals, and so on. If any cash advances were taken, they are associated with the expense report.

2. An expense report is submitted for approval and is routed through as many approval levels as needed. The approval rules can be configured based on an organization's policies. If expense report details are found to be satisfactory, it is approved by one or more relevant approvers.

3. The employee submits the receipts for all valid business expenses.

4. The expense department verifies the receipts and marks the expense report accordingly.

5. The expense reports are posted and accounting entries are created to recognize a liability for future payment due to the employee.

6. Once all the approvals are in place and receipts are verified, the expense report is staged for payment. The payment can be made through the Accounts Payable pay cycle or Payroll module.

7. Once the expense report is paid, payments are posted and accounting entries are created to record the payment and eliminate the earlier liability.

Note that this is a generic process flow and a particular organization may use a process with different steps. Now let's briefly discuss these processing steps.

Creating an expense report

It is important to create an expense report whether an employee needs to be paid by the organization or not. It is an important method by which employee expenses can be closely tracked to see whether they are following the organization's policies. Any deviations from the policy, such as use of a non-preferred merchant or claims that exceed prescribed expense limits, are automatically flagged by the system.

Follow this navigation to create an expense report:

Travel and Expenses | Travel and Expense Center | Expense Reports | Create

The following screenshot shows a sample expense report:

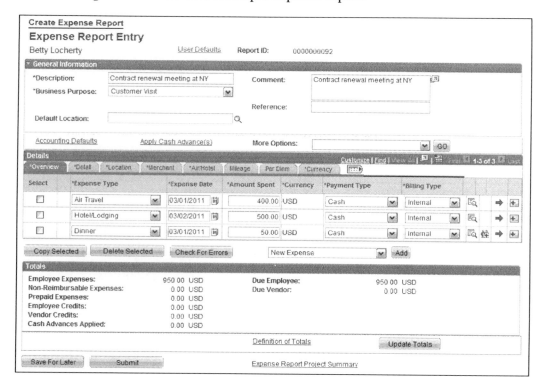

The Details section is used to record various expense transactions. For each of the expense lines in the report, additional details are recorded in subsequent tabs such as Detail, Location, and so on.

The Total section shows the summary of expense report.

Depending on the expense type of a line, the details that we need to provide will differ. For example, while location is a mandatory element for Hotel and Dinner expense types, it is not relevant for Air Travel. We will not discuss all the tabs here.

Click the Save For Later button if you wish to continue making changes to the report later before submitting it for approval. Click the Submit button to submit the report for approval workflow.

Verifying receipts

Organizations mandate that all expense reports be backed up by relevant receipts for each expense. The expense department verifies the receipts submitted by employees and marks the report accordingly.

Follow this navigation to verify receipts for an expense report:

Travel and Expenses | Process Expenses | Verify Receipts | Receipts Received

In our sample expense report, we can expect the employee to submit a total of three receipts for air travel, hotel bill, and dinner bill. The following screenshot shows how they can be verified:

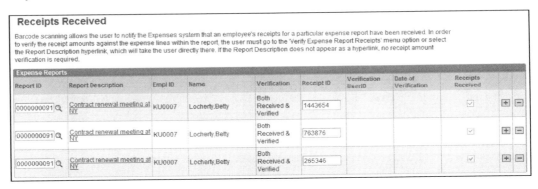

Enter the report ID and receipt ID in appropriate columns.

Running the expense processes

The PeopleSoft Expenses module offers a common page to execute all batch processes.

Follow this navigation to access the Expense Processes page:

Travel and Expenses | Process Expenses | Expense Processing

The following screenshot shows the run control page for the process:

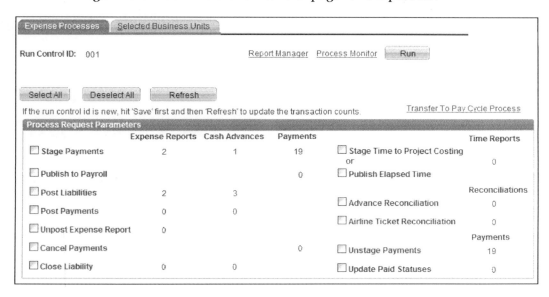

As you can see, this page displays all of the batch processes in Expenses module. The page also shows the number of transactions (such as expense reports, cash advances, and payments) that will be processed by a batch process.

- Publish to Payroll: This option creates an integration message to publish the expense data to PeopleSoft Payroll module.

- Post Liabilities: This option creates liability accounting entries for expense reports and cash advances. These accounting entries are stored in the EX_ACCTG_LINE table from where they can be picked up by the Journal Generator process to create journals.

- Unpost Expense Report: This option creates reverse accounting entries to nullify the original liability entries of an already posted expense report.

[A posted expense report must be first marked for unposting before it can be processed by this option.]

- **Close Liability:** We already discussed how to mark a cash advance for closing. This option creates reversal accounting entries to nullify the liability entries for selected expense reports and cash advances.

- **Stage Payments:** This option loads the data for approved expense reports and cash advances to the staging table to be picked up by the AP pay cycle or Payroll module.

- **Unstage Payments:** After a payment has been staged, if we wish to prevent it from being processed by AP or Payroll, this option can be used. It removes the payment data from the staging area.

- **Cancel Payment:** If a payment was created in AP and was subsequently canceled, this option creates reversal accounting entries for the payment. This option keeps the data in sync between AP and Expenses.

- **Post Payments:** This option creates accounting entries for payments made in AP or Payroll for expense reports or cash advances. These accounting entries are also stored in the EX_ACCTG_LINE table.

- **Update Paid Statuses:** After an expense report or cash advance gets paid, this process option changes their status to Paid.

- **Advance Reconciliation:** We discussed how cash advances are reconciled. Once an advance is reconciled, this process updates the expense report data with the respective cash advance details.

- **Stage Time to Project Costing:** The Expenses module offers a feature by which we can record timesheets for employees (we have not included this feature in our discussion). This option moves the timesheet data to a staging table from where it can be picked up by the Project Costing module.

- **Publish Elapsed Time:** This option creates a message to publish the timesheet data to the Time and Labor module.

Select one or more business units for which the expense transactions need to be processed on the Selected Business Units tab. Click the checkbox next to the desired process and click the Run button to initiate it.

 [PeopleSoft recommends that some processes should not be executed together. Please refer to the PeopleSoft documentation to know the invalid combinations.]

Payment processing

As mentioned in previous sections, payments for the approved expense reports and cash advances are handled outside the Expenses module, through the PeopleSoft Accounts Payable or the PeopleSoft Payroll (part of the Human Resource Management System) module.

If an organization wishes to use the Accounts Payable module, it is important to establish the employees as vendors in the PeopleSoft system. Once the expense reports and cash advances data are staged to the Accounts Payable module, we can use the Pay Cycle process to create payments for them. Note that we must use the values EXAD (Employee cash advances) or EXPN (Employee expense reports) for such Pay Cycle. Recall our discussion from the *Specifying payment selection criteria – Source / BU tab* section in *Chapter 6, PeopleSoft Accounts Payable Module*. These payments are then issued to the employees using the selected payment method.

On the other hand, if the approved expense reports and cash advances data are staged to the PeopleSoft Payroll module, the employee's payroll amount is adjusted accordingly.

Summary

PeopleSoft Expenses is an important module used to automate various employee transactions such as requesting and issuing cash advances, recording and processing expense reports for business purposes, recording time sheets, and reserving and booking travel requests.

We can design a wide range of approval rules using the **Approval Workflow Engine (AWE)**. PeopleSoft offers various pre-configured options which can be modified or new configurations can be created as needed. Based on an organization's requirements, we can configure which expense transactions need to be passed through an approval hierarchy, define various approval roles, specify chartfields for routing, and set up approval amount thresholds, among other things.

PeopleSoft Expenses is capable of integrating with external entities to import credit card transactions for employee expenses and benchmark data to establish expense reimbursement guidelines.

Cash advances can be requested by employees and, if necessary, payments issued for them. The Expense report is a flexible tool used to record employees' business expenses. We can apply cash advances to expense reports to prevent duplicate payments being issued to employees. Once approved, cash advances and expense reports details can be staged so that they can be paid through a PeopleSoft Accounts Payable pay cycle or PeopleSoft Payroll module.

9
PeopleSoft Commitment Control

Commitment Control is an optional feature of PeopleSoft used for enforcing budget control over an organization's spending. It enables an organization to perform what is known as "encumbrance accounting", or commitment accounting. Using this feature, organizations can define budgets for various categories of their spending and track each spending transaction against available budget amounts. Although commitment control configurations are part of the General Ledger module, it spans many more modules such as Purchasing, Accounts Payable, Expenses, Billing, Accounts Receivable, and so on, which are responsible for creating transactions for spending as well as generating revenue.

In this chapter, we'll cover the following important topics:

- Understanding commitment control
- Commitment control configurations
- Entering and processing budgets
- Handling commitment control exceptions

Understanding commitment control

Before we proceed further, let's take some time to understand the basic concepts of commitment control.

Commitment control can be used to track expenses against pre-defined control budgets as well as to track recognized revenue against revenue estimate budgets. In this chapter, we'll concentrate more on the expense side of commitment control, as it is more widely used.

Defining control budgets

An organization may draw budgets for different countries in which it operates or for its various departments. Going further, it may then define budget amounts for different areas of spending, such as IT hardware, construction of buildings, and so on. Finally, it will also need to specify the time periods for which the budget applies, such as a month, a quarter, six months, or a year.

In other words, a budget needs the following components:

- **Account,** to specify expense areas such as hardware expenses, construction expense, and so on
- **One or more chartfields** to specify the level of budget such as Operating unit, Department, Product, and so on
- **Time period** to specify if the budgeted amount applies to a month quarter or year, and so on

Let's take a simple example to understand how control budgets are defined. An organization defines budgets for each of its departments. Budgets are defined for different expense categories, such as the purchase of computers and purchase of office supplies such as notepads, pens, and so on. It sets up budgets for each month of the year.

Assume that following chartfield values are used by the organization:

Department	Description	Account	Description
700	Sales	135000	Hardware expenses
900	Manufacturing	335000	Stationery expenses

Now, the budgets are defined for each period and a combination of chartfields as follows:

Period	Department	Account	Budget amount
January 2012	700	135000	$100,000
January 2012	700	335000	$10,000
January 2012	900	135000	$120,000
January 2012	900	335000	$15,000
February 2012	700	135000	$200,000
February 2012	700	335000	$40,000
February 2012	900	135000	$150,000
February 2012	900	335000	$30,000

Thus, $100,000 has been allocated for hardware purchases for the Sales department for January 2012. Purchases will be allowed until this budget is exhausted. If a purchase exceeds the available amount, it will be prevented from taking place.

Tracking expense transactions

Commitment control spending transactions are classified into **Pre-encumbrance**, **Encumbrance,** and **Expenditure** categories. To understand this, we'll consider a simple procurement example. This involves the PeopleSoft Purchasing and Accounts Payable modules. In an organization, a department manager may decide that he/she needs three new computers for the newly recruited staff. A purchase requisition may be created by the manager to request purchase of these computers. Once it is approved by the appropriate authority, it is passed on to the procurement group. This group may refer to the procurement policies, inquire with various vendors about prices, and decide to buy these computers from a particular vendor. The procurement group then creates a purchase order containing the quantity, configuration, price, and so on and sends it to the vendor. Once the vendor delivers the computers, the organization receives the invoice and creates a voucher to process the vendor payment. As discussed in an earlier chapter, voucher creation takes place in the Accounts Payable module, while creation of requisition and purchase order takes place in the Purchasing module.

In commitment control terms, **Pre-encumbrance** is the amount that may be spent in future, but there is no obligation to spend it. In the previous example, the requisition constitutes the pre-encumbrance amount. Note that the requisition is an internal document which may or may not get approved, thus there is no obligation to spend the money to purchase computers.

Encumbrance is the amount for which there is a legal obligation to spend in future. In the previous example, the purchase order sent to the vendor constitutes the encumbrance amount, as we have asked the vendor to deliver the goods.

Finally, when a voucher is created, it indicates the **Expenditure** amount that is actually being spent. A voucher indicates that we have already received the goods and, in accounting terms, the expense has been recognized.

To understand how PeopleSoft handles this, think of four different buckets: Budget amount, Pre-encumbrance amount, Encumbrance amount, and Expenditure amount.

Step 1

Budget definition is the first step in commitment control. Let's say that an organization has budgeted $50,000 for purchase of IT hardware at the beginning of the year 2011. At that time, these buckets will show the amounts as follows:

Budget	Pre-encumbrance	Encumbrance	Expenditure	Available budget amount
$50,000	0	0	0	$50,000

Available budget amount is calculated using the following formula:

Available budget amount = Budget amount – (Pre-encumbrance + Encumbrance + Expenditure)

Step 2

Now when the requisition for three computers (costing a total of $3,000) is created, it is checked against the available budget. It will be approved, as the entire $50,000 budget amount is available. After getting approved, the requisition amount of $3,000 is recorded as pre-encumbrance and the available budget is accordingly reduced. Thus, the budget amounts are updated as shown next:

Budget	Pre-encumbrance	Encumbrance	Expenditure	Available budget amount
$50,000	$3,000	0	0	$47,000

Step 3

A purchase order can be created only after a requisition is successfully budget checked. When the purchase order i created (again for $3,000), it is once again checked against the available budget and will pass due to sufficient available budget. Thus, once approved, the purchase order amount of $3,000 is recorded as encumbrance, while the pre-encumbrance is eliminated. In other words, the pre-encumbrance amount is converted into an encumbrance amount, as now there is a legal obligation to spend it. A purchase order can be sent to the vendor only after it is successfully budget checked. Now, the amounts are updated as shown next:

Budget	Pre-encumbrance	Encumbrance	Expenditure	Available budget amount
$50,000	0	$3,000	0	$47,000

Step 4

When the voucher gets created (for $3,000), it is once again checked against the available budget and will pass, as the available budget is sufficient. Once approved, the voucher amount of $3,000 is recorded as expenditure, while the encumbrance is eliminated. In other words, the encumbrance amount is converted into actual expenditure amount. Now, the amounts are updated as shown next:

Budget	Pre-encumbrance	Encumbrance	Expenditure	Available budget amount
$50,000	0	0	$3,000	$47,000

The process of eliminating the previous encumbrance or pre-encumbrance amount is known as **liquidation**. Thus, whenever a document (purchase order or voucher) is budget checked, the amount for the previous document is liquidated.

Thus, a transaction will move successively through these three stages with the system checking if available budget is sufficient to process it. Whenever the transaction encounters insufficient budget, it is flagged as an exception.

So, now the obvious question is how do we implement this in PeopleSoft? To put it simply, we need the following building blocks at the minimum:

- Ledgers to record budget, pre-encumbrance, encumbrance, and expenditure amounts
- Batch processes to budget check various transactions

Of course, there are other configurations involved as well. We'll discuss them in the upcoming section.

Commitment control configurations

In this section, we'll go through the following important configurations needed to use the commitment control feature:

- Enabling commitment control
- Setting up the system-level commitment control options
- Defining the commitment control ledgers and ledger groups
- Defining the budget period calendar
- Configuring the control budget definition

- Linking the commitment control ledger group with the actual transaction ledger group
- Defining commitment control transactions

Enabling commitment control

Before using the commitment control feature for a PeopleSoft module, it needs to be enabled on the **Installation Options** page.

Follow this navigation to enable or disable commitment control for an individual module:

Setup Financials / Supply Chain | Install | Installation Options | Products

The following screenshot shows the **Installation Options – Products** page:

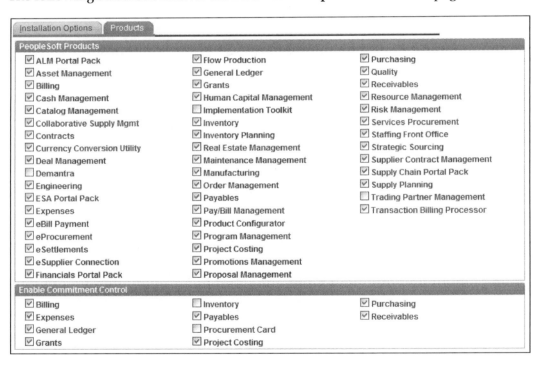

This page allows a system administrator to activate any installed PeopleSoft modules as well as to enable commitment control feature for a PeopleSoft module.

The **PeopleSoft Products** section lists all PeopleSoft modules. Select the checkbox next to a module that is implemented by the organization.

The **Enable Commitment Control** section shows the PeopleSoft modules for which commitment control can be enabled. Select the checkbox next to a module to activate commitment control and validate transactions in it against defined budgets.

Setting up system-level commitment control options

After enabling commitment control for desired modules, we need to set up some processing options at the system level.

Follow this navigation to set up these system level options:

Setup Financials / Supply Chain | Install | Installation Options | Commitment Control

The following screenshot shows the **Installation Options – Commitment Control** page:

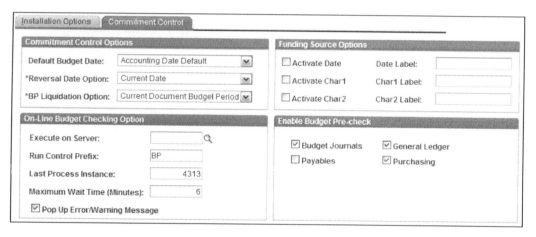

- **Default Budget Date**: This field specifies the default budget date that is populated on the requisitions, purchase orders and vouchers. The available options are **Accounting Date Default** (to use the document accounting date as the budget date) and **Predecessor Doc Date Default** (to use the budget date from the predecessor document). For example, the purchase order inherits requisition's budget date, and the voucher inherits the purchase order's budget date.

- **Reversal Date Option**: There are situations when changes are made to an already budget-checked transaction. Whenever this happens, the document needs to be budget checked again. This field determines how the changed transactions are posted. Consider a case where a requisition for $1,000 is created and successfully budget checked in January. In February, the requisition has to be increased to $1,200. It will need to be budget checked again. The available options are **Prior Date** (this option completely reverses pre-encumbrance entries for January for $1,000 and creates new entries for $1,200 in February) and **Current Date** (this option creates additional entries for $200 for February, while leaving $1,000 entries for January unchanged).

- **BP Liquidation Option**: We already saw that system liquidates the pre-encumbrance and encumbrance amounts while budget checking purchase orders and vouchers. This field determines the period when the previous amount is liquidated, if the transactions occur in different periods. The available options are **Current Document Budget period** (liquidate the amounts in the current period) and **Prior Document Budget period** (liquidate the amounts in the period when the source document was created).

- **Enable Budget Pre-Check**: This is a useful option to test the expense transactions without actually committing the amounts (pre-encumbrance, encumbrance, and expenditure) in respective ledgers. We may budget check a transaction and find that it fails the validation. Rather than budget checking and then handling the exception, it is much more efficient to simply do a budget pre-check. The system shows all the potential error messages which can help us in correcting the transaction data appropriately. Select the checkbox next to a module to enable this feature.

Defining commitment control ledgers and ledger groups

We have already discussed concepts of configuring the ledger templates, ledger groups, and ledgers in *Chapter 1*, *PeopleSoft Financials Fundamentals*. These ledgers are used to record actual accounting transactions. We also need additional ledgers to record commitment control transactions similar to the illustrative example we saw previously.

We briefly mentioned that dedicated ledgers are needed to record amounts from each bucket (that is, Budget, Pre-encumbrance, Encumbrance, and Expenditure). Thus, in order to use commitment control, we need at least one ledger group containing four commitment control ledgers. A sample ledger group may be configured as shown next:

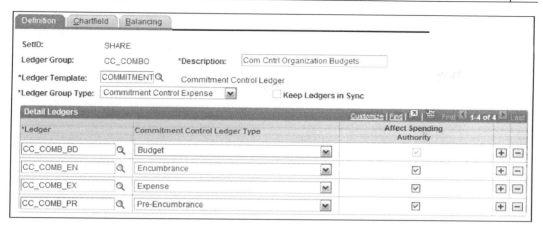

As you can see, the CC_COMB_BD ledger will store the budget amounts, the CC_COMB_PR ledger will store any pre-encumbrance amounts, and the CC_COMB_EN ledger will record encumbrance amounts, while the CC_COMB_EX ledger stores the expenditure amounts.

Select the ledger value and its purpose in the **Ledger** and **Commitment Control Ledger Type** fields respectively.

We have already discussed the configuration options on the Chartfield and Balancing tabs in Chapter 1, so we'll not go through them again.

> Ensure that the commitment control ledger group contains four ledgers with the types as shown. The Ledger Group Type field value must be **Commitment Control Expense** or **Commitment Control Revenue** as the need may be. The Ledger template used must be the one specifically used for commitment control.

Defining commitment control budget calendars

Note that calendars are created irrespective of whether an organization uses commitment control or not. They are mandatory for any PeopleSoft financial system. However, PeopleSoft uses different pages to build budget calendars. Depending on how an organization creates its budgets (monthly, bi-monthly, quarterly, and so on, we need to create appropriate budget calendars. There are various ways in which an organization may define its budgets.

For example, an organization may define its budget of $1,000,000 for IT hardware procurement for an entire year with no restriction on when this amount should be spent. Or it may decide to budget $250,000 for each quarter of the year. Thus, in the first case, it may spend up to $1,000,000 in the first month of the year itself. On the other hand, in the second case, it can spend only up to $250,000 in the three months of a quarter.

Follow these navigations to create new budget calendars:

Set Up Financials/Supply Chain | Common Definitions | Calendars/Schedules | Budget Period Calendar

Set Up Financials/Supply Chain | Common Definitions | Calendars/Schedules | Budget Period Calendar Builder

Set Up Financials/Supply Chain | Common Definitions | Calendars/Schedules | Summary BP Calendar

The following screenshot shows a sample quarterly budget calendar:

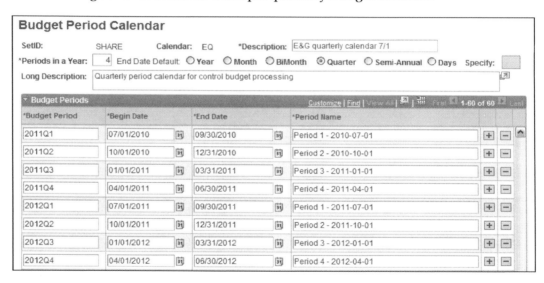

As you can see, we can specify the number of periods in a year, type of calendar (Month, Bimonth, Quarter, and so on, and **Begin Date** and **End Date** for each budget period. You can probably appreciate the fact that there will be 12 budget periods in a year if monthly budgets are defined, four budget periods in a year if quarterly budgets are defined, and so on.

Configuring tree definitions

Usually when budgets are set up, they are set up at a higher (summarized) level. For example, when an organization decides to set up budgets on the basis of departments, it may not establish budgets for each department. Instead, it may set them up for a group of departments. This will need a hierarchical structure of a desired chartfield known as **Tree**.

Note that Department is just an example how budgets are defined. An organization may decide to use any other chartfield or a combination of chartfields to define its budgets.

Follow this navigation to create a tree:

Tree Manager | Tree Manager

The following screenshot shows a sample tree created for grouping Department chartfield values:

As you can see, the tree has four levels of Department values. Thus, we can specify budgets for the Administration, School of Medicine, Sales Admin, and Manufacturing Support groups of departments. This approach greatly reduces the manual configuration effort by summarizing the budget amounts at a higher level.

When we budget check a transaction for department 15000, the system refers to this tree definition and checks the available budget for its rolled-up value (that is, Department group 14000) to decide if the transaction should go through or fail.

The creation and maintenance of trees is an exhaustive topic and will not be discussed due to page constraints of this book.

Configuring control budget definitions

This is one of the most crucial configurations for commitment control which sets up various processing options for a commitment control ledger group. Before discussing this configuration, we'll take some time to understand a few concepts.

- **Ruleset**: Budget definitions usually have multiple processing rules for different scenarios. For example, in our sample budget determined by Department value, we may have different processing rules for different groups of departments. For example, budgets for Sales and Manufacturing departments should be tracked by an additional parameter (Product) which may not be needed for other groups. Thus, any transaction with Sales and Manufacturing departments must have the Product chartfield value as well, while it is optional for other departments. These subsets of processing rules are known as **Rulesets**. The chartfield whose value determines which processing options, or, in other words, which ruleset, should be used is known as **Ruleset Chartfield**. In this example, Department will be the Ruleset chartfield.

- **Controlling options**: PeopleSoft offers the following options to decide how the expense transactions should be processed by the budget processor:

    ○ **Control**: This option validates each transaction amount (such as requisitions, purchase orders, vouchers, and so on) against budgeted amounts. If transaction amount exceeds the budgeted amount, it is flagged as an exception.

    ○ **Control Initial Document**: This option validates only the initial document against budgeted amounts. If the amount of the initial document exceeds the budgeted amount, error messages are issued. If an initial document successfully passes the budget check, all subsequent documents automatically pass the budget check. Thus, if a requisition passes budget check, the resulting purchase order and voucher will pass the budget check even if sufficient budget is not available at that time.

- ° **Track with Budget**: This option keeps track of all expense transactions; however, it does not issue any error messages like the previous option. All transactions for which a budget exists (even for a zero amount) are passed. If the transaction amounts exceed the budgeted amount, only warnings are issued but the transaction can proceed. Note that the presence of a budget is necessary.

- ° **Track without Budget**: This option tracks transactions even if no budget exists. If a budget exists and the transaction amount exceeds the budgeted amount, warnings are issued. If no budget exists, no warning is issued.

If necessary, we can specify that all transactions for some specific departments (or any other chartfield) should have an option of 'Control', while transactions from other departments should have an option of 'Control Initial Document'. A chartfield whose values control how the transactions are processed is known as a **Controlling Chartfield**.

Follow this navigation to create or modify a control budget definition:

Commitment Control | Define Control Budgets | Budget Definitions | Control Budget Options

The following screenshot shows a sample budget definition:

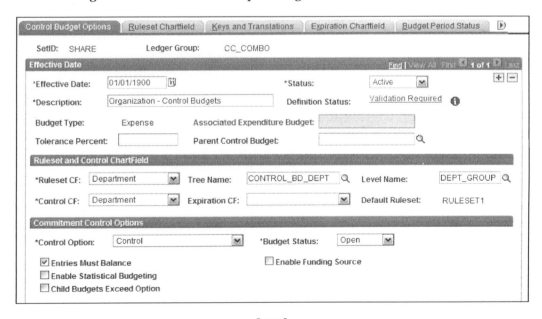

As mentioned previously, we are essentially setting up the processing options for the CC_COMBO commitment control ledger group in this configuration.

- **Budget Type**: The system automatically displays a value Expense or Revenue, depending on the Ledger Group Type selected for this ledger group.

- **Associated Expenditure Budget**: If we are configuring a revenue budget, it can be linked to an expenditure budget in this field.

- **Tolerance Percent**: This field is used to specify a percentage by which transaction amounts can exceed the budget amounts without triggering an error message.

- **Ruleset CF**: This option specifies the ruleset chartfield as discussed earlier. The value of this chartfield will determine which processing rules are to be used.

- **Tree Name, Level Name**: This specifies the hierarchy tree details for the ruleset chartfield that we discussed previously.

- **Control CF**: This specifies the control chartfield as discussed earlier. The value of this chartfield will determine how transactions with specified chartfield values will be processed.

- **Commitment Control Options - Control Option**: This specifies the processing option for this budget ledger. The available options are the same as we discussed previously: **Control, Control Initial Document, Track with Budget, and Track without Budget**.

The following screenshot shows the **Ruleset Chartfield** tab:

This tab is used to define one or more processing rules (rulesets) for different ranges of values of the Ruleset Chartfield. As we specified **Department** as the ruleset chartfield in the previous tab, we can specify various ranges of Department values to define different processing options for them. As you can see, we have defined two rulesets based on department values. Note that only one ruleset can be designated as the default.

In the next tabs, we'll define options to decide how we can process transactions differently for these two groups.

The following screenshot shows the **Keys and Translations** tab:

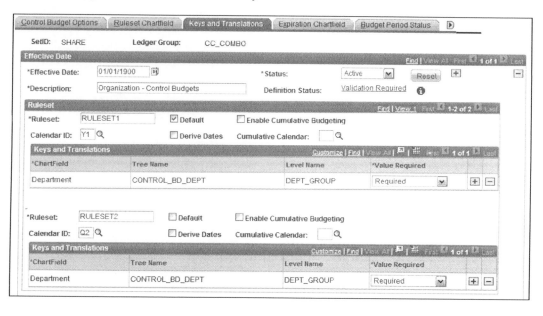

This is the tab where we can specify various processing options for the different rulesets. As you can see, the page shows two different sets of options for RULESET1 and RULESET2 that we defined on previous tab. Note that all of the options discussed next can be set up differently for different rulesets.

- **Enable Cumulative Budgeting**: Let's say we use a budget calendar with 12 periods, one corresponding to each month. Thus we define budget amounts for each period. Normally a transaction will be checked against budget amount defined for the month in which it was created. However, PeopleSoft offers an option to use cumulative periods using cumulative calendars to determine budget amounts. Thus, if each month's budget amount is $1,000, and we enable cumulative budgeting with a quarterly calendar, transactions will be checked against the cumulative budget of $3,000 (for three months). As a result, irrespective of the monthly budget amount, a transaction is validated against the available budget for a quarter and not an individual month. This is known as cumulative budgeting. Select this checkbox to use this feature.

- **Cumulative Calendar**: Specify a cumulative calendar if cumulative budgeting is used. This is a calendar with period larger than the regular calendar. For example, if regular budget calendar is monthly, we can use quarterly, semi-annual, or any other calendar with period larger than a month.

- **Calendar ID**: Specify the regular budget period calendar that we discussed earlier.

- **Keys and Translation**: This section lists the chartfield keys that are needed to track budget amounts. Thus, if we need to track **Sales** and **Manufacturing** department transactions by product, add the **Product** chartfield as the additional key to the appropriate ruleset. If a budget is defined at a higher level for a chartfield, specify the details in **Tree Name** and **Level Name** fields.

The following screenshot shows a part of the **Control Chartfield** tab:

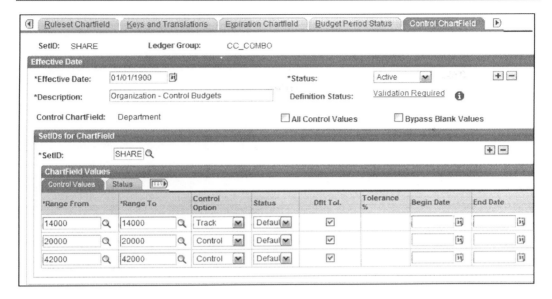

Earlier, we discussed how budget control options work. In the first tab, Department was specified as the control chartfield. Thus, this tab allows various ranges of Department values to be defined and corresponding control options specified. As shown in the given screenshot, we can specify different control options for different ranges of the Department value.

We'll not discuss the remaining tabs (Offsets and Excluded Account Types) in detail but quickly get an overview of their purpose.

The **Offsets** tab is used to specify the offset accounts for budget entry. Budget amount entry is done through online budget journals, which we'll see in a short while. This tab also records the offset account to be used for each source transaction that is budget checked.

The **Excluded Account Types** tab is used to specify which account types or specific account values should be excluded from budget check. Recall that PeopleSoft delivers the account types Assets, Liabilities, Equity, Revenue, and Expense. If we are using commitment control for tracking expense transactions, we can specify Assets, Liabilities, Equity, and Revenue account types for exclusion. If required, we can also specify individual account values that need to be excluded from budget checking.

Linking the commitment control ledger group with actual ledger group

So far, we have discussed various configuration options to ensure that all things are in place to record the budget amounts and track expense transactions against them. You may recall from Chapter 1 that we define various ledger groups for a business unit to track the actual accounting transactions. Now we need to establish a link between the ledger group that records the actual transactions and the ledger group that is used to track commitment control balances (budget, pre-encumbrance, encumbrance, and expenditure).

This is done on the 'Ledgers For A Unit' page.

Follow this navigation to access the page:

Setup Financials / Supply Chain | Business Unit Related | General Ledger | Ledgers For A Unit

This page shows all the ledger groups used by a business unit. Open the **Commitment Control Options** tab.

The following screenshot shows a ledger group **RECORDING** used to record actual accounting transactions:

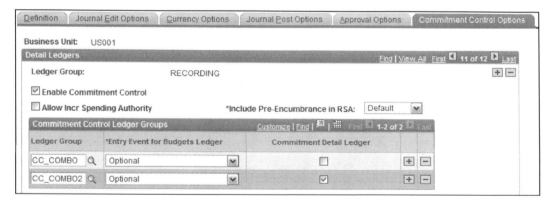

- **Enable Commitment Control**: Select this checkbox to indicate that the actual transactions recorded in this ledger group need to be tracked against defined budgets.

- **Ledger Group**: Select a commitment control ledger group against which the transactions need to be checked. Note that we can select multiple commitment control ledger groups here. This is relevant when an organization is using expense as well as revenue budgets or if budgets are defined for different levels.

- **Commitment Detail Ledger**: We saw earlier that budgets are usually set up at a higher (summarized) level by default. Therefore, when the budget processor validates the transactions, pre-encumbrance and encumbrance entries are recorded at the summarized level. If we wish to record these entries at a detailed level with actual chartfield values, we need to use a separate commitment control ledger group. Select this checkbox to indicate that a ledger group will track detail commitment control activities. In the given screenshot, the CC_COMBO ledger group tracks pre-encumbrance and encumbrance balances at a summarized level, while the CC_COMBO2 ledger group tracks them at a detailed level.

Let's consider our earlier example of Department tree to understand this. We mentioned that departmental budgets will be set up at the higher level, that is, for the following department values:

Department	Budget amount
90200 (School of medicine)	$1,000,000
14000 (Administration)	$1,500,000
20000 (Sales)	$2,000,000
42000 (Manufacturing)	$2,500,000

In the department tree, department 14000 contains various detail (child) department values such as 15000 (Business Services), 10500 (Benefits), and so on.

Now, when a requisition for department 15000 is created and budget checked, the pre-encumbrance ledger will record a balance for department 14000 (summarized or parent value) and not the department 15000 (detail or 'real' department value). When the purchase order is created from this requisition, again the encumbrance ledger will record the balance for department 14000 (summarized value). We can use a different ledger group to track detail department values by selecting its Commitment Detail Ledger flag. The Pre-Encumbrance and Encumbrance ledgers in this group will record balances for department 15000 for which the actual transactions are created.

Using commitment detail ledgers is optional. Organizations may decide to use it for better reporting. If tracking pre-encumbrance and encumbrance balances at a summarized level is sufficient, this feature is not required. Whether we use commitment detail ledgers or not, actual transactions are still recorded at detail level in the actual ledgers.

Defining commitment control transactions

During our discussion so far, we have already seen that a requisition, purchase order, or voucher are examples of commitment control transactions that get validated against budgets. PeopleSoft delivers a group of transactions which are recognized by the budget processor.

Follow this navigation to view/ modify the source transactions:

Commitment Control | Define Control Budgets | Source Transactions

The following screenshot shows a sample delivered transaction – Purchase order:

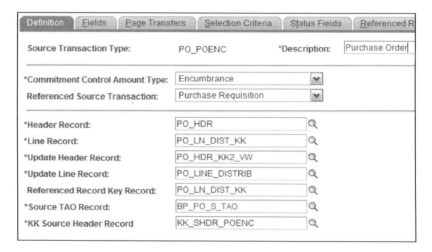

The following table lists various commitment control transactions delivered by PeopleSoft:

Source transaction name	Description
AP_ACCT_LN	**Voucher (gain, loss, close)**
AP_ACCTDSE	**Voucher (discount earned)**
AP_VCHR_NP	**Voucher (non-prorated item)**
AP_VOUCHER	**Voucher**
AR_MISCPAY	**Direct Journal Payments**
AR_REVEST	**Receivables**
BI_INVOICE	**Billing Invoice**
CM_TRNXTN	**Cost Management Transaction**
EX_EXCLOSE	**Close Expense Reports**

Source transaction name	Description
EX_EXSHEET	Expense Sheet
EX_TRVAUTH	Travel Authorization
GENERIC	Generic Transaction
GL_BD_JRNL	General Ledger Budget Entry
GL_JOURNAL	General Ledger Journal
GM_FA	Facilities and Administration
GM_FA_UPG	Facilities and Administration (for Upgrade Budget Processor only)
HR_PAYROLL	Payroll Transaction
PC_BUDGET	Project Budget
PC_JOURNAL	Project Journal
PO_POENC	Purchase Order
PO_POENCNP	PO (non-prorated item)
PO_PROCARD	Procurement Card
PO_RAENC	Receipt Accruals – Encumbrance
PO_RAEXP	Receipt Accruals – Expense
REQ_PRECNP	Purchase Requisition - Non-prorated
REQ_PREENC	Purchase Requisition

 It is very rare that we would need to change the delivered definitions of commitment control transactions. For most of the requirements, the source transactions can be used as delivered.

Entering and processing budgets

Now that we have familiarized ourselves with the necessary configurations to use commitment control, we'll now move on to the next stage. In this section, we'll discuss how we can create, transfer, and process budgets.

Entering budget journals

We already saw that the budget ledger in the commitment control ledger group stores the budget amounts. These budget amounts are entered using budget journals. In *Chapter 7, PeopleSoft General Ledger Module*, we saw how to create journals and post them to the ledger. The process to enter and post budget journals to commitment control ledgers is more or less similar.

Follow this navigation to enter a budget journal:

Commitment Control | Budget Journals | Enter Budget Journals | Budget Header

The following screenshot shows the **Budget Header** tab of the budget journal:

- **Ledger Group**: Select the commitment control ledger group that should record the budget amounts. Recall that we specified the CC_COMBO ledger group to business unit US001. When this journal is posted, the budget amount is posted to the ledger designated as 'Budget' in the CC_COMBO ledger group.

- **Budget Entry Type**: This field has two possible options: **Original,** if this is a new budget entry, and **Adjustment,** if this is an adjustment to an existing budget.

Note that the journal ID shows as **NEXT**. When journal is saved, the system automatically generates a journal ID.

The following screenshot shows the **Budget Lines** tab of the budget journal:

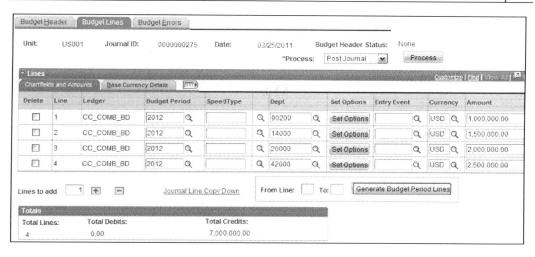

This is the tab where we enter the planned budget amounts. Note that the options we specified for the control budget definition (such as chartfields, calendar, and so on) determine the options on this page. In this example, we have specified the budget amounts for the groups of departments as shown in the table on page 18 for the year 2012. The reason we see only one budget row for 2012 is that the calendar we selected for the CC_COMBO budget has only a single period (corresponding to the whole year). If we had wanted to specify monthly budgets, we could have used an appropriate calendar on budget definition and entered monthly budget amounts for each department on this page.

Budget Header Status: This field shows the status of the budget journal. The following table shows various status values that a budget journal can have:

Status	Description
N	None: The journal has been created and no processing has taken place
S	Security Error: The journal has encountered an error due to violation of security rules
B	Balancing Error: The journal has encountered an error as it is not balanced
E	Error: The chartfield combination is invalid
P	Posted: The journal has been successfully posted
U	Unposted: The journal has been posted and then subsequently unposted

- **Totals**: The section at the bottom of the page shows the summary of the budget journal. Currently it has a credit total of $7,000,000. The balancing debit line for this journal will be created using the offset account for the budget entry that we specify on the Offsets tab of control budget definition.

- **From Line, To, Generate Budget Period Lines**: If we use cumulative budgeting, we can use the fields and button to automatically generate budget lines for each budget period in the cumulative date range.

- **Process**: This field in the top right corner of the page is used to specify the processing options for this budget journal. The available options are **Delete Journal**, **Copy Journal**, **Refresh Journal**, **Edit Chartfields** (which checks if the chartfield combinations on this journal are valid), **Budget Pre-Check** (which performs the budget checking without posting the amounts to the ledger), and **Post Journals** (which edits the journal and, if valid, posts to the ledgers in the specified ledger group). Select the appropriate option and click the **Process** button to take that action.

- **Budget Errors**: This tab displays any error messages related to security, balancing, and so on for this journal.

Transferring budgets

Organizations may face situations where amounts need to be transferred from one budget to another. Consider a scenario where a reorganization results in the merging of two departments to create a new department. In this case, as the old departments don't exist any more, their available budget amounts must be moved to the newly-formed department.

The PeopleSoft pages used to perform budget transfers are exactly the same as those used for budget entry with very minor differences.

Follow this navigation to enter a budget transfer journal:

Commitment Control | Budget Journals | Enter Budget Transfer

On the **Budget Header** tab, the **Budget Entry Type** field shows the options **Transfer Original** (if this journal is to transfer an original budget amount) and **Transfer Adjustment** (if this journal is a transfer of an adjustment made to an original budget amount).

The remaining pages are similar to what we have discussed previously.

Performing budget checking for transactions

In our illustrative example, we saw that transactions such as purchase requisitions, purchase orders, vouchers, and so on are processed to check if a sufficient budget amount is available. Depending on the result and the processing option specified, the system passes a transaction, flags it with an error, or ignores it by simply generating a warning message.

PeopleSoft offers a batch process called **Commitment Control Budget Processor (FS_BP)** to perform these functions. As we discussed earlier, there are various source transactions from different modules that can be budget checked by the Budget Processor.

Each module enabled for commitment control provides the ability to budget check its transactions. For example, the Expenses module gives an option to budget check expense reports, while the Accounts Payable module offers an option to budget check vouchers.

The budget processor also liquidates any previous pre-encumbrance or encumbrance balances for the transaction that it processes and successfully validates.

Handling commitment control exceptions

In this section, we will discuss the common solutions for resolving the transactions that are flagged as exceptions by the Budget Processor.

Typically when a transaction fails budget check, there are two ways to resolve it: adjust (reduce) the transaction amount or adjust (increase) the budget amount.

Option 1: Adjusting the transaction

Scenario	Resolution
There is not a sufficient budget amount available for the transaction.	Reduce the transaction amount sufficiently so that it can pass the budget check.
There is not a sufficient budget amount available for a given combination of chartfields. Assume that budgets are set up for different Department and Product combinations.	Change the chartfields and perform a budget check. For example, we can purchase a computer for a different Department which has a sufficient budget amount.
There is not a sufficient budget amount available for a budget period. Assume that an organization has monthly budgets.	Cancel the transaction, recreate it in the next period and perform a budget check.

Option 2: Adjusting the budget

Scenario	Resolution
There is not sufficient budget amount available for the transaction.	Increase the budget amount sufficiently so that the transaction can pass the budget check.
	Increase the budget tolerance limits so that the transaction can pass the budget check.
Transaction failed because the budget was closed.	Reopen the budget and perform the budget check.

Option 3: Overriding the budget exceptions

This option should be evaluated carefully before giving the users the option to override the budget exceptions. If it is granted, certain authorized users can override the error messages and force a transaction to pass.

Summary

Commitment control is a useful optional feature used by organizations to enforce budget controls. PeopleSoft offers the ability to define budgets and track transactions against these budgets. Budgets can be defined for both expense and revenue amounts. Dedicated commitment control ledgers are used to track the various types of commitment control transactions.

Budget, Pre-encumbrance, Encumbrance, and Expenditure ledgers are required in a commitment control ledger group. Commitment control budget definition determines the processing options for a ledger group. Rulesets specify processing rules for various groups of designated chartfields. A commitment control ledger group is linked to an actual ledger group for a business unit so that an association is made between the actual transactions and their corresponding budgets.

Budget amounts for necessary chartfield combinations are entered using budget journals. These journals are then posted to the appropriate commitment control ledger group. The budget processor batch process is used to validate transactions from various modules against defined budgets.

Based on user preferences, a user can be given the ability to override commitment control exceptions. Otherwise, the system prevents these transactions from proceeding. Organizations can decide whether to use this feature or not. If it is used, it can be enabled for select modules.

Index

fund code chartfield 10
operating unit affiliate chartfield 11
operating unit chartfield 10
PeopleSoft chartfield 14
product chartfield 10
product costing business unit chartfield 10
program code chartfield 10
project id / grant chartfield 10
required chartfield 14
scenario chartfield 11
source type chartfield 10
standard chartfield configuration 12, 15
statistics code chartfield 11
subcategory chartfield 10
chartfield value sets
creating 300, 301
chart of accounts 8
Chart of Accounts (COA) 9
class field chartfield 10
closing 296
closing process
chartfield value set, creating 300, 301
closing process group, configuring 303, 304
closing rules, configuring 301-303
configurations 300
group, configuring 303
running 304, 305
Closing Record Names 26
closing rules
configuring 301, 302
Combo Data 25
commitment control
about 355
budget calendars, defining 363, 365
configurations 359
control budget definitions, configuring 366, 370
control budgets, defining 356, 357
enabling 360, 361
expense transactions, tracking 357-359
ledger group, linking with actual ledger group 372, 373
ledger groups, defining 362, 363
ledgers, defining 362, 363
system level commitment control options, setting up 361, 362

transactions, defining 374, 375
tree definitions, configuring 365, 366
commitment control exceptions, handling
about 379
budget, adjusting 380
budget exceptions, overriding 380
transaction, adjusting 379
control budget definitions, commitment control
calendar ID 370
configuring 366
controlling options 366, 367
cumulative calendar 370
enable cumulative budgeting 370
keys and translation 370
ruleset 366
control budgets
account component 356
one or more chartfields component 356
time period component 356
cost types, asset management module
configuring 208
credit card data
importing 342, 343
current assets 199
customer correspondence, accounts receivable module
about 188
customer statements 188
customer payments, accounts receivable module
electronic payments 173, 174
Excel spreadsheet payments 176-178
express deposits, entering 171, 173
lockbox payments 174-176
payments, entering manually 168
receiving 168
regular deposits, entering 168, 169
regular deposits, reference information section 171
customer statements, customer correspondence
about 188
multi-process job, running 190, 191
statement ID, configuring 188, 189
statement print multi-process job, running 191

D

DD 142
DDS, transaction type 102
deferred revenue processing
  about 115
  account entries 116
  bills entering, process 117
department chartfield 10
depreciation
  depreciation calculation process, running 226
  information for assets, previewing 226-228
  processing 225
depreciation conventions, asset management module
  configuring 210, 211
  convention builder 211, 212
depreciation limits, asset management module
  configuring 213, 214
depreciation schedules, asset management module
  configuring 212, 213
discount user preference 65, 66
distribution codes
  configuring 120, 121
DM 142
DS, transaction type 102
dunning letters, customer correspondence
  about 192
  AR Dunning process, running 196-198
  dunning ID, configuring 193-196
  Dunning letter print process, running 198
  letter codes, configuring 192, 193

E

Electronic Fund Transfer (EFT)
  about 141
employee profiles, cash advance feature
  employee data, loading from PeopleSoft HRMS 320, 321
  employee data, manual update 318, 319
  maintaining 317
encumbrance 357
encumbrance accounting

about 355
  expenditure 357
expense location amounts, expense report feature
  configuring 326
expense processes
  running 351, 352
expense reports
  creating 349
  expense processes, running 351, 352
  payment processing 353
  processing, steps 348
  receipts, verifying 350
expenses approvals
  about 328
  approver profile, configuring 336, 337
  approver profile, defining 341
  approver routing lists, configuring 339, 340
  approvers, assigning to approver profile 338-341
  approver types, defining 329-341
  configurations 329
  privilege templates, defining 335-341
  refining templates, defining 334-341
  transaction definitions, defining 331-341
expenses processes 316
expense transactions, tracking
  encumbrance 357
  expenditure 357
  pre-encumbrance 357
expense types, expense report feature
  Benchmark Threshold % 323
  configuring 322
  expense type edit 324
  expense type group 325
  GL chartfield setup 325
  gross up indicator 324
  items with tax implications 324
  required fields 323, 324
expneses
  external data, interfacing with 341
EXSD, transaction type 102
external banks 52

F

FC 142
flat file journal entry 292

values, defining 95

Thank you for buying
Oracle PeopleSoft Enterprise Financial Management 9.1 Implementation

About Packt Publishing

Packt, pronounced 'packed', published its first book "Mastering phpMyAdmin for Effective MySQL Management" in April 2004 and subsequently continued to specialize in publishing highly focused books on specific technologies and solutions.

Our books and publications share the experiences of your fellow IT professionals in adapting and customizing today's systems, applications, and frameworks. Our solution based books give you the knowledge and power to customize the software and technologies you're using to get the job done. Packt books are more specific and less general than the IT books you have seen in the past. Our unique business model allows us to bring you more focused information, giving you more of what you need to know, and less of what you don't.

Packt is a modern, yet unique publishing company, which focuses on producing quality, cutting-edge books for communities of developers, administrators, and newbies alike. For more information, please visit our website: www.packtpub.com.

About Packt Enterprise

In 2010, Packt launched two new brands, Packt Enterprise and Packt Open Source, in order to continue its focus on specialization. This book is part of the Packt Enterprise brand, home to books published on enterprise software – software created by major vendors, including (but not limited to) IBM, Microsoft and Oracle, often for use in other corporations. Its titles will offer information relevant to a range of users of this software, including administrators, developers, architects, and end users.

Writing for Packt

We welcome all inquiries from people who are interested in authoring. Book proposals should be sent to author@packtpub.com. If your book idea is still at an early stage and you would like to discuss it first before writing a formal book proposal, contact us; one of our commissioning editors will get in touch with you.

We're not just looking for published authors; if you have strong technical skills but no writing experience, our experienced editors can help you develop a writing career, or simply get some additional reward for your expertise.

Oracle E-Business Suite R12 Supply Chain Management

Drive your supply chain processes with Oracle E-Business Suite R12 Supply Chain Management to achieve measurable business gains

Muneeb A. Siddiqui

[PACKT] enterprise

Oracle E-Business Suite R12 Supply Chain Management

ISBN: 978-1-84968-064-6   Paperback: 292 pages

Drive your supply chain processes with Oracle E-Business R12 Supply Chain Management to achieve measurable business gains

1. Put supply chain management principles to practice with Oracle EBS SCM

2. Develop insight into the process and business flow of supply chain management

3. Set up all of the Oracle EBS SCM modules to automate your supply chain processes

Getting Started with Oracle BPM Suite 11gR1

A Hands-On Tutorial

Learn from the experts – teach yourself Oracle BPM Suite 11g with an accelerated and hands-on learning path brought to you by Oracle BPM Suite Product Management team members

Foreword by Michael Weingartner
Vice President, Product Development, Oracle Corporation

Heidi Buelow   Manoj Das   Manas Deb   [PACKT] enterprise
Prasen Palvankar   Meera Srinivasan

Getting Started with Oracle BPM Suite 11gR1 – A Hands-On Tutorial

ISBN: 978-1-84968-168-1   Paperback: 536 pages

Learn from the experts – teach yourself Oracle BPM Suite 11g with an accelerated and hands-on learning path brought to you by Oracle BPM Suite Product Management team members

1. Offers an accelerated learning path for the much-anticipated Oracle BPM Suite 11g release

2. Set the stage for your BPM learning experience with a discussion into the evolution of BPM, and a comprehensive overview of the Oracle BPM Suite 11g Product Architecture

3. Discover BPMN 2.0 modeling, simulation, and implementation

Please check **www.PacktPub.com** for information on our titles

**Oracle Business Intelligence:
The Condensed Guide to
Analysis and Reporting**

A fast track guide to uncovering the analytical power of Oracle
Business Intelligence, Analytic SQL, Oracle Discoverer, Oracle
Reports, and Oracle Warehouse Builder

Yuli Vasiliev

**The Business Analyst's
Guide to Oracle Hyperion
Interactive Reporting 11**

Quickly master this powerful business intelligence product

Edward J. Cody

Oracle Business Intelligence :
The Condensed Guide to Analysis
and Reporting

ISBN: 978-1-84968-118-6   Paperback: 184 pages

A fast track guide to uncovering the analytical power
of Oracle Business Intelligence: Analytic SQL, Oracle
Discoverer, Oracle Reports, and Oracle Warehouse
Builder

1. Install, configure, and deploy the components
    included in Oracle Business Intelligence Suite
    (SE)

2. Gain a comprehensive overview of components
    and features of the Oracle Business Intelligence
    package

3. A fast paced, practical book that provides you
    with quick steps to answer common business
    questions and help you make informed business
    decisions

The Business Analyst's Guide
to Oracle Hyperion Interactive
Reporting 11

ISBN: 978-1-84968-036-3   Paperback: 232 pages

Quickly master this extremely robust and powerful
Hyperion business intelligence tool

1. Get to grips with the most important,
    frequently used, and advanced features of
    Oracle Hyperion Interactive Reporting 11

2. A step-by-step Oracle Hyperion training guide
    packed with screenshots and clear explanations

3. Explore the features of Hyperion dashboards,
    reports, pivots, and charts

Please check **www.PacktPub.com** for information on our titles

Made in the USA
Lexington, KY
14 July 2012